The Third Tower Up from the Road

The Third Tower Up from the Road

A Compilation of Columns from
McSweeney's Internet Tendency's
*Kevin Dolgin Tells You
About Places You Should Go*

Kevin Dolgin

SANTA
MONICA
PRESS

Published by:
Santa Monica Press LLC
P.O. Box 1076
Santa Monica, CA 90406-1076
1-800-784-9553
www.santamonicapress.com
books@santamonicapress.com

Printed in the United States

Santa Monica Press books are available at special quantity discounts when purchased
in bulk by corporations, organizations, or groups. Please call our Special Sales
department at 1-800-784-9553.

ISBN-10 1-59580-043-3
ISBN-13 978-1-59580-043-5

Library of Congress Cataloging-in-Publication Data

Dolgin, Kevin, 1964-
  The third tower up from the road : a compilation of columns from McSweeney's Kevin
Dolgin tells you about places you should go / by Kevin Dolgin.
  p. cm.
  ISBN 978-1-59580-043-5
  1. Voyages and travels. 2. Dolgin, Kevin, 1964—Travel. I. McSweeney's. II. Title.
  G465.D655 2009
  910.4092—dc22
                  2009002314

Cover and interior design and production by Future Studio

CONTENTS

INTRODUCTION

There's no reason to travel, or so I've been told. You can learn anything you need to know by electronic means, thereby avoiding all the messiness and fatigue of actually carting your carcass around the globe. What's more, there are no differences anymore, everyplace resembles everyplace else, and everyone eats at McDonald's, wears jeans, and wants to drive a Mercedes. All that remains to be seen are ruins of differences past and these will soon be perusable via high-tech virtual-reality gizmos that will directly stimulate our neural networks . . . not that anyone will want to visit the pyramids when they can visit the twisted dungeons sprung from the mind of a programmer working for Nintendo (and where you have the added benefit of crafting yourself the body of a Greek god and granting yourself powers of which Superman would be jealous).

I must admit that it has occurred to me, as I walk the streets of Amman or Tokyo, that the planet has been subjected to a heavy blanket of sameness when compared to the extraordinary diversity of attire and architecture that once typified it. A painting on the wall of my hotel room in Istanbul, depicting the city as it was a mere 100 years ago, once brought this home to me like a slap in the face. Today, most of Istanbul (aside from its extraordinary monuments) does look rather like most of a lot of other cities, whereas when my own grandfather was born it was still a vision out of the *Arabian Nights*.

But these similarities are, in many ways, cosmetic, and the expectation of a kind of planetary culture only makes the truly profound differences all the more striking. What's more, I do think that the above is true not only of the state of the world's *places* but also fundamentally of the world's *people*: we are all, really, the same—we are all *homo sapiens*, after all—however, we do come from different cultures and different histories, we react in different ways and have entirely different points of reference. This interplay between similarity and difference is fascinating, so fascinating that it's kept me traveling for over 20 years.

Most of my travels were made possible/obligatory by my business, but that's actually not such a bad thing. When you travel for business you almost inevitably end up having some kind of local contact, often (although not always) these people are themselves interesting and are pleased when you show interest in their home and their background. As such, you can often become immersed in local history and culture more easily than if you are traveling as a tourist. So while my business has kept me on the road, I must admit that often I just travel for the hell of it. For that matter, while I treasure the variety of cultures to be found on the planet, I deplore the presence of borders and cross them whenever possible, sometimes just to spite them. My professional travels have tended to take me to cities, and I've sometimes felt as though I've been collecting them, adding them to a little glass-topped case stowed away in the den of my soul.

When, after a few years of trying to be a musician, I decided to focus my creative instincts on writing, it seemed natural for me to stop hoarding my memories of the world's cities for myself, and to begin committing them to paper. I therefore took some time away from creating my own strange little fictional worlds in short stories and novels to report on the worlds I regularly visited on my various journeys. I was encouraged in this by a group of writer friends and acquaintances I had met via Francis Ford Coppola's Net-based Zoetrope writer's workshop.

My first foray into the domain of travel writing began with a piece that I wrote for the literary magazine *Hobart*, about a search for the Corsican Swallowtail butterfly that I undertook with my two sons one summer. Much to my surprise and gratification, not only was this well received, but it was nominated for a Pushcart Prize. As such, I was encouraged to continue in the same direction. I therefore contacted McSweeney's and pitched to them the idea of writing a regular travel column, which they thought might not be a bad idea, promptly naming it "Kevin Dolgin Tells You About Places You Should Go in Europe" in a fit of ironic realism (realistic because it's pretty damn straightforward, ironic because I've never been particularly limited to Europe). My first McSweeney's column appeared around the end of 2003, and I've been writing them ever since.

I quickly found that writing about traveling is much better than traveling on its own. I'm not at all a visual person, and I never take pictures of anything. If I do, they turn out to be thoroughly uninteresting. The postcards sold on the street, all nicely arranged in their big revolving racks, are always nicer than any picture I could ever take (not that I buy the postcards), and it's not as though I or anyone I know could actually feature in any pictures, since I almost always travel alone. I also have to confess that I can't stand looking like a tourist, and as soon as you stop to take a picture you either look like a tourist or like a photographer: the former if you don't know what you're doing, the latter if you do. It is always blatantly obvious that I don't know what I'm doing when I take a picture (to the point of holding the camera the wrong way around). Instead of taking pictures, I have always simply counted on the formation of memories, sitting back from time to time just to reminisce about a place in all its lush (or squalid) detail. Writing became the perfect way to solidify those memories, to capture something about a place and carve it into stone. Or at least ink.

What's more, it soon became apparent that scribbling notes on a piece of paper gives you a certain mystique. There's an underlying although inevitably unasked question about what, exactly, you're doing and why you're scribbling the aforesaid notes. After a while, I found that it also gives you an excuse to talk to people—by introducing yourself as a travel writer you gain access to all kinds of stories, and sometimes even to normally inaccessible rooms, tunnels, and byways in castles or museums or grocery stores.

In this book, you'll find almost all of the dispatches that I wrote for McSweeney's between 2003 and 2008, as well as a fair amount of material written specifically for this book. The dispatches are prefaced by the original piece about the Corsican Swallowtail from *Hobart*. I've also included a few comments on some of the dispatches where I felt that either an update or some explanatory remarks were warranted.

Far be it from me to suggest how someone else should read a book (or taste wine or make love or engage in any other of the myriad wonderful and intimately personal things one can do). However, I can't help but think that the dispatches in this book might best be read like one eats peanuts: a couple here, a couple there, lick your fingers and put them away for a while then take them out when you feel like it, perhaps in the middle of the night when you can't sleep and you need a distraction. There's not really much of a flow here: although the very last dispatch should definitely be read last, the others are really in no particular order, beyond that in which they appeared on McSweeney's. It's true that there's a certain evolution, particularly with respect to the conceit that the column was supposed to be about Europe (for the first couple of years, I facetiously tried to justify any dispatches that dealt with destinations outside of Europe, but then I pretty much threw in the towel and wrote about wherever I happened to be, regardless of the continent), but I find that there's a certain pleasure to be taken by reading something in a relatively chaotic fashion.

For those of you who are familiar with the column via Mc-Sweeney's . . . well now you have it all on paper, which makes it so much more real somehow. There are also a number of dispatches here that have not appeared in McSweeney's; notably, the last one, and a series of dispatches about a long trip through the American West. You also may be interested in my comments surrounding some of the McSweeney's dispatches.

For those of you who are unfamiliar with my travel writing, please do understand that you'll get pretty much no practical advice whatsoever in these pages. I've probably mentioned more street vendors than proper restaurants and any tourist attractions are more likely to be described for their smell or the way the fountain outside splashes than for their actual contents. These vignettes are impressions—I've tried much harder to portray the spirit of these places than to describe where one can get a good hot dog (although I do have some suggestions about french fries in Bruges). So if you're looking for actual travel tips, you'll be disappointed. For that matter, most of this is, of course, out of date—for all I know, someone may have taken down Frank Zappa's statue or changed the opening hours of Lenin's mausoleum; I've made no effort to verify these things in the intervening months or years. Three cheers for practicality! However, if you're looking for a *reason* to travel then perhaps this book might provide what you need.

I've received many comments and emails since I began writing the McSweeney's dispatches, including two or three in which young American readers have indicated that my columns helped convince them to spend a year abroad. There is no more satisfying thing to me than to imagine that someone out there has decided to broaden their horizons at least partly due to something that I've written. I sincerely hope that this book will help broaden some more, whether by enticing you to travel or helping you remember the travels you've already taken.

Bon voyage!

THE CORSICAN SWALLOWTAIL:
CORSICA, FRANCE

This was my first attempt at travel writing. It was originally published in Hobart *magazine. Ever since writing it, I have kept an eye out for the Corsican Swallowtail whenever I'm in Corsica, but I have yet to see one (I think).*

"In these impossible dreams of his he visited the Islands of the Blessed, where in the hot ravines that cut the lower slopes of the chestnut- and laurel-clad mountains there occurs a weird local race of the Cabbage White; and also that other island, those railway banks near Vizzavona and the pine woods farther up, which are the haunts of the squat and dusky Corsican Swallowtail."
—Vladimir Nabokov, "The Aurelian"

I n "The Aurelian," Nabokov wrote of Paul Pilgram, who dreamt of traveling the world in search of exotic butterflies but never left his native Berlin: a lot of searching, but no traveling. I have often found myself in the opposite situation—all travel, no searching. My own travels are the result of my professional life, and also of an ardent thirst for discovery, but I rarely travel because I'm looking for something specific.

Pilgram had always struck me as one of the more pathetic of

Nabokov's many pathetic characters. A frustrated little man cooped into a small shop in Berlin, he dreamt of the far north and its Arctic bogs, of Italian gardens in the twilight of summer evenings, of the white heathered hills of Madrid. Among these unrealized dreams were the pine woods and the railroad tracks of Vizzavona, in the center of the most beautiful island in the Mediterranean; an island he would never see.

An island I know very well, and one that continues to entrance even after all these years.

There may be other places that rival Corsica in terms of natural beauty, there are certainly other islands that feature mountains plunging into the sea (But what mountains! What a sea!), yet there are precious few that also feature medieval villages clinging to the sides of forested ravines and ancient walled cities perched on cliffs guarding secret ports. In the end, it comes down to taste—after all, there are those who prefer concrete hotels and beaches with garbage cans.

My own familiarity with the island is largely due to my having married a woman whose father is Corsican. Every summer, my wife, my two boys, and I leave our home near Paris and come to be revivified by the heady Corsican air, splash around in the sea and climb around on the mountains. While on a map Corsica looks very small, there are whole worlds packed into that island and all my varied Corsican travels had never taken me to Vizzavona. This, I like to think, was about all I had in common with Paul Pilgram.

One day last summer, I decided to go on a treasure hunt, to travel in search of something specific. But what? Since I wasn't really missing anything, and since I was already in Corsica, I thought I'd go searching for Paul Pilgram's butterfly. There are those who scatter the ashes of their loved ones on the unvisited seas of their desire, and while Pilgram only ever lived in Nabokov's imagination, he was such a sorry figure that I thought he needed a bit of symbolic burying as well. What better way than to sprinkle the ashes of his memory among the pine trees of Vizzavona? So on a hot Saturday afternoon, the boys and I set out to drive north from our summer home near Porto-Vecchio to the mountain town mentioned by Nabokov.

We took the road inland from the coast town of Ghisonaccia toward its sister town, Ghisoni. For centuries, people on the east coast of Corsica spent the summer in the mountains then drove their animals down to the coast during the winter. Most towns therefore have their "sea" and "mountain" incarnations. The mountain village was usually the larger and more important of the two, although the tourist trade has tended to reverse these roles.

Ghisoni is the "mountain" of Ghisonaccia and is reached by a near-normal road, a rarity in Corsica, where it is far more usual to find roads that are more like glorified, semi-paved mule tracks. The only spot on the road to Ghisoni that is difficult is in the Défilé de l'Inzecca, where enormous rock outcrops crowd the two narrow lanes. This is not really a problem, though, since we stopped every few meters to get out and gawk.

At this point, the road somehow clings to the side of a sheer gorge, at the bottom of which is the Orbu river. The Défilé de l'Inzecca consists of the gorge and the granite spires that thrust out from either side. The narrowness of the road poses no problem because *everyone* slows down or stops to gawk, even the natives.

After Ghisoni, a fair-sized town high on a mountainside, the road becomes much more typical, with sheer drops on either side of a tiny shoulder-less track and each hairpin turn brings new thrills as you wonder whether some hotheaded Corsican is going to come barreling around at you. Livestock is a problem as well, since the Corsican method of raising cattle and pigs consists of allowing them to roam free until it's time to bring them to market, meaning that the mountains are home to half-wild cows and semi-feral, hairy pigs, not to mention a large population of wild boar. Any of these animals can occasionally be seen lounging on the road.

For all its dangers, the road is spectacular. Corsica is like a gift from the sea to the sky—its mountains burst from the Mediterranean, reaching dizzying heights of up to 8,500 feet. In the interior, the island lies in green and brown folds, blanketed with a thick, dry vegetation known as the "maquis." This is an impenetrable tangle of thorns and spices, all of which fills the air with a distinct, sweet smell. From the road above Ghisoni, the maquis is spread out underneath—far underneath—and can be fully enjoyed, particularly if one is not prone to vertigo.

Finally, the road meets RN 193, the main road running from Bastia to Ajaccio. Geographically, historically and practically, Corsica is divided by a line of imposing mountains running from northwest to southeast. The major city in the northern half is Bastia, while the major city in the southern half is Ajaccio, Napoleon's birthplace. Vizzavona is near the pass where RN 193 crosses from north to south over the mountainous spine. After meeting the main road, the town of Vizzavona is only a few kilometers on, just north of the pass.

We parked near the somewhat improbable train station. (In reality, everything in Vizzavona is near the train station. It is not a large town.)

In the late nineteenth century, the French government decided to build a railway between Bastia and Ajaccio. On a Corsican scale, it was a feat as impressive as the linking of the Atlantic and the Pacific (and was probably inspired by the same) because of all those mountains. Needless to say, the railway was to follow the road that had, from time immemorial, connected north and south, via Vizzavona.

In 1889, the link was completed and Vizzavona became a popular mountain resort for the Corsican gentry. Today, the railroad continues to stop there, although the passengers who debark at Vizzavona tend more to be hikers than dilettantes.

As we got out of the car, I wondered whether Nabokov had ever actually been here. I was unable to find any reference to a trip to Corsica in my research but how else could he have described the railroad tracks and the pine woods? We decided to go to the train station itself both to ask about it and to ask questions about Nabokov and butterflies. Inside, we found the stationmaster/ticket seller/cleaning person/doer of whatever else needs to get done.

It turns out that she and her husband were also the proprietors of the restaurant/general store that is next to the station. She informed us that the railway is a thriving line, with four trains in each direction daily—six during the holiday season. Each train has three passenger cars and there were 40,000 passengers in all last year. This was all recounted with evident pride and then she left her post at the station to slip on an apron and help cook in the restaurant since the next train was not for some time. We asked whether she knew anything about butterflies or about Vladimir Nabokov.

She did not.

We decided to have lunch in her establishment, but first we made the acquaintance of her husband, who was manning the counter in the general store. The store is roughly the size of a typical American kitchen but it has one whole glorious aisle stocked with local sausage and cheese. Corsica produces excellent sausage and excellent cheese, although they are not for the weak of palate. He, too, knew nothing about butterflies or literary lepidopterists but he did sell us a book about Vizzavona that informed us, among other things, that there are 29 buildings in the town and even taught us the history of each and every one of them.

Our bellies full, we set out to hike along the railway tracks and soon left them to venture into the pine woods farther up. In fact, there is a clearly marked trail that leads not to the haunt of the Corsican Swallowtail but instead to a cave where real cavemen used to live.

"Real cavemen?" asked my youngest son.

"Yup."

"Cool!"

So we began trekking through the woods towards the real

caveman cave, our eyes peeled for the Corsican Swallowtail.

At this point it must be clearly admitted, for the record, that neither I nor my sons know anything about butterflies. We had a picture of the Corsican Swallowtail and had vainly assumed that we could just recognize it, but the problem with butterflies is that they fly. Or rather, they flutter all over and it's not easy to see all those markings. All this is to say that we don't *think* we saw a Corsican Swallowtail on that path but we aren't exactly sure.

We did see a plenitude of beautiful little blue-gray or whitish-gray butterflies and also some magnificent orange-brown ones but no dusky yellow and black ones with white undersides: the seemingly elusive Corsican Swallowtail.

We also found a lot of trees. When Nabokov wrote of pine woods he didn't prepare us for the size of the trees. These are trees that have stood watch over Vizzavona for hundreds of years and have reached prodigious heights. Above them all towers Monte d'Oru, a 7,800-foot mass of pink and brown granite.

At the end of the path, the three of us stood near the entrance of the caveman cave and imagined what it must have been like back when Neolithic Corsicans hunted the same wild boar with flint arrowheads. Then we decided to go farther up, to the pass itself.

We made our way back to the car and said goodbye to the town of Vizzavona, then drove a couple of kilometers up to the pass. The little book we had purchased told of a fort that had been built just above the pass. We found a trail of some sorts that led up to it and made our way to the fort of A Foce.

The eighteenth century saw not only America's struggle for independence but also Corsica's, first from the Genovese and later from the French. The Corsicans were less successful. The French built the fort in 1776 to control the crucial pass at Vizzavona and split Corsica in two. Those who controlled the fort controlled virtually all communications between the two halves of the island.

The fort is now in ruins and is rarely mentioned in guidebooks. It is not a very impressive fort as ruined forts go but it did cause us some excitement since there we saw a beautiful black and white butterfly, which unfortunately sported no yellow and therefore probably wasn't a Corsican Swallowtail. We did manage to get very close to it, though, and so were able to admire it more than had been the case with our earlier finds.

After visiting the fort, we decided to go farther down. In fact, we decided to go to the Manganellu river, which runs down the valley near the tiny town of Canaglia.

Canaglia is so small that it makes Vizzavona seem like Manhattan, but the village itself is of less interest than the river that runs near it. Once we managed to park the car, we followed a forest trail for about 45 minutes until we reached the Manganellu, a little stream that has scooped a number of pleasant pools out of the mountain. Two other families had found the same pool as the one we happened upon and were lounging on the smooth rocks near the water or jumping from the boulders into the stream. We quickly changed into our bathing suits and jumped in, thrilling to the cold water under the 90° air.

I wish I could say that we kept a keen eye peeled for Corsican Swallowtails but alas, this was not the case. By then, Paul Pilgram had been temporarily forgotten and we were fully given over to climbing on the rocks and swimming in the clear waters of the stream. Finally, we decided to make our way back to Porto-Vecchio, where my half-Corsican wife was expecting us home in time for dinner (grilled fish stuffed with fennel that grows wild near the house).

I don't think we found the Corsican Swallowtail (which is endangered, by the way) but we all agreed that the day was worthwhile. We had discovered a corner of Corsica that we hadn't known and had been further reassured in our belief that Corsica is, indeed, the most beautiful place in the world. I also discovered that while travel is sometimes an end in itself, searching for something— anything—can make it richer. I also somehow imagined that I had

scattered some of Pilgram's fictional ashes in the pine woods of Vizzavona.

As we ate our fish on the terrace, the warm Mediterranean
breeze played with our napkins, and I remembered Pilgram's dreams
of the far north, where the Arctic bogs produce delicate downy butterflies. Perhaps next, we'll go look for those.

THE FIUMICELLI RIVER:
CORSICA, FRANCE

This was the first column posted at McSweeney's. I hadn't quite figured out the extent to which they would allow me to write what is essentially the antithesis of a typical travel column, so it ends with a few practical points about traveling to Corsica. These were pretty much the last practicalities I ever included in any columns.

This dispatch also initiated the tradition of a yearly column on the island of Corsica. There is a very good reason for these yearly Corsican dispatches: with the exception of 2008, my family and I have gone to Corsica every summer for the last 20 years or so.

I would point out that my family and I go to the Fiumicelli just about every year, and whenever we have friends who have made the eminently wise decision to come to Corsica over the summer, we take them there as well.

The island of Corsica is a pile of mountains trying to plunge into the sea. Corsica is famous for its mountains (although its greater claim to fame is as the birthplace of Napolean— who, it would seem, had a very small penis according to other McSweeney's writers, but that's another story). The mountains sport neat little beaches at their feet, beaches crawling with half-naked Italian and French tourists on their summer holidays. Higher up, though, the mountains are crisscrossed with streams. These streams are the only parts of the mountains that actually do manage to get to the Mediterranean.

Increasingly, the streams are visited by people who spend their time either climbing up or sliding down them. Canyoning is becoming an acceptable leisure activity in Corsica, although the most interesting way to do it is to avoid the groups and the guides and simply find yourself a stream and attack it.

One such stream is the Fiumicelli, which flows into the Solenzara river near the Bavella Pass. In order to reach it, you have to drive inland for about a half hour from the east coast town of Solenzara (one of the least interesting towns in Corsica) along the D288 towards Bavella. While the D288 is currently being enlarged, in many stretches it retains its charming mule-path character, meaning that it is very difficult for one car to pass, let alone two, which sometimes leads to spirited negotiations about who has to brave 300-foot drops with no guardrails while driving in reverse to the nearest passing point. It should be driven with care.

After one such stretch, the road crosses the Fiumicelli on a tiny bridge in a hairpin left turn. This bridge is relatively new, the Fiumicelli having eaten the old one during a particularly violent but not uncommon spring flood eight or nine years ago (it should be noted that spring is not a good season to go canyoning in Corsica). The river can be reached by climbing down from the bridge on the near side, to the right. Jumping from the bridge is ill-advised, since the stream is about four inches deep at that point—sometimes six if the water is high. From there, the best direction is up.

One of the good things about canyoning is that you can't actually get lost in the traditional sense of the word. You can go farther up the river than you planned, but aside from that, even the most addled hiker can usually manage to stay within sight of water. You can therefore enjoy the scenery and the river itself without messing with things like maps and compasses.

Corsican scenery is like no other scenery. Even while deep in the mountains, the sea is ever present, as though it has dissolved itself into the air. For that matter, Corsica is worth a visit even if only as a kind of breathing excursion. A particular kind of vegetation coats all those mountains—the French call it "the maquis"—and it consists of an assortment of thorny bushes dotted with wild pigs. The scent of these plants (minus that of the pigs) mixed with the sea air makes an olfactory tonic. As for the views . . . the Fiumicelli runs through hulking boulders and scoops deep pools into the mountain itself. At one point, the river has formed a perfectly round, deep pool of about 50 feet in diameter with a waterfall pouring down one side. It's as though Walt Disney designed it—minus the guffawing dogs and learned mice. The hike consists of a bit of clambering (not-quite climbing) and a fair amount of swimming. In one or two places it is convenient, not to mention fun, to plunge into the river from the edge of a cliff (a few spots offer plunges of 10 to 20 feet). The whole is framed by pine forests and distant vistas of towering rose-colored mountains.

After three or four hours, the river crosses a hiking path heading south. Theoretically, the path can be identified by looking for a sandy area to the left. This trail eventually reaches the road, after about 35 minutes. A walk of another two kilometers down the road will bring you back to your car. Or, for that matter, you can simply slide down the river the same way you went up, which when all is said and done is by far the most agreeable way to go and which will probably be necessary anyway since it is virtually impossible to identify the correct sandy area and therefore find the hiking path. Alternately, hikers can simply sleep in the forest, which is illegal. What's more, the forest is policed by the wild pigs. The pigs won't hurt you, but it can be a traumatic experience to be awakened at 3:00 AM by a hairy snout snuffling around your head trying to find the source of that Camembert odor that unfortunately is still on your breath. Believe me.

Corsica can be reached by air from either France or Italy. Air France, Air Littoral and Alitalia all have frequent flights from many major cities. It can also be reached by ship from Marseilles, Nice and Toulon, as well as from Genova and Livorno. Just about everyplace on the island is worth a stay, although the stretch from Bastia south to Solenzara is best avoided. While there is no public transportation to the Fiumicelli, hitchhiking is easy in Corsica, especially during the tourist season. Note that while there is an independence movement on the island that has a reputation for blowing things up, they have never yet blown up a tourist (they know who pays the bills). They have been known to put an RPG into the occasional RV if it is parked illegally, but never without politely evacuating the occupants first and explaining the philosophical rationale for their actions (it would seem that people who vacation in RVs don't spend enough money locally and they ruin the landscape if they park illegally). If you don't plan on parking a three-ton truck on the flowers, you'll be fine. Much better to sleep under the stars with the pigs next to the burbling Fiumicelli.

THE PRIVATE TOUR OF TOPKAPI PALACE'S HAREM COMPLEX AS CONDUCTED BY JOHN-WITH-A-C: ISTANBUL, TURKEY

A brief aside: I know now why John is spelled with a c in Turkish. It's for the same reason that Dolmabahçe is spelled with a c.

In 1453, once the Turks had finally defeated the Byzantine Empire, Mehmet the Conqueror decided he needed a palace in Constantinople, so he set out to build Topkapi, which means something in Turkish. It remained the palace of the Turkish sultans until 1856, when Sultan Abdülmecid I decided to be a cool, cosmopolitan kind of sultan and build a new, more modern and thoroughly boring palace called Dolmabahçe in a hipper neighborhood on the other side of the Golden Horn (it is utterly uninteresting, don't even bother to tell the taxi driver to slow down as you pass it). This is yet another sorry example of mankind's race to trash what is beautiful and charming in a misguided quest for modernity. It is the same impulse that leads us to cover up cobblestone streets with asphalt and make plastic Christmas trees that dance when you clap.

But I digress.

For 400 years, Topkapi was the power center of the Ottoman Empire (and therefore of a fair chunk of the world), and the power center of Topkapi was the harem complex—a mysterious jumble of buildings, corridors and courtyards in which the royal family lived. That is to say, the sultan, his mother, his hundreds of concubines, his official wives (those concubines who had borne him a son), a couple of hundred eunuchs and the odd janissary (no, they did not mop the floors—they were an elite corps of soldiers, and they were restricted to the outer buildings of the harem).

Today, you can visit the harem complex, and the best way to do so is to avoid the official harem tours and find yourself a certified freelance guide. This is easy to do, since you will be assailed by any number of them as you enter the outer courtyard of the palace. They will guess your main language and immediately speak to you in it. They rarely get it wrong, although if you happen to be multilingual you may want to engage in the sport of language-baiting, which can always be a pleasant diversion *("Ah, vous êtes donc français?"/"Non plus. Sono forse italiano."/"Allora italiano?"/"Nein.").* Avoid the young ones, the eager ones, the handsome ones, and try to find John-with-a-c.

"Your name is John?"

"That's right."

"That's not a very Turkish name, is it?"

"It is a very Turkish name. It's not spelled the same, though. It's spelled with a squiggly *c.*"

Where, exactly, one is supposed to put the *c*, squiggly or otherwise, in the name "John" is beyond my limited Turkish, but this is unimportant, for John-with-a-c is not only a fully certified guide, he is also a fully certified harem guide and he has been guiding people through the harem for over 30 years. As he will gladly tell you, there are two castes of guides at Topkapi: you need to get your Topkapi certification in order to acquire the right to bother tourists at all, but if you want to lead them through the warren of the harem then you need a special harem certification. Back when the sultan lived there, you needed to get castrated, but it would seem the certification process has been simplified somewhat.

The harem can only be visited with a guide, but most visitors use the official guides and go around in large groups bulging with Dutch and Japanese tourists speaking their terminally unmusical tongues and taking pictures of everything. John-with-a-c will take you places they don't go, brushing off the protests of the security people with a flick of his wizened hand and squeezing through one half-opened, exquisitely carved wooden door after another in an effort to get you thoroughly and delightfully lost, all the while giving you not only the history of the place, but the half-whispered gossip of centuries past. He will show you the apartments of the sultan's mother—according to John-with-a-c, the real power behind most of the sultanate thrones—and the courtyard of the favorites. He will take you into small rooms, large rooms, too many rooms to remember, tiled with blue ceramic and leafed with gold. Your eyes will spin, and you'll hear the womanly voices of all those ghosts (which might actually have been the group of Dutch tourists around the corner, come to think of it). He'll tell you, as you stand on the upper terrace near the empty pool where the concubines once bathed, how those who wished to attract the sultan's eye would pay attention to the way they climbed dripping out of the pool (undoubtedly in a bid to attain wifehood by enticing him to participate in a bout of hopefully male conception), and as he speaks you can see a dreamy glint in his old eye. Eventually, he'll lead you back through the quarters of the black eunuchs out of the harem and into the palace courtyard.

The harem tour will only last an hour or so, leaving you ample time to visit the rest of the palace, which is enormous. The Ottomans didn't build palaces like those you'll find in Western Europe. Palaces and castles in the West were apparently built to impress the visitor with the sheer weight of stone used: "grovel, or we'll drop all this rock on you" they seem to threaten. Topkapi impressed foreign ambassadors and potentates with its mystery and its sheer beauty—elegant courtyards dotted with small white buildings boasting gilded roofs; every door carved with flowing designs; window grates so delicate they seem to be made of wooden lace. This palace cowed visitors with an unavoidable impression that whoever lived there must be so much *cooler* than they.

Try to hang on to John-with-a-c while visiting the rest of the palace, at least for a while. He can explain everything. You can also buy a guidebook at the kiosk where you get your tickets (note that the harem requires a separate ticket). After your visit, don't hesitate to go to the restaurant, which has a terrace overlooking the Sea of Marmara and is surprisingly good as tourist restaurants go. Try the lentil soup.

Istanbul as a whole is a fantastic city to visit, especially if you're interested in history. You'll want to avoid the trendier areas of the city, such as Taksim Square (although do take a walk down Istiklal Caddesi one night—a street worth a column in its own right), and try to stay in the Sultanahmet district, near Topkapi, the Hagia Sophia, the Blue Mosque, the Grand Bazaar, etc. You might want to stay at Yesil Ev, a wonderful little hotel in a historic, nineteenth-century wooden building just behind the Blue Mosque in a neighborhood that was restored to its former glory about 30 years ago. The hotel also has a restaurant that is one of the best deals in Istanbul. The only drawback (well, in truth there are several drawbacks if you're anywhere near picky) is that it has no air conditioning, meaning that if you go during the summer you must sleep with the windows open, and since you're near the Blue Mosque this means that you will be awakened by the cry of the muezzin announcing morning prayers at an ungodly hour (unless you actually plan on praying then, which would make it more of a godly hour—although I doubt God is up that early. If I had even a smidgen of omnipotence then I, for one, would immediately apply it to making sure I no longer had to get up early). Otherwise, if you're obscenely rich, the Four Seasons is just down the street. One supposes you can close the windows there and not have to listen to the sounds of the city. Which might not be such a good idea, because it is such an interesting city after all.

THE DALMORE DISTILLERY:
SCOTLAND

T he word "whiskey" comes from the Gaelic *"uisge beatha,"*
which means "the water of life." You squeeze life, whiskey
comes out. At least it does in Scotland. It's probable that the
stuff was first discovered (great things are never invented, they lie in
waiting in some pre-invention limbo for a genius to come along and
stumble upon them) when some genius stumbled upon the bright
idea of distilling ale. He undoubtedly realized immediately that this
was just the stuff to make the Scottish climate bearable.

Today, there are about 100 distilleries in Scotland, and many
of them can be visited. The tours of the distilleries inevitably include
a visit to the wash tuns, which are very, very, very big barrels (in the
way that whales are very, very, very big dolphins) where snickering
tour guides invite unwary visitors to get a nose full of carbon dioxide,
and a visit to the warehouses, where the casks are kept for anywhere
from three years (cut-rate blended swill) to thirty years or more (for
the unmentionably expensive contents of special commemorative
bottles and the like). In between is a visit to the pulsing heart of the
distillery—whatever distillery it might be—the still room, consisting of a number (usually four to eight) of stills. These are elegant
contraptions, up to eighteen feet tall, made of gleaming copper and
sporting swanlike necks that taper away in alcoholic elegance. The
heart of the still room is the spirit safe, a clear glass cabinet through

which the distilled spirits flow in charming little waterfalls under the gaze of the master distiller. The spirit safe is locked with an official padlock from the Customs and Excise authority. This is always a big, flashy affair with all kinds of official-looking things engraved onto it. Lions and such.

Some distilleries have made their tours into genuine tourist attractions. Glenmorangie is an excellent Highland whiskey, the most widely drunk single malt in Scotland and one of the few that doesn't lend its wares to the blenders. Incidentally, it's pronounced "GlonMORangie," as in rhymes with "orangey," and accepts buses full of tourists, escorting them around with full-time guides and leaving them in the distillery's shop where one can buy all kinds of twee little things, like Glenmorangie hats and T-shirts, as well as enough whiskey to get Inverness drunk. No easy task, that.

Some distilleries, though, haven't worked out the tourist thing. They don't seem to grasp the business potential here. This is a good thing. There's a place for the big tourist gigs—after all, one really should go up the Eiffel Tower once. However, there's also a place for the non-tourist thing (which, in a fit of semantic existentialism, therefore becomes the tourist thing, but such reasoning leads to headaches). Mr. Sinclair, at the Dalmore Distillery, has not figured out the tourist thing, and the Dalmore should therefore be visited.

The Dalmore makes a dark, solid whiskey. Some whiskey drinkers find it relatively unexceptional, though very pleasant, but according to *Nessie's Loch Ness Times* in 2002, a group of unspecified whiskey experts declared its 21-year-old as the best whiskey in the world over 12 years of age. I wouldn't know, I can't afford stuff that old. Either way, it's not the whiskey itself so much as the place.

Mr. Sinclair is the manager of the Dalmore. He has been working there for over 35 years, and is now a shareholder in Dalmore's parent company, Whyte and Mackay, which also owns a few other distilleries. He is the kind of older gentleman whom you would peg as a genteel Scotsman from across the street in Katmandu. It's not that he wears a kilt or a tam-o-'shanter, it's just that he radiates a certain Scottish aura. Kind of like fog.

Since there are no tour guides or buses or visitors' centers (not to mention shops) at the Dalmore, Mr. Sinclair himself will take you around to visit the distillery—a place that is clearly as dear to his heart as the Sistine Chapel is dear to the heart of the pope. He will show you the stills with their unique water jackets, he will discuss the intricacies of different types of wash tuns, he will take you to the warehouse, where he seems to know the history of each cask, and may even take the stopper out of a cask of 40-year-old whiskey so you can smell it (not taste it, mind you). Then he will take you back up to a wood-paneled living room to sample a few of the distillery's creations.

There, if you're very, very lucky, he may let you in on a neat trick. Mr. Sinclair can show you how to make money in bar bets by saying that you want your whiskey in a glass with water (a sin in normal times) but you don't want them mixed because you'd like to drink the water first and then the whiskey. Upon hearing that this is impossible, you then proceed to pour it yourself, for there is a way to do so in which the whiskey floats on top of the water, with a clear line dividing them. You can then stick a straw through the whiskey, drink the water off, then down the dram. The best part about this trick is that once you've fleeced your barmates you can say, "Och aye, 'twas Drew Sinclair up at the Dalmore who showed me that. Fine man, he is." Or, you can just send me five bucks and I'll tell you how to do it, and then you can lie about Mr. Sinclair.

The only thing that jars a little bit about the distillery, which is set in a series of low, gray buildings overlooking Cromarty Firth, is the oil rigs. OK, they're not exactly in front of the distillery, but a bit down the road towards Invergordon. I, for one, had always been of the impression that offshore oil rigs were to be found a little farther off the shore than these, which are almost onshore oil rigs. You drive right past them to get to the distillery (assuming you've first gotten lost) and one can hardly help but stop and gaze at them in horrified wonder as they squat menacingly in the water—as though they just needed to run into the surf to take a giant steely pee. They spoil an otherwise perfect view, but then again, they are filling the tank of the car you've so flippantly driven around to do nothing more important than visit a charming little distillery and learn a neat trick from dear Mr. Sinclair.

THE SPANISH KING
OF BRUSSELS, BELGIUM

Europeans cities are built around Squares . . . or "Circles" or "Places" or "Piazze" or "Platzes" or whatever you want to call them. For the sake of convenience, we'll refer to them here as "Places" with a capital *P*, because that's what they call them in France and that's where we live. Anyway, every city in Europe boasts numbers of them and each claims that one or another of them is the most beautiful Place in the world. There's Paris's Place de la Concorde, Milan's Piazza del Duomo, Madrid's Plaza Mayor—even London sometimes laughingly tries to get into the picture with Piccadilly Circus or some other equally unlikely entrant. In general, though, there are two that tend to stand out. One of these is understandably Venice's Piazza San Marco, and the other can surprise many people who don't know it, because it's in Brussels.

"Brussels," you say. "Isn't that a vegetable?" No, it's the capital of a confusing little country where everyone is capable of speaking three languages but refuses to speak more than one depending on whom they are talking to (usually one you don't speak, like Flemish, which is Dutch in disguise). It is also generally considered to be the capital of Europe because it is swarming with bureaucrats who work in ugly buildings far from one of the most beautiful Places in the world.

The Place in question is in the very center of the city. In a burst of creative inspiration, it was named La Grande Place, which means "The Big Place," but don't let the simplicity of its name fool you. La Grande Place dates from a long, long time ago (note the stunning depth of research that went into this column), but the buildings that currently surround it generally date from the seventeenth century. At the time, they consisted primarily of guild halls. The guilds were groups of craftsmen and merchants who formed tightly woven associations to protect their trade and better wield their considerable influence. Each guild went to great lengths to build impressive halls in a kind of competitive architectural potlatch that gave rise to the understandably flamboyant but surprisingly homogeneous architecture around La Grande Place—the whole of it capped off by the city hall, which is undoubtedly one of the most beautiful town halls in the world.

When you put that all together, you get one hell of a Place. You have to stand in the middle, in a lake of cobblestone, and slowly turn, taking in all of these tall, skinny, elaborate buildings, their walls and roofs studded with statues. There is a kind of game you can play with some of them—one statue of the pregnant Virgin Mary seems to be pointing at a statue of a man across the Place, who is pointing to another, who is himself pointing to another, and so on, in an apparent paternity dispute. The chain ends with the statue of an archangel pointing to the sky as if to say, "No, it was *him*." Furthermore, the city recently cleaned most of the façades and statues so that their bronze shines in the all-too-rare Belgian sun. If you keep on turning you will eventually come across the Spanish King.

Le Roi d'Espagne used to be the guild hall of the bakers' guild, but it is now a beer hall, which is a nice, Teutonic way of saying "a bar." In the summer (a 48-hour period in mid-August), there are tables outside on a kind of wooden dais, but you want to go inside.

Rare are the bars that boast stuffed horses in their entrance. Rarer still are bars that boast stuffed horses *and* a view of one of the most beautiful Places in Europe. Le Roi d'Espagne is unique in this respect, and it further offers a wide selection of Belgian beers. You may think that Germany is the *Vaterland* of beer (you and 80 million Germans) but Belgians would dispute that. For some reason, Americans think of waffles when (if) they think of Belgium, but if you ask a Belgian to name his country's defining foodstuffs he would probably say french fries (which are certainly not named "french" fries in Belgian . . . nor are they named "freedom" fries, for that matter, but that's another story), mussels, chocolate and beer. Not the best combination, grant you, but taken individually (paying particular attention not to mix the chocolate with the mussels and the french fries) their gustatory excellence is undeniable. It is in beer, however, that there is the greatest variety, including lambic beers, which are still brewed by letting wild yeast spores drift in through open windows. These beers are lovingly concocted by fat, jolly trappist monks. Or so I've always imagined it.

Anyway, the place to drink these beers is in Le Roi d'Espagne. There are simple wooden tables available downstairs, near the horse, and supposedly a special basement bar that is reported to be somewhat hipper, but the best part of the establishment is the upstairs. This is a mezzanine-type area with tiny windows that open up to La Grande Place. It's generally less crowded up there, and it's often possible to get a seat near one of these windows, where you can sip your lambic beer and gaze out on La Grande Place. This is the ideal spot in Brussels to sit and study your very slim tourist guides to the city, planning which of the three sites you'll be visiting in which order. Incidentally, plan on spending a good 12 minutes at the statue of Manneken Pis, a minuscule bronze of a small boy peeing into a fountain that is the universally acclaimed mascot of the city of Brussels. It seems the little tyke once tried to help put out a fire in this way a couple of centuries ago and thereby saved the city. It's worth a laugh, and it's only five minutes by foot from Le Roi d'Espagne, and if you're lucky he'll be dressed up as anything from a medieval pikeman to Elvis Presley. The residents of Brussels get their kicks as best they can. It should also be noted that the renowned inferiority complex of Brussels with respect to Paris can be summarized by the fact that Paris's defining symbol is a 990-foot-tall tower of iron, while Brussels boasts a three-foot-tall bronze sporting a one-inch dick. Great Place, though, and the best place to relax while considering it is in Le Roi d'Espagne.

THE WATERFOWL
OF WINDSOR, ENGLAND

Eton and Windsor sit across the Thames from each other. Eton considers Windsor, undoubtedly thinking, "Ah yes, that is what I shall be when I grow up." The two towns almost ache with the kind of snobbish understatement that renders stereotypical the image of landed British gentry. Even the signs on the shops seem to smile that annoying little wry smile at you. "American, are you?" I don't know how the signs can tell, but they can. They don't mock my British friends, only me.

Needless to say, both towns are cute, pretty, "twee" as the British would say and are worth a visit. For that matter, the entire Thames Valley, west of London, is worth an extended visit. In this part of England, the Thames itself is a charming little river, the kind of river that trees simply love to hang over, shedding leaves into its placid waters and providing shade for walkers. One does feel that if all were truly right in the world, those who strolled along the Thames near Eton would be wearing waistcoats or Victorian dresses, carrying shiny black walking sticks or frilly parasols as the case may be, but don't let this stop you from enjoying the river's banks even in sweats and sneakers.

Don't let it stop you from staying there, either. In fact, one of my favorite hotels in the world is in the Thames Valley—the Monkey Island Inn, in Dray, which sits all by itself on an island in the

Thames, accessible only by footbridge. The English have a knack for making the impractical enjoyable.

But I digress. Our subject for the moment is not the river itself, nor its banks, but its inhabitants. Namely, its birds.

The Windsor Bridge was built in 1823, replacing an earlier wooden structure. At the time, it was a toll bridge (it cost sixpence to cart a corpse across it, for instance) but today one can walk across it freely, with or without a cadaver. One can no longer drive across it, because it's a bit iffy, but one can walk across it, and it's a good place to start observing the birds.

There are hordes of waterfowl living in the Thames near the Windsor Bridge. Preponderant among them are the swans. Swans are very large, beautiful, and exceedingly nasty creatures that float around like they own the world, bullying lesser birds such as ducks and gulls in order to come as close as they can to anyone who seems likely to want to give them something to eat. While you're still up on the bridge, they don't deign to take notice of you, but once you go down to the riverbank, the fun begins.

I suggest the Windsor side. The Eton side does boast a better view (of Windsor and the castle), but the Windsor side has a nicer walking path. If you walk slowly looking at the birds, they will immediately assume that you're going to give them some bread, and they'll start gliding over to you. It takes them a while to realize that you're not giving them anything to eat. Foolish birds.

I remember being a young child and thinking that swans moved through the water propelled by some kind of magic, or a magnetic force. I was disappointed when I first saw their big gnarly feet paddling underneath the surface. It was as though they were cheating. The Thames is muddy enough, though, that the illusion can often hold, and the swans simply glide around, snapping out at the ducks. I'll pause here to head off a potential avenue of complaint, for I can already imagine notes from irate British duck enthusiasts saying that these are not, in fact, ducks, they are really Speckled Russian Gribbens, or some equally obscure fowl. Cut me some slack, I know nothing about such things and anything that has wings and says "quack" is and will always be a duck to me.

I recently counted over 40 swans in the Thames near the bridge, and countless ducks, speckled gribbens, whatever. I also noticed some very particular behavior that should undoubtedly be researched by people interested in such things. Notably, I saw a swan waterskiing. This is the truth. The thing flapped and ran along the water in that ridiculous way swans have of trying to take off, until it got a little air, then it flew in a wide, low circle, stuck out its legs, webbed toes splayed, and went SWISH . . . . . . on its feet along the water's surface for a good 10 meters, wings spread and neck craned. It looked like great fun, exactly the kind of thing I would do if I were a swan. I expected it to stop and say, "Dude, that was righteous," but it didn't. It just folded up its kit and bobbed around with a mischievous glint in its beady black eye. I waited a good 15 minutes to see if it would do it again, but it had decided to engage in that favorite swan sport of being mean to other animals and so was distracted from extreme skiing.

A good place to stay on a waterfowl observation outing is Christopher Wren's house, which is now a hotel right near the bridge, on the Windsor side. It doesn't have the outright charm of the Monkey Island Inn, but it's not quite so isolated and I think it's supposed to be haunted. Christopher Wren is a fun historical figure, because you've probably heard of him, yet have no idea what he did. I had a vague impression he had something to do with Winnie the Pooh, but it turns out he was an architect. Anyway, if you decide to check out the birds, you should probably bring some bread. For that matter, bring some extra and feed them for me, I owe them.

TOM TIT'S EXPERIMENT: SÖDERTÄLJE, SWEDEN

This column prompted a number of responses from Swedish readers, explaining that my Swedish was incorrect, both in terms of grammar and with respect to the various bits and squiggles that modify the letters. I had tried hard to get all the bits and squiggles right, and after these undoubtedly deserved criticisms I gave up entirely, for all languages.

This is a very bad time of the year to visit Sweden. It's dark all day and really cold. That's a shame, since Sweden is otherwise a very nice place to visit, and Stockholm is a truly wonderful city, with lots of the windy little cobblestone streets that so many other cities misguidedly ripped up in the great modernization movements of the first half of the twentieth century. Furthermore, Stockholm is a water city, like Venice, or Copenhagen, or Hong Kong: a city that seems to be in a kind of perpetual fusion with the sea. Water cities are always interesting.

As off-the-beaten-path as Stockholm is, Södertälje is even more so. This is understandable, since there is almost no reason whatsoever to go to Södertälje. In fact, just about the only reason one could possibly have to go to Södertälje can be summarized in the words "Tom Tit's Experiment."

Tom Tit's Experiment is a kind of museum, of the type that were popular in the '80s, in which one could get one's hands on the exhibits and experiments . . . particularly well suited for little hands. There are many of these kinds of museums around the world, and I suppose that if push came to shove one wouldn't really have to go to Sweden to find a good one, but there is something about Tom Tit's Experiment that is different.

Perhaps it's the informal nature of the place. It seems kind of slapped together. In the United States, museums such as these are often well thought out, carefully designed and studied to produce a pre-calculated result on some gradient of fun. Tom Tit's Experiment is the kind of place your nice and somewhat ditzy aunt would put together if she had the money and the inclination.

For example, the most popular experiment is the great soap-bubble maker thing (so it was translated to me). This device can create soap bubbles big enough to stand in. As a special McSweeney's exclusive feature, the actual formula for the soap-bubble liquid is here revealed:

> 16 parts of very soft water
> 4 parts of "Yes" detergent, easily purchased in any Swedish supermarket
> 1 part glycerol
> A pinch of sugar

This will make bubbles big enough to encapsulate a typical Swede.

Other experiments include the world-renowned rat circus. This incomparable spectacle is held in the Periodic Table Theatre, in which each seat is labeled and arranged according to one of the elements. Try to get something around atomic number five, six or seven (boron through nitrogen) as these afford the best views.

The rat circus is highly informative. There, you can observe female rats as they exhibit their resourcefulness (no male rats, since they pee all over everything). You can also learn how to say "*min råtta äter min kåka,"* which means "my rat ate my cookie," which may one day prove useful. You never know. An inside tip—if you can get one of the Swedish children sitting near you to bet his afternoon snack on the rats, you'll garner some easy Wasa crispbread and cheese by betting on Ingrid. Very smart rat.

Another cool thing is upstairs, where there are scale models of fetuses in various stages of development, nestled into scale models of the parts of women that typically surround them. If, like me, you've never really been able to grasp how a baby could actually have been all scrunched up inside your wife (or inside of you, if you're a mother), and if that image has grown increasingly difficult to understand as the baby in question grows up and starts climbing trees and stuff, then these models are very useful. You can take the baby out, unfold it, then fold it up again and put it back in and see how it works (which is unadvisable otherwise).

Lastly, who could possibly skip the device into which one can stick one's head and scream as loudly as possible? Screaming as loudly as you can is a releasing activity that is generally frowned upon in other circumstances, particularly if you spend as much time in hotels as I do. Definitely worth a trip to Södertälje.

Tom Tit's Experiment is named after a fictional character, the alter ego of a French scientist who wrote books and articles about science for children some 100 years ago. It seems that these were very popular in Sweden, and they tickled the imagination of Klas Fresk, who was a teacher and who dreamt of creating an experiment center for schoolchildren. In 1987, he finally convinced some people with money to fund the conversion of a factory that had previously made machines to separate milk from cream, and hence Tom Tit's Experiment was born.

It must be confessed that it's probably not worth going all the way to Sweden just to visit Tom Tit's Experiment. However, it is certainly worth going to Sweden to visit Stockholm, and if your children get too bored visiting the wonders of the city (make sure to see Alfred Nobel's house), a day trip down to Södertälje is just the thing for them.

Otherwise, they may never know how to say "*min råtta äter min kåka.*"

A mind is a terrible thing to waste.

THE BEST FALAFEL
IN THE WORLD:
BEIRUT, LEBANON

Given the strife that has befallen Beirut since I wrote this dispatch, I have checked up with my friend there to find out what's happened with Sayoun's. The falafel stand has stood firm despite all the turmoil, but he informs me that the two brothers who ran it had a falling out, and one of them has actually opened a competing falafel stand right next door, likewise called Sayoun's. So now there are two Sayoun's falafel stands selling the same falafel, with the same recipe and the same name. I wonder how people choose?

There are always people buying falafel at Sayoun's. This means that the entire shop—all 10 square meters of it—is constantly full of customers, night and day. Some of them eat it there, leaning against the wall, popping the skinny green hot peppers that are provided in stainless steel bowls while they munch their falafel sandwiches. Others buy bags of the sandwiches, or just the falafel itself, and take them out to their cars, in which there is inevitably someone else waiting, then drive away and eat them in their homes. They come in sleek black Mercedes and they come in rickety old cars of indeterminate make, but no matter who they are, they come to Sayoun's to get their falafel.

In case you've never been east of Cleveland, falafel is a vegetarian dish, looking like a brown meatball, but far less dense. In reality, it's made from a mixture of ground chickpeas and/or fava beans, shaped into a ball (actually, it's kind of a flattened sphere, which would make it an oblate, so I'm told), and deep fried. That may not sound appetizing, but believe me, you wouldn't want to hear how Cheetos are made either. Falafel is a staple food in all of the eastern Mediterranean and beyond, and it has started to make inroads in other countries as well.

I have been a fan of falafel ever since I discovered Mamoun's, on Thomson Street in the West Village, back in the early '80s. There was a time when I lived solely on a diet of blues, alcohol and Mamoun's falafel. Falafel is well-known in France, since they used to try to run Lebanon (with about the same success as everyone else who has since tried), and my falafel education was thus further advanced after moving to France 20 years ago. However, once I started traveling in the Middle East, I discovered that I had been eating ersatz falafel all along. So, when I found myself recently in Beirut and a Lebanese friend suggested that we go to the best falafel shop in the world, I jumped at the chance.

Sayoun's is on Damascus Road, just up from Martyr's Square. If it weren't for the crowd of hungry people hanging around outside, it could be easily missed. You have to look for the hungry people, the idling cars, and a blue sign that says "M. Sayoun" in both English and Arabic. This stands for "Mustapha Sayoun," who opened the shop in 1935. It is currently run by his sons.

If you were to take a giant magnifying glass and focus it on Beirut, you would do worse than to focus it on Sayoun's falafel shop. In it you'll find people of every age, class and religion, all there to buy falafel. It's not that there's a great variety of falafel. In fact, you have very little choice at all. You can choose whether or not you want hot sauce, but that's about as far as it goes. One way or another, you'll end up with a sandwich of falafel, with tomatoes, sliced radish, mint and parsley. The sandwich will be wrapped in a thin piece of paper and presented to you in haste, as the sandwich maker goes on to the next one. If you're thirsty as well, you can choose between water and a narrow variety of sodas.

The best way to eat a Sayoun's falafel sandwich is to stand around in the shop, popping an occasional hot pepper while you eat. When you take a pepper, you'll have to reach around someone else who is also eating a falafel sandwich, but this is not rude. You'll probably also have to put down your soda on the little metal ledge, hoping no one bumps into it while you're getting your pepper. No one will. You will then need to grasp frantically for the soda again after eating the pepper because it's considerably hotter than you thought it would be, but that shouldn't stop you from taking another after you regain feeling in your tongue.

During all this, you can check out the little blue tiles in the wall and the certificate from the health inspector, but this is nowhere near as interesting as watching them make the falafel. One man comes from the back of the store (an area that appears to have the floor space of a phone booth) with a big bowl full of batter. Another man takes a special little scoop thing and begins using it to make balls of batter, which he plops rapidly into a large vat of hot oil. After only a few seconds, he fishes them out and places them on the rim, where they drain. Once they're ready, they go into a stainless steel tray and are quickly snatched up by the sandwich maker proper, who has already prepared an array of pitas, onto which another man has sliced tomatoes and yet another has dealt parsley and mint leaves like a vegetable croupier. The sandwich maker distributes the balls of falafel while the boss himself hovers over the nascent sandwiches, slicing radish against his thumb in a feat of manual dexterity I never plan on trying myself. The sandwich maker adds the sauce and wraps up each sandwich, which he then places into a tangle of eagerly waiting hands before starting the whole process over again with a new batch.

Sayoun's has been in the same place ever since its opening. I asked the proprietor (through my friend, who translated) if the store had stayed open all that time. He smiled and shook his head, then pointed to the building across the street. The structure across the street had been an office building, but now it is a shell. Its exterior walls are gone; they now make up the pile of rubble restrained behind a fence that fronts the sidewalk. "We closed during the war," he said. "It would have been impossible to stay open."

Damascus Road was on the green line, the frontier between Beirut's warring factions from 1975 to 1990, while Lebanon was torn apart by a vicious civil war with few rules and little hope. Before the war, Beirut had been known as "the pearl of the Middle East"—a cosmopolitan city of striking beauty. In those 15 years, though, the city was destroyed, almost entirely razed.

Before 1975, Beirut was a hub for commerce and travel in the Middle East. People came from around the world to enjoy Lebanon's surprisingly diverse countryside, its 5,000 years of history, and the stunning beauty of its capital. The war changed all of that. But today, more than a decade after peace finally came, the city has been rebuilt, with only the occasional blown-out hulk of a building to mark those spots that haven't yet been renovated. Beirut has almost regained the glory of its past, and is just as cosmopolitan as before. In fact, in many respects it is a very European city. (Please note that the preceding sentence is necessary so that this column will sneak its way past the editor, since I am supposed to be writing about Europe, and Beirut is not technically in Europe. Per se.)

After your falafel, I suggest going off to the Petit Café in the Raouché neighborhood. There you can have tea and a shisha—a water pipe in which you smoke flavored tobacco while men with funny trousers mess with your coals. Shisha smoking is a particular vice of mine that may warrant a column of its own one day, but that either way should not be missed while in the Middle East. The Petit Café affords a magnificent view of the Pigeon Rocks, a set of things that are either very small islands or very large rocks, depending on your point of view, standing just offshore in a cliff-lined cove. The rocks have natural arches, through which the Mediterranean comes and goes while birds circle overhead. If it's nice out, you can go on the café's terrace, which is built into the top of one of the cliffs, and admire the rocks and the birds and the sea while you make bubbly sounds with your shisha.

Go to Beirut. There you can see evidence that buildings, cities, countries, lives and even falafel shops can be rebuilt. That is a good thing to know.

USEFUL PHRASES

This was probably the most popular of the McSweeney's columns, at least as measured by the fan mail and the reactions in the blogosphere. Since having written it, I've added greatly to my repertoire of useful phrases, which now include (with varying degrees of proficiency):

> *"My father has ten toes" in Chinese*
> *"Barking dogs never bite, but you can't be sure about meowing cats" in Turkish*
> *"My horse may be ill" in Navajo*
> *"Watermelons don't bounce" in Korean*
> *And the phrase about not having cows but rather an octopus, in Arabic, mentioned in another column.*

I thought I would take a pause from interesting places and share some interesting phrases instead.

Long ago, I determined that there are three broad categories of linguistic fluency. The first is the perfectly comfortable level, ranging from your native language to any language in which you can converse with ease, although at the lower end of this scale you probably have a headache at the end of the day. The second category consists of those languages in which you can generally make yourself understood with the aid of sweeping gestures and meaningful grimaces. The third category is comprised of languages that are a complete mystery to you.

I'm fortunate to have three languages in the first category and one or two more in the second. This means, though, that every other language is in the third category. I have a theory about these. For me, these languages are either/or affairs. If you travel to a country in which the principal language is a category III language then either you work on it enough to get it to category II, or you learn only how to say "please," "thank you," "excuse me," and one phrase that is perfectly nonsensical.

The principal reason for the nonsensical phrase is that it's a sure conversation opener. No one will imagine that the only thing you know how to say in their language is "my hovercraft is full of eels" (to borrow someone else's nonsensical phrase) and therefore an immediate cultural exchange will ensue. Really, this works.

I thought I would give you a number of these, in case you plan on traveling to countries with category III languages. I've given them to you in the languages in which I use them, but you can use the same nonsensical phrase in a variety of languages, and I confess that I have learned the first phrase I cite in four or five different languages, ranging from the original Swedish to Cantonese. I'll also point out that for the most part, I'm not trying to spell these words properly. I'm using approximate spellings, as if they were spelled the way one would expect (or at least the way I would expect), and not with silly squiggles and such. I'm doing this because the last time I tried to write something in Swedish in a column (about Ingrid the intelligent rat), I was informed via email that I had not gotten it right at all, so I'm not even going to attempt it anymore.

Enough of the preliminaries, let's get to the useful phrases.

"My hedgehog isn't stupid." In Swedish: "*Min igelkot e inte dum.*"

This was my first nonsensical category III phrase. I used to hang around with a Swede, who decided to teach me some of the language, which was a thoroughly frustrating exercise for us both. Eventually he gave up and suggested, "Learn to say *min igelkot e inte dum* and no one will expect it's the only thing you can say." I therefore learned this and we tested it out on a couple of friends of his who came from Gothenburg to visit. When I met them, I rose, shook their hands, explained about my hedgehog and smiled. They looked very surprised and started speaking rapid Swedish to me. I protested, explaining that this was all I knew, which they refused to believe, and a long conversation ensued (in English), which quickly veered to more interesting topics. Hence was born my theory about nonsensical phrases.

This phrase has served me well and long. I even employed it when giving a speech to 350 Swedes, with much the same effect (at a ski resort in the middle of Sweden, but that's a story for another column). The most convincing example, however, did not occur in Sweden at all, but in Massachusetts of all places. I was in a bar one evening with a couple of Americans and a very unusual Argentine who had a French name and lived in Mexico. He was part pharmaceutical executive, part fashion photographer and part party organizer, and he had been telling us a highly embarrassing story about an incident involving 50 cardiologists, an airport security system and a nipple ring (I won't get into the details, but it ended with his assertion that it would have been much worse had he been wearing his *other* body jewelry). Anyway, at that point, a young man entered the bar accompanied by two young ladies. They had apparently stepped in out of a commercial for the World Wrestling Federation, because he was certainly built like a member of that esteemed organization and was glowering as well. For all I know, he was indeed a wrestler—"Nick the Neanderthal" or something. He looked around the bar and disappointment registered on his prominent brow ridges, probably because there weren't enough people around to admire his upper arms and the women clinging to them. The three of them sat near us and ordered something (champagne for the girls, warm blood for him). We ignored them and continued our revelry.

Before long, the wrestler muttered something, ostensibly for the benefit of his companions, calling into question the masculinity, or at least the heterosexuality, of our Argentine friend, who luckily didn't understand it (he was just crazy enough to challenge this guy to a duel or something). I, therefore, hastily took the floor in our little group and began expounding on my theory about category III languages and nonsensical statements (see above). In the course of explaining this, I taught them all how to say "*min igelkot e inte dum.*" Immediately, the two girls sitting with fireplug-man squealed, leaned over, and said, "*Din igelkot e inte dum!?*" Then started speaking in rapid Swedish. I stopped them, explaining that this was all I could say, they didn't believe me . . . etc. The normal routine.

They left their companion and came to join us, asking all the while about how I had learned to say this, and who we were, and what we planned on doing later that evening. Needless to say, this annoyed the inert mass of muscle with whom they had entered the bar, but he was too confused to do anything about it except grunt "let's go" to them. They replied with what I assume was a Swedish insult, and he left, after making a rude gesture at us all.

"There is a penguin in my closet." In German: "*Da ist ein Pinguin auf meinem Schrank.*"

German is, in fact, more of a category II language for me, but it's pretty low on the scale, and besides, this is a great phrase to use in German. I particularly recommend it for hotels, if you'd like to get to know the staff. This will also provide you with an introduction to the word "*bitte,*" which will inevitably be the response of any German to this phrase. *Bitte* is a great word. It can mean many things, depending on the intonation. It can mean "please" or "thank you" or "are you out of your mind?" Needless to say, it's in the latter sense that it's generally employed when responding to the phrase, "There is a penguin in my closet." Of course, you don't want to be nasty, so you need to explain rapidly to the hotel staff that there is not, in fact, a penguin in your closet, and that you were just employing your single phrase of German. If you do not explain this quickly, then, being German, they will dutifully send someone to remove the penguin from your closet, and that would not be a very nice thing to do to the cleaning staff.

"I would like a large chessboard." In Spanish: "*Quiero un gran tablero de ajedres.*"

This actually began as a useful phrase, since I really did want to buy a large chessboard (in Toledo, if I remember correctly, which is a beautiful city that you should definitely visit). I wandered around asking for large chessboards, and did indeed end up buying one (upon which I regularly play). However, I have since employed it as a nonsensical category III phrase.

This has come in handy in a number of instances. One comes to mind from an evening in Barcelona (which reminds me that I'll have to write about Barcelona soon. How I love Barcelona!). I was having dinner on the terrace of one of the delightful restaurants near the navy museum, on the harbor. I was alone, which is unfortunate in a city like Barcelona. Anyway, the waiter was a very pleasant gentleman who spoke to me in Catalonian, and then in Spanish. I speak neither, and I explained this to him in slow Italian, but then told him that I wanted a large chessboard in Spanish. He was perplexed; he shook his head and pointed at the menu, apparently reiterating that this was a restaurant and that chessboards were not food. I tried again to explain, in Italian, that this was all I could say. He eventually understood and was intrigued.

It was a slow night in the restaurant, and the waiter, who it turns out was an avid chess player, sat down after a while and we engaged in a spirited conversation about chess (specifically about the king's gambit opening), in a mix of Catalonian, Spanish and Italian. A wonderful evening.

"Is that a kind of frog?" In Japanese: "*Koreiwa kairu no ishu des ka?*"

The whole "*koreiwa* (thing) *no ishu des ka?*" construction can be very useful. For instance, if you replace *kairu*, meaning frog, with *sakana*, meaning fish, then you can pretty much know what can and can't be eaten in Japan, which is handy, since you can't even make the usual supposition that things must first be dead, let alone cooked, before you eat them. If it's a kind of fish, though, then you can eat it, even if it's trying to swim or crawl away. However, the frog phrase will get you more conversational mileage, at least partially because the answer is rarely, "Yes, that is a kind of frog" (*"Hai, korewai kairu no ishu des"*).

This particular phrase has actually proved most useful to me in Paris. I once saw a young Japanese man standing on a street corner on the boulevard Sevastopol, studying a tourist map. He had a backpack on, and sewn onto the backpack was a cartoon character that seemed to be a kind of frog. With no introduction I said, *"Sumimasen* (excuse me), *koreiwa kairu no ishu des ka?"* This was one of the few times that I have actually been able to stun a Japanese person. *"Hai!* (yes)," he replied. I nodded significantly and walked away.

It should also be added that the way one comes out with the words is important in Japanese. If you are a man, you should spit the syllables out as though you were expelling vile-tasting marbles from your mouth. If you are a woman, you should murmur them demurely, while behind them you suppress something between a giggle and a plea. I confess that I would hate to have to be a woman in Japan.

"I love you, I want to spend my life with you." In French: *"Je t'aime, je veux passer ma vie avec toi."*

French is a category I language for me, and this is hardly a nonsensical phrase, but I thought I should include this one all the same, not for its shock or conversational value, but rather because it's possible that if you live abroad for a while you may end up needing it. Of course, by that time, I assume French (or whatever the language of your host country might be) would be category I for you as well, but you should be warned about this one either way. I suggest you think twice before saying it—use the utmost discretion, because it can have a profound effect on your life. However, if used in the right circumstances, and especially with the right person, then I can tell you from personal experience that this phrase is capable of bringing you unspeakable joy.

LJUBLJANA CASTLE:
LJUBLJANA, SLOVENIA

The reaction to this column was rather surprising for me, since a number of Slovenes sent me emails about it. The Internet is weird: you sit alone behind your computer and send dispatches off to California, but you never really know how many people read the things (McSweeney's doesn't follow readership details on the individual features). While the reaction from Swedes to the column about Tom Tit's Experiment proved to me that there were people outside the States reading the columns, the fact that there were actual Slovenes reading them was a bit of a jolt. I mean, there are only about two million people in the entire country, after all.

From time to time, I've fantasized about coming from an obscure country. Perhaps this is because I come from the least obscure country in the world, but I've always thought that it would be cool to come from someplace that most people haven't heard of, and have as a native tongue a language that no one else speaks.

Slovenia is such a place. I know that among the readers of this piece will be Slovenes and people of Slovenian descent who will take umbrage at my calling their homeland "obscure," but rest assured that this is not a slur on Slovenia, but on the geographic ignorance of the rest of the world. And let's face it, many people, particularly those who don't live on its borders, simply don't know where Slovenia is, or even that it exists. This may change in a few months, as Slovenia enters the European Union, but its obscurity is pretty well established (which is probably a paradox).

As further proof—look at the people on Slovenian banknotes. Most countries put their most famous historical figures on their banknotes (except for Great Britain, which uses the same lady over and over). Slovenia does the same, and hence its banknotes are graced by such people as Janez Vajkard Valvasor, Primoz Trubar and Joze Plecnik (all missing some squiggles in their letters, but I do not have a Slovenian keyboard). What? You've never heard of these individuals? You're probably not alone.

Slovenia does have an excuse. Up until recently, it hadn't existed as an independent country since . . . well forever, really. It had been part of Yugoslavia until 1991, and before that, part of the Austro-Hungarian empire. Always, though, Slovenia had its own character, people and language. And it has a capital city with a really cool name . . . Ljubljana, which is pronounced just like it's spelled (if you think of the *j*'s as being kind of like *y*'s but not really).

Ljubljana is a pleasant little city, as capital cities go, and it is dominated by a castle. I love castles. Not your Renaissance fancy-house-type castles, like those along the Loire, but your hulking "just try to invade" castles, with turrets and moats and slits through which you can shoot crossbows. It's just a thing I have. I have spent many happy hours crawling around on the ruins of fortifications throughout Europe and Asia, imagining armies of clashing steel, the despair of the siege, the "thunk" of the stones thrown by the siege engines. (A brief aside: at Urquhart Castle, in Scotland, they have a working trebuchet, in case you're interested.)

There aren't all that many cities around that have those kinds of castles in their center. Most of them were destroyed long ago to make the city more pleasant and less menacing, and because their military significance was, for the most part, eliminated by the perfection of artillery. Ljubljana, though, kept its castle, on a hill dominating the city. Even the city flag features the castle, plus a big green dragon. Dragons are cool, too.

So, when I was recently back in Ljubljana for the first time in 10 years, I decided to go visit the castle, which I had never done before.

To get to the castle, you can either drive, if you have a car, or walk. If walking, you need to cross the triple bridge (more on that later), head left, then go up a small street whose name I failed to note, but you can't miss it. Actually you can, but just ensure that the street you take is a tiny thing with a record store selling only reggae CDs. Shortly after the Bob Marley poster, the street peters out and is replaced by a footpath that climbs up the hill.

At the top squats the castle. From the outside, it's all browns and whites, with lots of holes through which you can fire crossbows and cannons at any Ottoman armies that happen to be about. It's not extremely large, and you can walk around the whole thing, admiring it and the commanding view of the city, except that it might be snowing on you (depending on the season). Since it was snowing on me, I went in the courtyard rather quickly.

The castle is currently being renovated, but at the level of the courtyard, most of the renovation is done, and there are many of those natty stainless steel wire hand things to keep you from falling into holes and walking on the 400-year-old vine and such. I actually like those things—they're far less ostentatious than metal rods or other similar tourist-control mechanisms. Even the main door to the castle has been seconded by a door-like arrangement of the metal wires and posts, which gives a very nice, airy feel to the old fortification. In fact, the whole renovation process seems to have gone very well. The buildings and towers of the castle are well restored, painted a pleasant white and the woodwork, though simple, has been redone. The courtyard itself has been repaved where one would expect it to be paved, and little steps help you to get around.

There are also some concrete stairs that lead down. Although I expected nothing more than a washroom, I headed down them as well, because I can't resist exploring holes and passages in old castles, and because it was still snowing on me.

Underneath the courtyard I found an Escheresque medley of steel pillars, concrete slabs and old rock, with three or four stairways, some of which seemed to lead nowhere. It took me some time to figure out what was going on, and I eventually surmised that the renovation work wasn't quite finished and that all this would probably be replaced with walls and doors and architecture. That's kind of a shame, because if you just dress the mess up a little then it could serve as a kind of polar opposite to a Zen rock garden—a place to come and screw up your head.

While I was admiring it all, a gray cat trotted along and looked at me. I didn't say anything to the cat because I was taking notes, but the cat kept on checking me out, so I ended up checking it out as well. I must have passed some kind of test, because it came and started rubbing itself against me and meowing a little. It looked like a pretty well-fed cat, and I explained that I had no food, but it stayed there all the same while I looked around. Maybe it just knows that I like cats. Cats can sense these things. I assume the cat lives there, and since no people do anymore, it's probably the closest thing to a king the castle has.

A woman came down one of the confusing staircases and stood there looking appropriately bewildered. I suppose she hadn't been expecting to find The Labyrinth of the Steel Posts, and she tried retreating up another staircase, but that one went nowhere. The cat and I both watched her until she found the right way out. I followed her, saying goodbye to King Cat, and made my way across the courtyard to the castle tower, where one can enjoy a quaint 3-D audiovisual thing that shows the history of Ljubljana via a presentation that kind of looks like a video game. After the show, you can climb up some wonderful wrought-iron spiral stairs, each step of which has the image of a dragon worked into it, to the top of the tower, where you get a view of Ljubljana all spread out below. You can admire the red tile roofs of the buildings. It's amazing how distinct different cities are when you observe their roofs. Ljubljana has nice roofs.

Ljubljana is bisected by the Ljubljanica river. The side of the river with the castle is the smaller side, although it boasts some very nice buildings and statues, and the wonderful marketplace, designed by the architect Joze Plecnik (see the list of famous Slovenes above). The marketplace is very lively, a great place to visit. In fact, you should always check out the marketplaces of European cities. It is particularly appealing from the other side of the river, though, since it's riverfront consists of a beautiful arched walkway, all in white. You can hang out on the Petkovškovo Nabrezje and admire the view of the arcades, as well as the castle looming high above them. There are a couple of bars here where you may be able to find a window with a view to amuse you while you sample the local beers—which are well worth sampling.

To cross the river, you can take the triple bridge—a hallmark of Ljubljana because it's not just one bridge, but three. In all other respects, and even in that one, it is entirely unremarkable. You can also take the Dragon Bridge, which is just as unremarkable, but which has four scary dragons guarding it. The dragons are very scary.

Incidentally, I finally learned what it is that Ljubljana has about dragons. It turns out that legend says Ljubljana was founded by Jason (formerly of the Argonauts, before his solo career as Prince of Corinth). According to legend, Jason fled from Colchis and the pursuing King Aeetes by sailing up the Danube and down the Ljubljanica, founding Ljubljana on the way (assumedly during a rest stop). There, Jason battled a great monster, which is portrayed as the Ljubljana dragon.

So I guess that means there are a greater number of famous Slovenes than I had originally counted—they include Jason, Medea, and Hercules, for that matter, all of whom were on the *Argo*. I can't help but imagine they would be pleased if they were to visit today the city they founded then.

THE ANTIQUE CAROUSEL
OF THE PICCI FAMILY:
FLORENCE, ITALY

On the Piazza della Republica, in Florence, is a carousel with twenty horses and two gilded "king's carriages." The carousel is made of wood and is gaily painted in reds and blues. It also boasts two flowerpots with fresh flowers in them. This is the antique carousel of the Picci family (as is stated in a panel along the top), and it goes around and around every day from November through May, from about 10:00 in the morning to about 8:00 at night.

I assume I don't need to convince you to go to Florence. I also assume that before you go, you'll learn about all of the places you must see—the Uffizi and Pitti museums, the Duomo cathedral, the Baptistery . . . and so on. But if you have the good fortune of being in Florence outside of the tourist season, you should also visit the antique carousel of the Picci family.

The carousel is run by Carlo Picci, who represents the fourth generation of the family to run a carousel (the fifth generation is also doing so, and the sixth is still at the stage of riding carousels more than running them, but they seem to exhibit a healthy interest). The carousel in the Piazza della Republica dates from the beginning of the twentieth century, but has been lovingly restored.

The carousel is not too big, and at 20 horses it doesn't have much capacity, but that's all right with Carlo Picci. "This way," he says, "there's enough space between the horses that the mamas can stand next to the little ones while they ride. Otherwise they might be afraid." I observed a small girl who was obviously reassured by her mama's presence, and a small boy who clearly didn't want his papa standing next to him as he rode, then rode again, then capped it all off with a leisurely trip in one of the king's carriages, under a gilded crown with red and green gems in it. "A regular," Signor Picci informed me.

Along with the panel stating the carousel's ownership and antiquity, the top of the ride has paintings of different Italian cities. I recognized some: Pisa, Rome, Bologna, Parma, Venice, and some other places I haven't been but would now like to visit. There was no music, though, when I first visited. "It's a little late," said Signor Picci, "and we don't want to disturb the people around the piazza. But go, take a ride. Go ahead!"

The last time I had been on a carousel I too had been reassuring a young child, but that was several years ago. I chose a black horse and climbed up. The piazza went spinning about slowly, and as I came around, Signor Picci smiled and waved to me, as did his wife in the little ticket booth. I waved back. Signor Picci was right—it would have been difficult to describe the carousel properly without riding it. The horse went up and down and gently swayed forwards and backwards while the lights played over the paintings of Roman gods on the inside column. The cherubs painted on the ceiling flirted with each other. Then the music came on. "I put on the music for you!" yelled Signor Picci from the side, waving again. Accordion versions of Neapolitan ballads—sadly, recorded, but eminently appropriate.

My ride was better than a shot of Botox for injecting a little youth back into me. So much so that I decided I wanted some ice cream. I asked my ersatz grandfather where the best gelati in Florence was to be found, and he directed me to Vivoli at Santa Croce.

I like the Piazza Santa Croce, which is a large open space lined with typical Florentine buildings. Many of these are leather shops, most of which sell goods that are made next door to them. Vivoli itself is a small gelateria on a tiny street about 30 pleasant meters in from the piazza itself (I forgot to mark the name of the street, but just ask a local, they all know Vivoli). I must confess though that its gelati are a bit too creamy for my taste. I prefer the gelati on Via Calzaiuoli, nearer to the Piazza della Republica, and therefore to the Piazza del Duomo. Furthermore, Via Calzaiuoli is an interesting street, running from the Duomo down to the Ponte Vecchio, lined with expensive shops and boasting both an unfortunate Disney store and an innocuous private investigator's office. I assume that the PI probably spends his time in mundane jobs, tracking unfaithful spouses and the like, but I amuse myself by imagining him as a kind of Italian Sam Spade, uncovering all sorts of Machiavellian plots in the city of the Medici.

One other place I'll definitely suggest, and that otherwise may go unvisited in your more typical tours is the central market, in the Piazza del Mercato Centrale. The market is a large stone structure, with soaring iron pillars inside. The top floor is devoted to fruits and vegetables and the ground floor to meats, cheeses and . . . well, everything else. In the market you can find enormous sheets of raw tripe—a Florentine specialty—as well as buckets of pig ears and even pig faces. The market in Florence is the only place I have ever seen a tray full of pig faces (marked "pig faces" in Italian). An interesting sight. On a more practical note, this is the best place in the city to get good olive oil. There are almost as many types of olive oil in Italy as there are types of wine, and Italians get just as finicky about them. Here, you can taste the different oils before you make your selection and they are not absurdly expensive.

One of the few drawbacks of Florence is that it seems to be overrun with American students who roam the streets in large, loud groups, jostling and joking with each other and pushing themselves into the bushes (OK, there are no bushes, but if there were, they'd be pushing themselves into them). One wonders why they are living in Florence, since they apparently associate with each other, not with the Italians. Perhaps they like being among the pretty buildings? Even in restaurants they generally don't seem capable of ordering in Italian.

Only once have I heard Italian being spoken with an American accent by a young person, and this was in the marketplace (he wasn't buying pig faces, though, just cheese). Anxious to have my distasteful impressions dispelled, I approached the young man with the airtight excuse of being a writer ("Excuse me, can I ask you a few questions?—I'm a writer," which is a disturbingly easy way to insinuate yourself into someone's day). The young man told me that he was a student of economics who was spending a few months in Florence to learn Italian. And because it's Florence, after all. Upon expressing my admiration of his having learned passable Italian in such a short period, and asking if this was the norm, he admitted that it was rare. He had taken a small apartment in the middle of town, and tried to mingle only with Italians, but then he said that he liked languages, spoke Russian at home and could also speak Spanish. Many American kids don't even bother to take Italian classes, he said, since you can get by in Florence speaking English.

Alas. If any among you are American students considering some time abroad, I'd like to give you some unasked-for advice: Definitely go, live somewhere else for at least a year, but follow this young man's example. Shun other Americans, try to blend in, find a small shabby apartment in the middle of town, buy second-hand clothes and dress like local students, learn the damn language . . . keep in mind that the best way to accomplish all of this is to have a passionate love affair with someone from your host city. While you're at it, don't fall in love with another student, instead find a person with a dramatically different lifestyle and background to enhance your spirit-bending adventure, and make sure this person doesn't speak a word of English. Learn your new language in terms whispered over a pillow and you'll learn things you never would have expected. For example, you might consider falling in love with a local ballerina. Be careful, though. If you do undertake all of this then your life might turn out far different from what you had originally imagined and you may end up 20 years later reminiscing about it, wondering how a kid from Queens managed to deserve all this while you write curmudgeonly advice in a travel column for a nonexistent person named McSweeney.

THE BASEL RATHAUS:
BASEL, SWITZERLAND

Switzerland is a small country. According to the CIA World Factbook (a surprisingly useful source of country information, available on the Net), Switzerland is slightly less than twice the size of New Jersey. One can't help but wonder how this particular unit of measurement came about. Americans often measure land in state equivalents, and the "Rhode Island" is almost a standardized unit, but why use the "New Jersey"? Why not simply say that Switzerland is 28% bigger than Maryland? Or 65% as large as West Virginia? Then again, who knows how the CIA reasons?

But I digress already.

For its small area (roughly half the size of South Carolina), Switzerland is amazingly diverse. The country has four distinct official languages: German, French, Italian and Romansh, and many citizens speak only one of them . . . and all this in a country that's only 1/3 the size of Mississippi. Of greater interest, though, is the fact that every Swiss city is different, with an entirely different architecture, history and overall feel to it. There's the serene majesty of Geneva, the calm beauty of Lugano, the soothing air of Lausanne, and the downright boring streets of Montreux. Let's face it, as different as they are, most Swiss cities are pretty dull. True, Zurich and Berne have a bit of life to them, but on the whole, it's not a swinging country, except during jazz festivals, of course. That's not to say these cities shouldn't be visited. After all, boring places have their stories to tell too, and when all is said and done, a place is as exciting as you make it. It's simply a question of how hard you have to work at it. You have to make a conscious effort to be placid in cities like Amsterdam, Rome, or New York, whereas if you want to have your heart race in most Swiss cities then you'd best take along some artificial stimulants.

Basel is no different: boring but interesting. It's situated on the Rhine, and the city borders on both France and Germany. The residents tend to speak Schwiezerdeutsch, the difficult Swiss version of German. They tend *not* to speak French or Italian. Of course, this may be a lie. They may all speak these languages perfectly but are simply too amused listening to me try to speak to them in German. The Swiss get their kicks as best they can.

The old center of Basel is very pleasant. It's crisscrossed with tramways, for one thing. I like tramways. It also features a great market square, the Marktplatz, that has a nice little open-air market in it on most days. The square is dominated by the Rathaus, which is one of the reddest monumental buildings you're likely to come across. Delhi's Red Fort isn't as red as this building. The Moulin Rouge isn't as red as this place. It's the reddest.

The building houses the government of the canton of Basel. (Switzerland is divided into cantons. Who knows, maybe Swiss intelligence services measure areas in terms of multiples of cantons: "We have learned that their state of New Hampshire is as big as 30 Unterwaldens.") The cantonal government meets there regularly, and you can actually observe their debates! I discovered this quite by accident, while I poked around in the red courtyard of the Rathaus looking at the paintings and statues and the little unhappy faces carved into the window frames. At the end of the courtyard is a place to park your bicycle, and on the right, near a statue of a strikingly ugly man in Renaissance armor, is a door marked "Tribune." If you go through this door and climb a bunch of stairs then you'll come to a small gallery of what looks like church pews, overlooking the assembly room.

It's a nice room. The delegates (or whatever one calls people elected to a Swiss cantonal assembly) sit in a half circle arrangement facing a central podium, at which sit other people, who I assume have some even more significant function. All that is typical, as governmental assemblies go, but the room itself is worth a look and even the delegates themselves are a bit of a hoot.

Up in the gallery, you're treated to a good view of the ceiling, which is covered with images of plants and the people who make them grow. On the walls of the gallery are images of knights and ladies and, of course, a crossbowman or two (in case you didn't know, William Tell didn't shoot the apple off his son's head with a bow, but with a crossbow, and the weapon has always been dear to the Swiss). The main room boasts two rather modern paintings of Renaissance scenes. I couldn't help but think that the characters in the paintings looked very much like bankers wearing costumes, but perhaps I just wasn't in the right mood.

From up in the gallery, you can watch delegates read the newspaper while some other delegate drones on about something in Schwiezerdeutsch. While I was there, an animated man in a gray suit and a beard was going on about life sciences while the others read a variety of journals. He was eventually replaced by a less animated man with a gray suit and a shorter beard who seemed to be discussing the same topic, although whether he agreed or disagreed with the first man was beyond my powers of comprehension. Eventually, he was replaced by a man with no beard at all and an unusual blue suit with thin red crosshatching. The assembly seemed to be more abuzz while this last man spoke, but it may just be that they were tittering about his clothes.

Scattered around the assembly room are images of a strange creature. It looks like a cross between a chicken and a dragon. I came upon the same figure, or one of its evil cousins, spitting water into any number of fountains. Funnily enough, I had never noticed these things before, although I am often in Basel. I figured the best place to clear up the mystery was at the history museum.

The history museum of Basel is a great place. For one thing, it's in a big old converted church. For another, it has a collection of armor and weapons, which always interests me. Lots of pikes and crossbows, of course. It also has a collection of old globes, from as early as the fifteenth century. I love old globes. They're really wrong. But the history museum's greatest attraction is the "Dance of Death," a series of 19 fragments from a larger fifteenth century work. Each fragment corresponds to a dialogue between death and some individual, ranging from popes to pagans. For the most part, death is saying "it's time to go" and the individual is complaining about it.

I also managed to find out in the museum what the chicken-dragon thing is. It's a basilisk. Basel has long been associated with the mythical creature, which apparently is very different from J.K. Rowling's version. No one seems to know why the city was first linked to the beast; it may just be because the names are similar. It does go back a long time, though. In fact, in 1474, a rooster was publicly executed in the Münsterplatz because it was purported to have laid a basilisk egg. (Yes, basilisks are born of eggs laid by roosters. You learn something new every day.) I think it was hanged, which seems a very complicated way to kill a rooster, but the Swiss are sticklers for rules, and if you lay a basilisk egg, you get hanged.

No basilisks haunt Basel today. It's a very calm place. The worst you have to fear is long-winded Swiss politicians, but brave them and check out the cantonal assembly in the Rathaus. It's true they govern an area that's only 1/6 the size of Rhode Island, but that's still 12% bigger than Liechtenstein.

IN SEARCH OF FRANK ZAPPA: VILNIUS, LITHUANIA

In May 2008, a group of Lithuanian artists decided to make a copy of Zappa's statue and present it to the city of Baltimore (Zappa's hometown). Vilnius's mayor, Juozas Imbrasas, said of the gesture: "I hope that replication of the original statue of Frank Zappa in Vilnius and bringing it to Baltimore will perpetuate the memory of one of the greatest artists of the century." I suppose that means I'll now have to visit Baltimore as well.

In 1995, a group of fans in Vilnius set up a statue of Frank Zappa near the center of town. It was sculpted by Konstantinas Bogdanas, and it is the only public statue of Frank Zappa in the world. Previously, Bogdanas had spent a great many years casting busts of Lenin, who was nowhere near as good a guitarist as Zappa. It should be pointed out that Frank Zappa never had anything to do with Vilnius, never set foot in Lithuania, and had not a smidgen of Lithuanian heritage. Needless to say, as I was to be in Vilnius, it was evident that I must find that statue and pay homage to the great weird one.

I arrived in Lithuania exactly one week after the country officially joined the European Union, an event that was greeted with a mix of joy and a kind of vindication by most Lithuanians ("Yes, we are part of Western Europe. We've *always* been part of Western Europe and are no farther east than Finland, which *everyone* says is part of Western Europe"). Due to other commitments, it was a couple of days before I could set out on my Zappa quest, but when the time came I packed the necessary accoutrements (city map, sunglasses, pen and paper) and asked the hotel desk clerk where the statue was. She looked at me with her gray eyes (I have the impression that all Lithuanian women have gray eyes. The men may also have them, but I didn't really notice.) and sighed (I also have the impression that Lithuanians sigh a lot). She then took my map and indicated a spot just on the other side of the river.

"I think it's here," she said. Then she took the map again and indicated a different spot. "Or here. I know there's a statue there."

"Um, are you sure it's Zappa? American guitarist, big moustache?"

She said she was sure, but I wasn't so sure she was really sure. Anyway, what the hell. I set out across the river and walked up a pleasant, tree-lined street bordered by lots of trendy little shops. No Zappa. I decided to ask one of the gray-eyed ladies running a magazine kiosk. I began by asking her if she spoke English, or for that matter French, Italian or German, but she just sighed and shook her head. I asked about Zappa, but I believe she thought I was referring to yet another language (where would one speak Zappa?) and continued to shake her head.

This conversation was repeated many times. I ask a Lithuanian kiosk lady or taxi driver whether they speak some language I speak, the person sighs and shakes his or her head, then looks puzzled when I say "Frank Zappa?" while making a gesture near my upper lip that is supposed to indicate a bushy moustache. The problem is that many of these kind people so wanted to help me that they would take my map and indicate a place on it, although I'm quite sure they really had no idea what I was asking. It might be that the word "zappa" or something like it means "tree" or "grassy place" or "nondescript street corner" in Lithuanian, and these people thought

I was looking for the nearest one, because many of their directions led only to attractions such as these.

As such, I wandered around Vilnius, which when all is said and done is not such a bad fate. The core of the old city is very nice, with a faintly Germanic or perhaps Scandinavian feel to it—lots of neat stone buildings, quiet squares, pale beige and yellow façades. The city also seems replete with green spaces. These, though, are not the green spaces of London, with grass cut by fastidious English gardeners wielding scissors . . . no, these are nearly feral green spaces, with grass that is itching to be free, grass that wants to grow big and become fat with seed.

It's not that these little parks and such are sloppy, or anything so disagreeable as that. They seem like the parkland equivalent of a home owned by an interesting but not particularly organized family that might have a cat or two. No actual *dirt*, but not exactly a shine on the furniture and the odd sock on the back of a chair. One such park seemed to correspond more or less to a potential Zappa location indicated by a gray-eyed kiosk lady, and it did indeed contain a statue . . . of someone whose name might have been Petras Cirkej, if I read the rather unusual script correctly. Not a bad looking fellow, but most definitely not Frank Zappa.

However, near Petras I found someone who did speak a slight amount of English, which was refreshing. This young gentleman thought about it, then explained that Zappa was to be found in an area farther to the south, which he showed me on my map. I immediately struck out toward the area he had circled.

This brought me a little bit outside the city's charming center, into a neighborhood of drab Soviet-style apartment blocks, where slab-like brick buildings rise for a few stories out of concrete parking lots and expanses of dirt. I had vaguely heard that Zappa's statue was in a kind of self-proclaimed republic of weirdness within the city of Vilnius, with its own flag and schools, and I wondered if perhaps this apartment complex might not be it. Not that it looked all that counterculturish. I therefore wandered around the dirt paths looking for a little square that might house Zappa, but to no avail.

And then I heard a guitar riff, one that I thought I recognized as being from "Shut Up 'n Play Yer Guitar." Ah! This was undoubtedly coming from the boom box of a Zappa fan, probably sitting under the statue listening to old albums, just like all those sorry souls who desperately wished they had lived in the '60s and who linger at Jim Morrison's grave at Pére Lachaise in Paris. I slogged through the mud toward the sound, running into a dead end or two until I managed to get to the general area. By the time I got closer, it had stopped, and the statue was nowhere to be found. Who knows, maybe Zappa had been playing with my head from the great beyond, which is just the kind of thing you would expect his ghost to do if it could. Or perhaps it had just gotten late and I was tired and hungry and becoming disturbingly obsessive about the whole thing.

Given the latter possibility, I decided to eat and drink, so I headed back towards the town center to Zemaiciu Smukle, one of the few places that serves Lithuanian cuisine in Vilnius (as usual, I have left out myriad squiggles that my keyboard is incapable of reproducing). I had discovered the place a few days earlier, when a Lithuanian friend brought me there. When deciding on a restaurant he had asked, "What kind of food do you want to eat?"

"Lithuanian!"

"You're kidding, right?"

Despite his evident lack of enthusiasm for his native cuisine, we had gone to Zemaiciu Smukle, which I must say has excellent beer. One can also sample such delicacies as boiled pig ears, which is considered a pub snack in Lithuania, as well as "Zeppelins," which are so named because they are shaped like Zeppelins, although they are nowhere near as light. Zemaiciu Smukle is full of tourists, while the French restaurant next door is full of Lithuanians, which is kind of a hint, I suppose. The French place, though, does not have very cool little vaulted dining rooms spread throughout it, in which one sits at a heavy wooden table, nor does it have so much weaponry on the walls.

I've reached the conclusion there is a "weapons-on-walls" belt extending from the Rhine to the eastern edge of Europe. Restaurants east of the Rhine seem to have a penchant for hanging their walls with bows and swords and halberds and such. At the end of our small dining room hung crossed battle axes that were far larger than one would imagine necessary, while above my head hung a morning star that was not as securely fastened to the wall as would have been my wont. This is not uncommon once you cross into Germany and head east. I've never seen so much as a slingshot hanging on a restaurant wall in France or Italy.

While eating my duck soup (I just had to try duck soup—in homage to Groucho. It was not good.), I thought of asking the waiter about Zappa. His first response was that the statue was in Kaunas, not Vilnius, but I knew enough to insist that he was wrong. He therefore said he would ask his colleagues and get back to me. After a while he returned with a map. "Here!" he proclaimed with such confidence that it didn't even occur to me to doubt him. Since the here to which he referred was not that close to where I was, and since it was getting late, I hailed a cab and pointed out my destination on the map to the cab driver, who answered with an enthusiastic "Sure, boss!" and then sped off as though we were delivering a fresh heart to a waiting transplant patient. During taxi rides such as these, I have a personal survival strategy, which is to close my eyes. When you do that, the swaying of the car is actually quite relaxing, and while you are still just as likely to die in a horrific automobile accident, you are far less likely to develop stress-related chronic illnesses such as high blood pressure.

This time I found a statue of a man named something like Giurtonaz. He wasn't as good looking as Cirkej, but at least he had a nice big bushy mustache, which was a step in the right direction.

The next morning I had a very early flight home to Paris, and so I assumed that my Lithuanian trip would end without my having met Frank Zappa's bronze effigy. In one last desperate attempt, I asked the desk clerk as I checked out (a different desk clerk). He sighed, and explained exactly where the statue can be found, then asked which was my favorite Zappa album. (For the record: *Weasels Ripped my Flesh*, for the title as much as for the music.) I instructed the taxi driver to drive, slowly, to Zappa, then on to the airport, which he did, except for the part about driving slowly.

And there was Frank. The statue is a bronze bust on a high steel column just off of Kalinausko Street. Zappa seems a little too majestic, more like Rodin's *Balzac* than a man who named his children Moon Unit and Dweezil. But then, it must be remembered that Bogdanas had spent something like 50 years sculpting Soviet political leaders. The statue is appropriately surrounded by walls covered in artistic (and some less artistic) graffiti with musical themes (except for the South Park figure). There are a couple of small brown benches near it in case anyone gets pensive.

I had no time to sit, though—I was already running late and while Vilnius was actually a nice place to visit, it was about time to get home, put *Burnt Weeny Sandwich* in the CD player, and remember what Frank Zappa sounded like when he still graced the planet with his presence.

THE INSIDE-OUT HEART OF PARIS: BEAUBOURG, FRANCE

I should point out that I haven't run across the Crazy Dreadlocked Percussionist in years. I hope he's OK. However, there is a less crazy undreadlocked percussionist who's taken to hanging out on the platform for the RER (suburban trains) in the station at Les Halles late at night. He sits on the little plastic seats next to the westbound A line and he taps out rhythms with drumsticks on bits of plastic or wood, or on the seats themselves. He doesn't collect any money, he doesn't talk to anyone, he just hangs out and plays. Maybe he's the Crazy Dreadlocked Percussionist's protégé or something. I'll have to ask him.

C ities are strange mutant creatures, with multiple hearts. After all, where is the heart of New York? Is it Midtown? Downtown? The Village? Harlem? It all depends on who you are, I suppose. So it is with Paris. Trendy Left-Bankers will probably think of St.-Germain or perhaps somewhere in the 5th, around Luxembourg, whereas their children might talk about Montparnasse. Rich, trendy Right-Bankers will think about the businesses on the Champs Élysées, while rich, non-trendy, stuffy Right-Bankers will think of the various neighborhoods in the 16th, and artistic Right-Bankers will probably think about Montmartre or someplace in the 9th. (A brief aside: for those who have no idea what I'm talking about with all these numbers, Paris is divided into 20 "arrondissements," which are themselves divided into myriad more or less official neighborhoods.)

But there is an inarguable point of view that states that the true center of the city is, well, in the center, or at least near it. Historically, Paris has been centered on the Île de la Cité, and just north of the island is the Centre Georges Pompidou, an enormous inside-out building that sports its plumbing on its exterior in the form of bright red and blue pipes and girders and things.

The Centre Pompidou squats at the bottom of a broad, sloping plaza that reaches from the rue St. Martin (which was the main north-south thoroughfare in Paris during the Middle Ages) to the center's doors. This plaza is a kind of free, permanent outdoors theatre, a modern *Cour des Miracles*, where just about everybody imaginable comes to mix together in a riotous hubbub of art and music and street performances in general.

The plaza is Carnegie Hall for French street performers. It is the tops, the ultimate, the place with the biggest and most difficult crowd of all. The most coveted spot is about halfway down, on the right (as you face the Centre Pompidou), primarily because there is another plaza that does not slope down, but runs along the right side, forming a kind of extended terrace with a railing upon which people can lean and look down on the performers. This means that the "orchestra" spectators can sit on the cobblestone slope of the main plaza, while the "balcony" spectators can hang out on the right, making for a nice crowd and a vague impression that you're at a modern equivalent of a Roman amphitheater.

However, it's a safe bet that Roman amphitheaters had no performers like the Crazy Dreadlocked Percussionist. The Crazy Dreadlocked Percussionist sometimes plays the Beaubourg Plaza (note: the French call this whole area Beaubourg, after the old neighborhood), although his performances are sporadic at best. He has a kind of pushcart, with various accoutrements sticking out of it, which he bangs on with his drumsticks. None of these things were originally intended to be instruments, and they make an unholy racket. He pays homage to his racket by dancing around, his dreadlocks shaking. This is very impressive, since his dreadlocks are the kind that stand up, making his head look like a cross between a frightened hedgehog and a mop. Throughout it all, one cannot help but notice the banana hanging on a string from a metal rod extending above his pushcart, and one cannot help but wonder what, exactly, he is going to do with it. Well, this is the highlight of the show, the central theme, as it were, and the inspiration of his only lyrics, because after a while, the Crazy Dreadlocked Percussionist will holler "Banana!," in English, and then whack the banana once with a stick. In itself, this makes no noise, or at least none that can be heard by the spectators, but as of the third or fourth whack it does make an interesting visual effect, since the banana explodes in a gooey mess. Once this is accomplished the show is over, and the Crazy Dreadlocked Percussionist moves on to wherever he moves on to.

The Crazy Dreadlocked Percussionist is one of the more surreal acts at the Beaubourg Plaza. More often than not the show tends toward the theatrical or acrobatic. Entire theatre troupes have put on shows there, often drawing audience members into the act. Recently, my son and I watched five young circus performers juggle a whole mess of balls and pins and things while conducting a kind of dance with a big wooden pole, all this alternating with musical interludes played on a variety of instruments. As we left, the next act was warming up—some guy with a really tall unicycle.

Musicians play the plaza as well, but they don't make up as large a proportion of the performers as at other hot street performance venues, such as the plaza in front of the Orsay Museum or, especially, in front of the steps of Sacré-Cœur. Beaubourg is more for the performance artist. Sometimes, you'll even find modern dance.

There aren't many cities where you can collect money by performing modern dance in the street.

On the top of the plaza, running along the rue St. Martin, are sketch artists doing portraits and caricatures for the passersby, who are glad to sit still for the requisite time, watching the performers below. Behind them are shops that sell postcards, posters, and yes, the occasional cheesy Eiffel Tower model or "Paris" pen. Nearer to the Centre Pompidou itself are human statues, holding as still as possible in the hope that you'll drop some money in front of them. The latest trend seems to be for them to dress up as Egyptian sarcophagi, with gold-colored masks over their faces. I think that's cheating myself, since they assumedly can wiggle their noses and stuff under there. But then, I'm no judge of human statues.

Next to the Centre Pompidou, just to the south of it, in fact, is the world's most fun fountain. This fountain was designed by Niki de Saint Phalle and Jean Tinguely, and it celebrates the work of Igor Stravinsky. The fountain is a large basin with all kinds of cool things in it, most of them spitting water (although some just churn the water around, or spin in it and make little waves). There are 15 things in all, many of them (primarily those designed by de Saint Phalle) brightly colored constructions made out of resin. The others, primarily those by Tinguely, are more mechanical—machines that make a great effort to do their spitting and churning.

If you ever have to meet someone in Paris, this fountain is a great place to set up a rendezvous. For one thing, if you're late, the person can hang out at one of the cafés next to it, or simply stand and watch it. The fountain can provide a lot of entertainment. Furthermore, you can tell a great deal about a person by asking them which of the 15 things is their favorite. Will it be the big red lips? Or perhaps the scorpion-like machine? Maybe the elephant, or the little spirally thing that goes around and around, or maybe even the blue hat. I confess that I'm not exactly sure *what* you can tell about a person from their answer, but I'm convinced it's highly significant. A kind of watery Rorschach test.

If you find this beneath you, then feel free to set up your trysts at the Café Beaubourg, which is one of the trendiest places in the city. Last I was there (someone had told me to meet him there—which I regretted, I would have much preferred the fountain) it was all a mess because of some fashion shoot. An anorexic woman was twirling around for a black-clad photographer while the waiters tried to maneuver around those umbrella things that photographers use. One shouldn't have to wait too long for a $10 cup of coffee.

Parisians were quite upset when the Centre Pompidou was built, primarily because it's so damn ugly. However, it does grow on you, and when all is said and done, Beaubourg is a strange, avant-garde, artistic kind of neighborhood anyway, so a strange, avant-garde building in the center of it perhaps is not so out of place. And it should also be said that the ostensible reason why the building was designed this way was to save space inside of it, and the inside is certainly full of space. It's interesting space, too. The building houses a museum of modern art, as well as all kinds of cultural and educational resources that people really do use. It also tends to be not anywhere near as crowded with tourists as is the Louvre or the Quai d'Orsay. (A brief aside: my wife's grandfather used to carry luggage at the Quai d'Orsay back when it was still a train station.)

In the end, though, despite all of the interesting things inside the Centre Pompidou, the *most* interesting spectacle is outside of it, on the plaza. Next time you're in Paris, stop by and watch.

OF HERMITS AND SARACENS:
LE VIEUX NOYER, FRANCE

France seems small to American eyes. It's dinky, looks something like a state, all nestled in there among other countries with no room to stretch out (Napoleon notwithstanding). But for all its relatively small size, France boasts an incredibly diverse countryside. There are the flat plains of Picardy and the towering mountains of Savoie, the balmy sea coast of Provence and the stormy channel beaches of Normandy, the pleasant students of Toulouse and the snotty waiters of Paris.

In roughly the middle of the country, the plains turn into hills and the hills begin turning into mountains. This is just about at the same point that the cloudier northern disposition runs into the sunnier southern disposition. The net effect is beautiful and pleasant, with deep gorges cut into the landscape and little villages nestled here and there where one can actually get served with a smile.

I've never been too enthusiastic about French mountain villages (with the exception of those in Corsica). They have a tendency to be kind of drab, and French mountain dwellers have an inconvenient habit of roofing their buildings with corrugated metal, for the unconvincing reason that the snow slides off it nicely. How dare they ruin my aesthetic experience for the sake of mundane practicality!

Anyway, there are some very pretty villages all the same, and there are some very small villages and what must be the prettiest and the smallest is named le Vieux Noyer, population one.

Le Vieux Noyer stands on a jutting peak overlooking the new Noyer (Noyer sur Jabron). The village was built around AD 600, and it was abandoned by its inhabitants in the early part of the of twentieth century. The inhabitants left either to die in the First World War or to live in the new village at the bottom of the valley.

Why? The reasons are a little murky. It seems to have something to do with water, and with a general softening of the population, according to the village's sole inhabitant, whom I'll call "Pierre" in order to respect his hermitic lifestyle.

"In AD 800," Pierre explained, "this village held off the Saracens. There were 900 souls who lived here. You can still see the vestiges of the old fortifications. Back then, they weren't put off by hiking up and down the mountain and they didn't need any big roads. These days, though, people all want to be connected to each other, you know? So they moved down into the valley and founded the new village."

Well, *most* people want to be connected with each other. Pierre clearly does not. Although he is originally from Aix-en-Provence, he used to come to the Jabron valley with his parents on holiday. When he "retired" from his unnamed and probably not altogether existent career, he decided to live in le Vieux Noyer with his dog, in a little building that he estimates at about a thousand years old. It was probably a barn of sorts. A very, very small barn, maybe five meters on each side.

The building is a single room with a dirt floor and stone walls. On one side is a fireplace and a small gas cooker hooked up to a tank of propane. On the other side is Pierre's sleeping bag. Pierre has some shelves, which are populated by various things, including a cheese grater, a backpack, a pair of skis, lots of blankets and a couple of pots and pans.

Pierre is a wiry man, somewhere between 40 and 60 years of age, with striking blue eyes and a reddish dog. The building he lives in is near a small fountain, which serves as his water supply. For electricity, he improvises.

"I don't pay for electricity. I did it for years and I'm not giving them anymore of my money. I have an old car battery. It serves me fine. I just listen to the radio sometimes anyway. Don't need lights or anything."

Not that Pierre is anti-technology. He even participated in a film recently.

"They made a movie next door and they gave me a part to play." It should here be noted that the next door in question is an abandoned building, part of a medieval farmhouse that is half fallen down. "They wanted a real provincial look. It was supposed to take place during the First World War. I played a deserter from the army!"

Pierre was obviously very proud of his role, and it should be said that it's easy to imagine him flipping the finger at a draft officer in 1916.

Pierre's building and the fallen-down farmhouse next door are actually on the outskirts of le Vieux Noyer. Until recently, there was another hermit who lived in the very center of the abandoned town; an Englishman. Pierre thinks he's dead, since he hasn't seen him in a year or so and the house is locked up. He's not sure, though. Apparently, hermits don't lead an active social life, even when they are the only two inhabitants of a village.

The Englishman's house is indeed locked up. It also has the jawbone of a wild boar hanging on the doorway. This was either his way of warning people off, or he thought it was a fetching knocker. The world will never know.

Walking through the streets of le Vieux Noyer is a surrealistic experience. The village is a struggle between stone and leaf, as the local flora tries to take back the land. The main street, which isn't a street in the sense of anyone ever having driven a car along it, but more a street in the sense of a clear path along the rock, is lined with buildings whose great age coats their stones like ivy, their roofs and windowpanes and floors all gone, but their walls mostly intact. Plants have replaced people in the rooms of these buildings; through doorless doorways you can glimpse trees growing in living rooms and vines winding up interior walls. The trees outside are graced with the silk houses of tent caterpillars and small blue flowers dot the tall grasses.

In the summertime, the sun almost always shines on le Vieux Noyer, painting the church a bright white. The church is the only building that's been kept up, since a hiking trail goes by and since it's a church. More interesting than the church, though, is the graveyard, where long-forgotten people are buried in long-forgotten graves, hidden under tangles of grass and flowers. If you look closely, some of the gravestones are still legible. You can see "Marie, died on March 13, 1878, aged 27," behind a leafy vine and wonder who she was and what killed her so young, and in which of these majestic, abandoned houses she used to live.

And you can indeed see the vestiges of the fortifications, over on the east side of the town. It must have been a formidable stronghold, perched on the top of a rocky peak, overlooking the entire valley. What's left of the wall consists of some thick masonry and a gate of sorts. I'm glad to say that the place is still garrisoned. A ferret, or some other weasel-like creature, mans the ramparts and will stare at you menacingly with beady little eyes from a hole up in the arch if you approach too closely. I doubt he has any serious weaponry (but then I'm sure a vole would disagree), but he looks like the type that would gladly pour some boiling oil on you if given half a chance. Perhaps when the Englishman was still around he armed the ferret to keep away intruders, but these days he just tries to scare you away by staring at you. Saracens be warned.

If you want to visit the town, you're going to have to get to Noyer sur Jabron, most likely through Sisteron, which is a wonderful place to visit in its own right. You can see le Vieux Noyer from miles away, but the actual road up to it is unmarked and pretty much impossible to describe. Just keep trying to go up. If you're on foot, then you follow the hiking trail, and if you have a car, then you follow an impossible road that was never meant for motor vehicles but that will allow you to pretend you're on a cheap carnival ride as you bounce around, winding your way up to the top.

Just don't try to find Pierre. Having spoken to me for an afternoon, he's all spoken out and probably won't be receiving any visitors for a couple of years.

MICKEY MOUSE
AND MARSHAL ZHUKOV:
MANEZH SQUARE,
MOSCOW, RUSSIA

Beneath the towering walls of the Kremlin, Marshal Zhukov sits on a great bronze horse, trampling a swastika. In front of his statue, on a sunny afternoon in June, sat a full-size Mickey Mouse, available to have his photo taken with adoring Russian toddlers. Next to the man in the mouse suit stood another cartoon character, soliciting passersby for photo ops.

"What is that next to Mickey?" asked a Russian friend of mine, as we observed the scene.

"It's someone dressed up as a Teenage Mutant Ninja Turtle."

"Ah. And please to tell me what is mutant turtle?"

How can one be expected to explain Teenage Mutant Ninja Turtles to a middle-aged Russian woman?

"Let's just say that its presence is proof that you definitively lost the Cold War."

Moscow has changed a lot in the past 15 years. The Kremlin, of course, is still there, but then it's been there for over 500 years. St. Basil's Cathedral is still there as well, and a good thing it is, with its candy-colored cupolas piled all around. Many are surprised to discover that even Lenin is still there in his low red mausoleum, as well preserved as ever (he can be visited every day except Monday and Friday, between 10:00 AM and 1:00 PM). However, there are many new additions to the capital as well.

One of the more interesting of these is Manezh Square. Many years ago, the small Neglinka River served as a kind of moat for the northern approaches to the Kremlin (the much larger Moskva River constituted a natural defense on the other side). In the early nineteenth century, the Neglinka River was driven underground, running through a decidedly unromantic pipe beneath the pavement. During Soviet times, the area above remained relatively undeveloped. In the early '90s, the popular mayor of Moscow, Yuri Luzhkov, decided to renovate the area. He uncovered part of the river, transforming it into a long flowing fountain studded with bronze statues of Russia's favorite fairy-tale heroes. He also built Moscow's first modern shopping mall, complete with a food court serving all manner of junk, and he lined the newly uncovered river with a kind of promenade upon which one can find cafés and, in a final gasp of surrender, a McDonald's. At the far end of the whole shebang, he erected a fountain featuring three horses, with a little circular walkway around half of it, over which spout streams of water that are just unruly enough to get you seriously wet if you decide to walk underneath them.

This has become a Mecca for the youth of Moscow. While the shopping center is already somewhat passé ever since the creation of newer, larger temples to consumerism, the long fountain that is the Neglinka, and the cafés and restaurants that line it (including the McDonald's) serve as an evening meeting point for thousands. The majority of these seem to be between the ages of, roughly, 18 and 25. The men are accompanied by cans of beer and the women are accompanied by the men, who are doing the kinds of silly things that young drunk men do in an attempt to impress or at least capture the attention of young women. The young women seem to put up with this and even giggle from time to time, which spurs the men on to do even sillier things, such as wading out into the fountain to speak with a bronze Ilya Murometz, or some other fairy-tale figure.

It is an appealing fountain, this little stretch of the Neglinka River. The bottom is tiled with mosaics of fish, and groups of multicolored lights shine up through the water, giving the entire thing an otherworldly glow. The fairy-tale heroes strike interesting poses: crowned frogs confront witches, bears battle wolves, swans rise from the depths, and if one can ignore the drunk Russian males wading among them, they make a very pretty tableau.

Little marble staircases lead down to the water's edge, and the fountain itself is spanned by white bridges, leading over to the cafés. On the other side is a wooded park, between the fountain and the walls of the Kremlin. Between the trees are expanses of grass, upon which sit or lie couples in various stages of relationship-building, ranging from stilted conversation to sucking on each other's tongues. Either way, cans of beer are nearby.

At the end of the Neglinka fountain stands the fountain with three horses, with its spouting walkway. There's a little plaza here, where on two occasions I observed impromptu tattoo parlors, where a bare-chested man painted images onto those willing to part with a few rubles. (I had better things to do with my own rubles.) His patrons were generally well-pierced, sporting neo-punk hair. Behind them, people hesitated before walking along the curved walkway behind the statue, under the spouting arcs of water: some people squinched up their eyes and ran through, emitting little shrieks as they got wet; others hunched their shoulders and walked through forcefully; yet others (all males) pretended not to notice, sauntering along as if to prove their immunity to water. All of this is unnecessary, of course, since one can just as easily go around the fountain on the other side and not get wet at all.

There is a noticeable lack of older people at Manezh Square in the evening (not during the day, when the mix is more typical, and the shopping center is bustling with all kinds of consumers). Of course, all cities have their young spots and their old spots, places where the different generations go to lead their different lives. Moscow is, perhaps, somewhat extreme in this. It's been almost 15 years now since walls started falling, and many of the evening denizens of Manezh Square don't even remember what it was like when the dead man in Red Square was still a hero instead of simple tribute to the embalmer's art. They don't even recognize the irony of having a teenage mutant turtle slumming for rubles in front of Zhukov's statue. Just as my own generation became rapidly sick of hearing how tough things were during the Great Depression, they may be losing patience with their parents' tales of the Soviet era, and simply want to go someplace different to show off their latest eyebrow stud and get a picture of Elvis painted onto their calf. Who can blame them?

For a more mixed sampling of Moscow evening demographics, you may want to head over to Arbat Street, which is just a few minutes' walk from Manezh Square. Arbat Street is a pedestrian walkway leading out towards the west, ending at Smolenskaya Boulevard. It has always been a center for artists and the kinds of cafés they frequent. In fact, according to another Russian friend, some of the portrait artists have been plying their trade there for over 25 years. Governments may come and go, but the same artists will continue to take your money for a quickly sketched portrait. That kind of stability can be comforting.

Arbat Street is lined with pleasant places to have a coffee, as well as cheap restaurants, usually serving pizza, and, of course, there's another McDonald's. One Russian proudly proclaimed to me that Moscow is the site of the second biggest McDonald's in the world, which is further proof that they lost the Cold War, although in this case I refrained from pointing this out. Since Russians do not make good pizza, and since only tasteless rubes would eat at McDonald's while traveling to a foreign country (please excuse me if you're a tasteless rube—I meant no harm), you're much better off eating Russian food. Or, for a highly unusual treat, try a Georgian restaurant, where they will serve you a host of tasty dishes that are entirely unrecognizable, accompanied by lots of different kinds of leaves.

Arbat Street is not to be confused with *New* Arbat Street (or "Novyy Arbat Street"), which is an entirely different matter. New Arbat Street is a linear emporium of gambling parlors, electronics shops, a casino or two, and glitzy restaurants. There is also a sports bar/sushi restaurant, which is not an entirely reassuring combination. New Arbat Street was *the* place to hang out during Soviet times, as it contained restaurants and bars for foreigners, largely populated by the children of the diplomatic community (as explained to me by a Serbian who grew up in Moscow with his diplomat father and who had many unsavory and titillating experiences there). Today as well, New Arbat Street is a swinging place for Muscovites of all generations: the older generations (or at least those with money) frequenting the casinos and the younger generations skateboarding along the large sidewalks.

Whether at Manezh Square, Arbat Street or New Arbat Street, modern Moscow shows its face in the evening. It's still shaking off the torpor of 65 years of a decidedly un-fun system, but it is doing so with vigor and even a kind of frenzy. Who knows, maybe 15 years from now, next to the statue of Zhukov trampling a swastika will be a statue of Mickey Mouse trampling a hammer and sickle.

ODYSSEUS AND
GRILLED LOBSTER:
BONIFACIO, CORSICA, FRANCE

Odysseus was having a hard time of it. He had already dealt with the Lotus-Eaters and the cyclops, but his men had just opened the bag of winds given to him by Aiolos, blowing him back out to sea from within sight of his homeland. He now found himself approaching a "glorious harbor which a sky-towering cliff enclosed on either side with no break anywhere, and two projecting promontories facing each other running out toward the mouth..."

In the opinion of many scholars, this refers to Bonifacio, at the southern tip of Corsica. I agree, because Homer describes Odysseus as being someone of very good taste, in which case he could hardly have spent all those years gallivanting about the Mediterranean without having visited Bonifacio.

It is summer (or at least it is as I write this), which means that it is time for a column about Corsica, since this is where I go in the summer and since it is also the most beautiful place on the planet. This year, I'll write about Bonifacio (Bonifaziu in Corsican), which is one of those places you must see at least once. It is a small, imposing fortress of a city, built on a rocky peninsula with a stunning blue sea on one side and a deep, almost fjord-like cove on the other, serving as its harbor, as described by Homer. Back then, it was apparently inhabited by the Laistrygones, whose women were the size of cattle and who ate men for fun. Admittedly, modern Corsicans too are more renowned for their pride than for their hospitality, but cannibalism is no longer the norm and Bonifacio is worth the risk.

The city was probably founded in the ninth century, and was then elaborated by the Genoese in the twelfth. They had defense on their mind. There is only one gate, at the neck of the promontory. (In fact, another road has been cut into the bluffs on the inland side, allowing automobile traffic, but this is a modern convenience.) To walk up to the gate is a lesson in humility. You must imagine what an assailant would have felt, contemplating three successive gates, the last of which is approachable only by a narrow walkway. One would have been vulnerable to fire on one's right (the side upon which a medieval soldier bore no shield) from the massive wall above; from the front, where the imposing gate itself stood; and from behind, where yet another wall boasted two firing portals bearing archers, or later, cannons—all of that leading only to a drawbridge over a narrow, deep ravine. Even if that could be forced, the gatehouse within held yet more horrors and yet another thick door.

There is one other way up to the city, the famous "staircase of the king of Aragon," a narrow line cut into the cliffs on the seaward side at roughly a 45° angle, with big, nasty, slippery steps that until a few years ago offered no protection of any kind: no guardrail, nothing. You just did your best to climb up with a 100-foot drop ready to greet any slip on your part. In all fairness, there were signs on either end saying that it was dangerous. Sensitive to the public relations problems inherent in having tourists plunge to their deaths on the rocks below, the city of Bonifacio eventually built a retaining wall on the cliffward side, so that today you need only worry about slipping down the 187 steps.

Alfonso V, the king of Aragon, had the staircase built in 1420, after he had been besieging the city for five months (no way he was going to try the craziness of the main gate). Not a patient man, according to legend, he ordered the staircase built hacked into the cliff in one night, which is generally held to be the most strenuous night's work in history. Reality is more mundane, as the Bonifacians probably built the staircase themselves in order to better accommodate the small boats that came to provide much-needed supplies during the long siege. In either case, Alfonso eventually gave up and settled for conquering the rest of the western Mediterranean. This was probably for the best; most foreign powers who have tried to rule Corsica have eventually regretted it.

Today, Bonifacio draws invaders of another kind, as tourists come from all over the world to gawk at it and park their yachts in the harbor. Some of the most impressive yachts in the world come here, their passengers sitting in harbor-side cafés eating ice cream concoctions and comparing tans, or just lounging on the decks of their boats and reveling in the jealousy they produce in passersby.

Up in the old city, overlooking the harbor, tiny streets wind into each other, forming a twisting labyrinth. They are lined by ancient buildings with impossibly steep staircases. Stone arches traverse the streets high above, connecting the buildings on either side for no apparent reason in a style that is typically Bonifacian. The city ends somewhat before the end of the promontory itself, and the cemetery takes over. Given the rocky ground, it is Corsican custom not to bury the dead, but rather to inter them in mausoleums. Corsican cemeteries, therefore, look like little cities, and indeed it is said that when the Italians raided Bonifacio in 1940, they mistakenly bombed the cemetery instead of the city proper.

If you visit Bonifacio, you might consider having dinner at one of my very favorite restaurants in the world afterwards. You must leave Bonifacio and drive towards Ajaccio (one day I'll write about Ajaccio). After a few miles, you'll see a sign saying "A Tonna," which is Corsican for tuna, and refers to a minuscule hamlet that is a further couple of miles down a winding road with more character than pavement. At the end are three or four buildings, one of which is a restaurant named Marco, because it is owned by Marco.

A Tonna has a tiny little harbor, where a few rowboats are tied to a desultory pier. Years ago, men used to go out and fish for tuna in boats like these, which is why such a small place got a name at all. Today, it really only exists for the restaurant. But the harbor sits near the mouth of a large bay that faces almost due west. All of the bay and all of the opposite coast is visible, miles and miles of it. On this coast, you can see exactly zero buildings: it is all pristine, except for the restaurant itself, which is built jutting out onto the rocks, and where you should, of course, ask for a table on the terrace outside. At the end of the day, the sun is bound to set, and when it does you will see the sky explode in color while the waves break against the rocks beneath you and all that stark coastline turns different shades of gold until, finally, the sun disappears behind a distant horizon, causing you to go "ooh."

Marco has a pretty limited menu. You start with fish soup, and then either lobster or whatever fish they're serving that day, or bouillabaisse, which is really both. But it is very, very good soup and lobster and fish. You then get Corsican sheep cheese, served, as is local custom, with fig preserves, followed by *beignets de pomme*. Exactly the same limited menu has been served there for 35 years and it's not about to change, which is a very good thing. All the fish is caught locally and served the same day. The lobsters also come from the sea nearby, after which they live in a long stone tank that runs down the center of the restaurant until they are lifted from the water to give their lives for you.

Keep in mind that the restaurant is only open from April through October. I asked the head chef what he does the rest of the year. "Not much," he said. "I have a house in Morocco where I spend the winter. It's nice there." When I asked the others in the kitchen what *they* do, they smiled, "Sometimes we go to visit him."

The best way to experience Corsica is to marry someone of Corsican parentage: if possible, parentage that has bequeathed a house in Corsica overlooking an ancient Genoese guard tower and a secluded beach. If possible, I suggest the person in question also be a beautiful and very understanding ballerina, since that's kind of nice. To make it absolutely perfect, try to find a beautiful, understanding Corsican ballerina who doesn't drink, since this will allow you to accompany your dinner at A Tonna with plenty of heady Corsican wine (try a Fiumicicola) without having to worry about piloting a motor vehicle along the tortuous mountain roads afterwards. Your ballerina can drive while you just sit there patting your distended belly in a satisfied way.

You can even suggest to her that she head off to a spot you both know, from which you can walk down to a different secluded beach for a midnight swim. Midnight swims are nice anywhere, but nowhere more so than in Corsica. There are no big beaches on the island, only a succession of little coves, more or less difficult to access, most of which you really have to know about in order to reach. I know of several, and, of course, there's no way I'm going to tell you how to get to them. Anyway, if you do get to one (some of which are visible from the road), then you can stumble along the path with your ballerina, get to the empty beach, take off all your clothes, and dive into a universe of stars. The Mediterranean is full of little phosphorescent beings that you can't actually see during the daytime, but at night, if you swim in its warm waters, you will be surrounded by millions of tiny green lights that dance around with every movement you make. You can come up for air and look at the real stars in a cloudless sky, with the moon hanging over distant mountains. Then, of course, you can swim on over to your ballerina with a leer, because there is absolutely no experience on earth that is so romantic, not to say downright erotic.

I never did understand why Odysseus was in such a hurry to get back to Ithaca.

THE DOOR TO HELL:
PARIS, FRANCE

The title of this dispatch has caused no small amount of consternation, perhaps in keeping with its eerie subject. I pretty much automatically translated the words "La Porte de L'Enfer" as "The Door to Hell," whereas in English, the infamous portal is more commonly known as The Gates of Hell. (Note that in French, there is no specific word for "gate." You just use the word for door and make a kind of sweeping motion with your hands to indicate that you mean a really big one.) This has since been pointed out to me, and if the phrase strikes you as strange, do forgive me. I shall try to refrain from translating anything in the future, so with no further ado, lasciate ogni speranza voi che leggere.

Just off the rue de Varenne, in Paris's 7th arrondissement, stands the door to hell. You will be glad to know it is closed.

The door is a bronze sculpted by Auguste Rodin. This was the work of a lifetime: he began in 1880 and still did not consider it finished at the time of his death, in 1917. A number of his best-known sculptures were originally created to figure into this apocalyptic tableau. You will find, for instance, a smaller version of *The Thinker* (who was supposed to represent Dante—which is a kick-ass art trivia question), as well as Francesca and Paolo, the doomed lovers of *The Kiss* (not quite as good a trivia question, but still not bad).

You'll also find Ugolino as he crawls through the dust, his starving family clinging to his arms, and all kinds of other tormented sinners I won't describe, but rather leave you to discover on your own.

The door stands just inside the garden of the Rodin Museum. This is my favorite museum in Paris for a variety of reasons. First, it should be taken into account that I do not consider the Louvre a museum, but rather a kind of cultural mini-universe. Then there's the fact that I love Rodin. But most of all, it's because of the garden. You can get into the garden for only one euro if you just want to walk around without going into the museum proper, which is Rodin's former house and is well worth the other four euros. I would describe it for you, but you can find many descriptions of it in more traditional sources of information, so I'll just nip back to the door to hell.

There's a bench across from the door. I suggest you sit there and observe how people deal with this sculpture. A surprising number of people have their photos taken in front of the door to hell, either requesting this of their girlfriend/boyfriend, or pressing themselves upon strangers to take a picture of the two of them together, with the door to hell behind them. You have to wonder about this. It's quite possible that they don't actually know what the sculpture represents; there are no devils or pitchforks or anything. Or perhaps they like tempting fate, or are proud of the fact that they are on this side of the door (for now). Who knows?

Recently, I saw a sprite young Chinese tourist wearing an orange polo shirt and a floppy yellow hat. She was standing in front of the door smiling and fiddling with her hands, as one does when one is being photographed. Her boyfriend was kneeling, instructing her to move this way or that in Chinese (or so I surmise). In the meantime, tortured bronze souls reached out to her, imploring. She remained oblivious. There are legions of tourists getting their pictures taken by the door to hell, but the orange polo shirt and especially the floppy yellow hat seemed particularly out of place for me. This is not what you wear to hell.

I don't begrudge them their photos. It's a very impressive sculpture, and if you happen to be wearing a floppy yellow hat when you abruptly find yourself in front of the door to hell then you too may well forget to take it off.

You can't actually go through the door to hell. Rodin didn't sculpt it in such a way as to allow it to open. If this frustrates you then you may consider taking a walk south from the Rodin Museum to go through a different kind of door and descend into the Paris catacombs, which might suffice as a proxy for hell.

For centuries, the stone used to construct the buildings and monuments of Paris came from quarries beneath what is now the 14th arrondissement. The quarries have not been mined for many years, but all that digging left a vast network of caves and tunnels underneath the southern part of Paris. In 1786, the city decided to remove the Cemetery of the Innocents, in the center of town, after a nearby basement wall collapsed and a local bourgeois discovered some unwelcome and long-dead visitors in his cellar. One thousand years of constant use had filled the cemetery to well beyond its limits. This, however, presented the problem of what to do with all those bones. Someone then remembered the empty quarries and thought this would be a swell place for their dead ancestors. The corpses were deposited in the abandoned quarries, turning the caves and tunnels into bona fide catacombs.

For the following hundred years or so, the catacombs served as a repository for the bones of Paris. A number of cemeteries were decommissioned and the bones removed to the catacombs. In the catacombs themselves, the bones are generally arranged according to the cemetery of their origin, providing a kind of postmortem address to the inhabitants (although I suppose in this context, the etymology of "inhabitant" renders it inappropriate . . . but I digress).

You can visit the catacombs. There is an entrance near the Place Denfert-Rochereau. You go down a whole bunch of steps into an appropriately dank and dark tunnel through which you then walk for several minutes until you come to the catacombs proper.

You can't miss it. One minute you're walking along a tunnel, the walls of which are rock, and the next minute you're walking along another tunnel, the walls of which are femurs, with artistically placed rows of skulls, and rib-bone lattice work. The bones weren't just dumped here, they were arranged into patterns. Lots of patterns, because there are lots and lots of bones.

About six million Parisians reside beneath the city in the catacombs, all mixed up together in a classless mélange that is fittingly republican (in the French sense of the word). It's a chilling experience to go down and visit them. They are arranged neither by title, nor by station, nor even by gender, but rather by body part, apparently because it's easier to make really pretty designs by first sorting all the skeletons into relatively similar bones. So men, women, friends and enemies may well end up with their very bones all mixed together in the interest of visual effect, which is either uplifting and ultra-cool, or morbid and infinitely depressing, depending on your frame of mind.

Of course, there is far more to the catacombs than the part that is open to the public, and enterprising individuals—adventurers, thugs, resistance fighters, night owls, whoever—have always wandered around down there, much to the frustration of the Inspection Générale des Carrières, the city agency responsible for making sure that the south of Paris doesn't one day collapse. When you visit the bones, you can sometimes see dark gated passages running gloomily off into the distance. Spooky.

The Place Denfert-Rochereau is only a few minutes' walk from the rue de Varenne. You can therefore visit the Rodin Museum, finishing with a nice long contemplation of the door to hell—causing your mortality to begin knocking on the inside of your skull ("What, you forget about me?")—then head over to Denfert for a dip into the catacombs, where your mortality will do a veritable jig in your brain, all the while singing songs about dust. I agree it's not the most lighthearted day out in Paris, but if he were to really think about it, Dante would probably approve.

THE SUBMARINE SIGHTS
OF COPENHAGEN, DENMARK

A lot of cities have canals. There are, of course, the canals of Venice, but northern Europe has a wealth of wonderful canals, too. Flemish cities are crisscrossed with all kinds of canals, such as those of Amsterdam, Bruges, and even Utrecht (great canals, the ones in Utrecht). Paris has the Canal Saint-Martin, which Americans only learned about when Amélie Poulain skipped stones across it, and a number of German cities have canals lined with beer gardens that shouldn't be missed. None, though, have canals that are themselves as full of life as the canals of Copenhagen, which actually *pulse*.

Now, the reason Copenhagen's canals pulse is that they are full of jellyfish. On some days, there are so many jellyfish that it almost seems you could walk across the canals by stepping on them. (Beware! This is just an illusion.) I only noticed them for the first time when I returned to Copenhagen recently after several years of absence, and was drawn to the canal near the Christiansborg Palace by the sound of thousands of chanting voices and a bad rock band.

Neither the voices nor the music were produced by the jellyfish; they were instead produced by a host of unhappy students who were demonstrating against the government's unwillingness to provide sufficient funds for their education.

They say that the government has cut spending, even though

the government denies this. "Here, read this," said one very enthusiastic student to me, in his inevitably perfect English, after I asked
about the demonstration. "It's in Danish," I pointed out. "Oh yeah,"
he said. But then I assured him that I would be able to get it translated by my Pregnant Blonde Danish Friend (more on her later) and
he perked up. I took advantage of this to ask him and his numerous
friends about the jellyfish.

"Oh yeah, the jellyfish!" he said, glancing over the side of the
bridge upon which we were standing. "They're nice. I think it's mostly around this time of the year. There are almost as many jellyfish in
the canal as there are rusted bikes," he said, as his friends concurred.
"It's kind of a tradition to throw your old bicycles into the canal. You
do a kind of funeral thing." Another student interrupted, "It's also a
good place to ditch a bicycle you've stolen. Not that I've ever stolen
any myself, of course."

Of course.

The jellyfish all seem to be of the same species. They are
white, with a pinkish hue, and they have four little circles in their
bell. They just float along amidst the leaves and the bobbing bottles
of Tuborg, pulsating from time to time. They apparently lead relatively tranquil lives in the canals, probably because there are no sea
turtles down there to bother them.

There are, however, sculptures. Farther along on the same
canal is what must be the only maritime sign of its kind: "Attention,
sunken sculpture," evidently for the sake of any boaters who might
be taking an excursion. Near this sign is a buoy, and from the side
of the canal, if you look into the water near the buoy you can see
the vague forms of a sculpture entitled *Merman with Seven Sons*. The
merman and his sons seem to be having a parley of sorts, down there
among the gently pulsating jellyfish.

The canal in question is not too far from the Stroget (names
are, as usual, lacking the local squiggles and slashes—use your imagination), Copenhagen's fashionable shopping street. Along with

their canals, many cities also have fashionable shopping streets, but Copenhagen's manages to retain a particularly Danish charm, with pleasant pastel-colored buildings fronting a bustling pedestrian thoroughfare, where you can buy pralined almonds sold in rolled-up paper, and you can pop into a store for salty licorice.

A moment here on salty licorice. Danes love licorice (always black; they've never heard of red licorice). This is not particularly unusual, as many European cultures retain a particularly honored spot for licorice, including the French, who call it *réglisse* and suck on horrid little black licorice pastilles. Anyway, the difference in Denmark is that they put salt on the stuff (I believe they do this in Sweden, too). They make little fish out of black licorice, roll them in salt, then ask you to try it in the same sinister way that a Brit will give you bread with marmite. It is very, very nasty. Be warned.

Back to the Stroget. You can stroll down the Stroget for hours, unless you're as pregnant as my Pregnant Blonde Danish Friend, who gets tired from all that strolling and periodically has to stop in a shoe shop. Since I am nowhere near as fond of shoe shops as she is, this caused a degree of strain, so I did give in a couple of times and stood around while she looked at a special kind of boot, which I think were called something like "ooks." At least Danish stores on the Stroget have a charming habit of sometimes serving champagne and salty licorice in the evening. You can skip the licorice.

The Stroget boasts the Guinness World Record Museum, which I somehow suspect is not the only Guinness World Record Museum, nor, for that matter, even the flagship one, but which looks interesting enough from the outside. It certainly drew the attention of my Pregnant Blonde Danish Friend, primarily because the display window features what it claims to be the world's most expensive pair of shoes (or a copy of them). My Pregnant Blonde Danish Friend immediately disputed this, saying that the £13,500 cited in the display was nothing, and that Jimmy Choo has undoubtedly made more expensive shoes than that. I don't know who Jimmy Choo is, but I do know that I'll never be wearing any of his shoes.

Not too far from the Guinness World Record Museum is the Museum Erotica, which also has some shoes, I suppose. I didn't go in (not out of any puritanism, believe me, but rather because I had other things to do), but I did take a close look at their pamphlet. The Museum Erotica has Chinese silk screens, Indian etchings, a whole room dedicated to Marilyn Monroe, extremely lifelike rubber women, a large golden phallus, and pictures of people who probably could have qualified for inclusion at the Guinness World Record Museum down the street.

After a hard day of cultural enlightenment at Copenhagen's museums (there are others that are undoubtedly more cultural, although perhaps not as enlightening, but for those, just read a guidebook), you can relax at any one of the trendy cafés that line the Stroget, or its tributaries. Danish cafés are cool. Most things in Denmark are cool, for that matter. It must be faced: Danes are among the coolest people around, and anyplace full of Danes sipping coffee—or even hyldeblomst, a very Danish thing made of elderflowers—is bound to be relatively trendy, just because it's full of Danes sipping stuff. You can even sit outside on the terrace in October, since Danish cafés are kind enough to provide little blankets on every chair. I think that's just spiffy.

I can't proclaim with any certainty that the rest of Copenhagen's canals, inlets and bays are also full of jellyfish, because I didn't do a thorough census; however, they're worth a visit even if they're jellyfish-free. For that matter, even if you stay away from the water entirely, Copenhagen is worth a visit. You can dye your hair blonde, hang out in a trendy café with a little blanket over your shoulders, sip hot spiced wine . . . in summary, pretend you're Danish and be really, really cool.

THE THIRD TOWER
UP FROM THE ROAD:
HUANGHUACHENG, CHINA

A very brief aside: Roy Kesey no longer lives in China, but rather in Syracuse, New York. That's a shame, because I'm in Beijing far more often than I am in Syracuse.

It must be admitted that Huanghuacheng is not in Europe. Not by a long shot. As such, theoretically, it has no place in a column about places you should go in Europe. However, elsewhere on these pages (or screens, if you must be technical about it) one can find the work of Roy Kesey, describing China, and as I took a brief foray out of Europe and visited Roy in Beijing, he very kindly lent me a small part of his remit so that the editors would agree to let me write about the third tower up from the road at Huanghuacheng on China's Great Wall.

If you are reading this, you can safely assume that the editors swallowed this reasoning.

However, since China really is very firmly in Roy's domain, I shall not even mention the various interesting places in Beijing: not a word about the ladybugs at the Temple of Heaven, nor about the sorry-looking fish in the narrow hutongs, nor about the electric lines festooned with fried kites. No, I shall restrict my comments to the third tower up from the road at Huanghuacheng on China's Great Wall.

Most tourists visit the wall at Badaling, and it's likely that the pictures you've seen come from there. This is where Nixon visited the wall during his historic visit to China, during which he was heard to muse several times, "It is indeed a great wall," leading G.B. Trudeau later to wonder whether he was entirely sober before climbing up it. However, Badaling is full of nosy tourists and the wall there is fully restored, leaving little of its rustic splendor. Roy decided to bring me to see the wall in its splendidly rustic form at Huanghuacheng, a spot that had only recently been opened to the public.

Opened to the public is perhaps something of an exaggeration. The wall is there, but then it's in many places—at 5,000 kilometers long, it covers a lot of ground. There was a parking lot of sorts (i.e., a small patch of dirt by the side of the road) at which we retained the services of two ladies to watch over the car, and one or two shacks advertising rooms to rent, although that must have involved a definition of "room" with which I am unfamiliar. One of them, though, was on the far side of a really nifty bridge over a small river. The bridge was confected out of wires and some unconvincing wooden slats. Roy and I discovered that we had to walk out of step, otherwise the bridge took to swaying in a menacing manner.

Anyway, since this part of the wall is somewhat outside of officialdom, it is guarded by a small contingent of local villagers, each of whom tries to charge a toll for walking on his or her stretch of it. This, however, is illegal (as is clearly stated on a number of signs by the road), so following Roy's lead, I pushed past most of them . . . but we were stymied by the gatekeeper of the third tower up.

Studded along the wall are guard towers. These are generally square or rectangular structures with little openings on the sides; low archways to allow those walking along the top of the wall to traverse them, and small apertures on the sides to shoot at passing barbarians. (An aside: one wonders what occurred when the barbarians first came upon China's medieval version of the SDI. When you're in one of those towers looking over a formerly barbarian landscape, you can just imagine tittering as the Huns below ride past saying, in Hunnish, "We'll just go around it. This thing must end somewhere.")

Just before the third tower up, we ran across its self-proclaimed gatekeeper, a small, stocky woman of indeterminant age who held up two fingers and shouted at us in Chinese, demanding payment of two yuan apiece to enter "her part of the wall." "It's not your wall," Roy replied. "It's China's wall." (Another aside: I'm trusting Roy for the translations here—for all I know they could have been having a violent argument about ping-pong.) After this exchange, we continued forcefully, ignoring her blockade tactics and pushing into the tower. She somehow produced a three-foot-long plank and began waving it at Roy's calves. Roy, who is a paragon of physical courage, ignored her and began admiring the inside of the tower. The gatekeeper of the third tower up is, however, nothing if not tenacious, and she continued shouting at Roy, who escaped her pleas by climbing up a homemade ladder to the top of the tower. The ladder consisted of two large vertical branches with notches carved into them, into which were fitted a variety of planks, branches, sticks, bits of wire, whatever, to serve as rungs. It is further testimony to his courage that he climbed up this thing at all. The gatekeeper didn't hesitate, but climbed up right after him and sat herself down on top of the ladder, blocking his way. "Now you owe me two more yuan for climbing the ladder," she said.

I thought it prudent to stay on the ground, both to secure Roy's retreat if he ever made it back down the ladder, and because I didn't trust the sticks quite as much as he did. I therefore took a look at the inside of the tower.

The tower, like the rest of the wall, is made of large grayish stones that seem to fit each other perfectly. It's a reassuring structure, one I would appreciate having around me if I were under attack by barbarians. Its walls were covered in neat black official-looking graffiti, none of which I understood, of course, and near the ladder was written, in the same black paint but in English, "Climb ladder cost 2 Yuan."

Roy sat down next to the gatekeeper and began arguing with her again. He had the kindness to shout down translations to me.

"Everyone must pay two yuan," said the gatekeeper. "Even I must pay two yuan. Look . . . " at which point she removed two crumpled bills from one of the torn pockets in her gray jacket, and ceremoniously transferred them to another pocket. "You see, I must pay myself!"

I confess that despite the gravity of the situation, I found this highly amusing.

"But it's not your wall, really," said Roy. "It belongs to China. You're not allowed to extort money from people who want to walk on it."

"But it *is* my ladder!" said the gatekeeper. "I built it myself." She had him there.

"She has me on that one," Roy shouted down. He considered the ladder for a moment. "I doubt she actually hauled this up here herself, but maybe she paid someone to do it. It doesn't look like it was put here by the government."

I agreed, it certainly didn't look like a ladder designed by the Chinese government.

"OK," he said to the gatekeeper. "We'll pay you for using the ladder," at which point he gave her four yuan and motioned that I could come up. Unwilling to seem the coward and curious about the view, I climbed up the ladder, too, figuring that at worst I'd fall only two meters.

The view from the top of the tower was breathtaking. The thing about the Great Wall is that it's . . . well . . . it really is a great wall (maybe Nixon wasn't high after all). It just goes on and on, always on the crest of a ridge, and snakes like a dragon across the landscape. God knows I'm not the first one to make that remark, but sometimes clichés are so well-worn because they wear well. I won't describe it too much, though, because maybe Roy will decide to do that one day and I've used up enough of his remit already.

We stayed up there for a while, admiring China and talking about life and stuff. I find that when you're in the presence of ancient greatness, day-to-day concerns melt away and you're left talking about bigger things, like meaning, and art, and firecrackers.

Actually, firecrackers rarely come into it, but by now the stocky lady gatekeeper had climbed down her ladder and was shouting up at us that she had firecrackers to sell and wouldn't we like some? "No," Roy shouted down, "we don't want firecrackers." She then looked at me, pointed, and went "Boom! Boom!" I assumed that she was trying to sell me firecrackers as opposed to threatening my life, and since she was armed with nothing more than her plank, I figured a real threat would have been more along the lines of "Whump! Whump!" I therefore didn't panic but just shook my head.

Roy and I eventually climbed down the ladder and then back down the wall, having made our peace with life, China, and the stocky lady guarding the third tower up from the road. As we walked away, she stood there yet, her chin set and her plank at the ready, awaiting the next invasion of barbarians, as the last invasion had just retreated back to their car. I assume she's sitting there still, guarding the wall as her people have done for thousands of years. I strongly suggest you go and invade it for yourself.

WARNING:
THIS COLUMN CAN CAUSE
FETAL DEFECTS

It's always seemed to me that the anti-smoking lobby can get just a tad fanatical at times, and while this column was written in something of a spirit of reaction to that, it must be admitted that my shisha smoking did indeed turn problematic. I eventually realized that I enjoyed it far too much and missed it to an unseemly degree when I was traveling. This, coupled with some worrying things I read on the Internet, drove me to give it up. Unfortunately, after having given away my shishas, it struck me that I may as well have a cigarette from time to time . . . a habit I had quit some 10 or 15 years before. Alas! I quickly found myself smoking several a day and realized that I needed to smoke the damn things. In other words, I was once again hooked. This meant that I had once more to go through the whole "giving up cigarettes" process, which is not fun.

Far be it from me to promote smoking. I have no doubt that this would only further blacken my already black record in the great hall of American records. However, as I recently found myself back in Beirut enjoying one of my many vices, I thought the time had come to talk to you about the nargile.

The nargile goes by many names—shisha, hooka, even hubbly-bubbly—but no matter what it's called it provides the same sensory experience, namely: sweet, cool, fruit-flavored smoke that fills your mouth while you make gently gurgling sounds by drawing on a smooth wooden mouthpiece attached to a colored flexible tube that is sometimes pleasantly fuzzy. If you go back and count the senses in that sentence, you'll find that the nargile covers all five, hence its hedonistic allure.

So, what is the nargile doing in a travel column? It's here because there are many, many interesting places in which one can smoke a nargile. There is, of course, my house, which I at least find interesting and which boasts two nargiles, but there are also places like Beirut's Petit Café, which perches above the Pigeon Rocks and which I've mentioned before. For that matter, just about any restaurant or café in Lebanon will provide you with a nargile upon demand, and if you walk through Beirut's rebuilt "downtown" area in the inevitably lively evening, you'll be treated to a sweet atmosphere heavily scented with apple. Nargile smoke smells like nothing so much as incense.

You can also leave Beirut for a quick one-hour drive up the coast to Byblos, which is a beautiful little port that is the world's oldest continually inhabited town and where you can have fresh fish in a charming restaurant with both a view on the port and a cave in the back that was used by Phoenician smugglers.

Which allows me finally to respond to one disgruntled Ohioan reader: you may have falafel in Cleveland, but do you have Phoenician smugglers' caves?

Anyway, you can't actually smoke a nargile in the fish restaurant (although I may have convinced the owner to serve them in the future after breaking the ice with my new Arabic Useful Phrase: *"Ma aandi bachra, walla aandi djedj—aandi oktobut bas mano ma'I,"* which means "I do not have a cow and I do not have a chicken—I have an octopus, but not on me"); however, you can walk down a little farther to a café, which of course will serve you one.

Lebanon is far from the only place in which the nargile is widespread. Throughout the Arab world and well beyond, into countries like Turkey, cafés, restaurants and tea rooms offer nargile.

We can begin with the Pudding Shop in Istanbul. This café is on Hippodrome Square, or "Meydani," which used to be the Roman hippodrome, and which retains its ancient layout, although the vestiges of the stadium are gone. The Pudding Shop is always full of students smoking nargiles, playing backgammon and debating the state of the world. They will be very happy to have you come and join them. I assume there are also good places in Israel in which one can smoke a nargile, although I unfortunately haven't been there in a few years, and my own habit wasn't fully formed back then.

In Egypt, I must suggest the Sheraton hotel in Heliopolis. It's not very "earthy" nor is it a bastion of Egyptian culture, since it's inevitably stuffed with foreign businesspeople, but it must be admitted that they have a fantastic complex of outdoor cafés, pools and restaurants, as well as some of the best nargile service in the world. You can get a more "authentic" experience in the cafés near the great market, where you can smoke your nargile while listening to a musician with an oud lament about loves lost.

I have no qualms about authenticity when suggesting the Jumeirah Beach hotel in Dubai. There is no "authentic" Dubai, since the city itself is a modern invention. The Jumeirah Beach is part of the same hotel complex that boasts the Burj Al Arab, which proclaims itself to be the world's only seven-star hotel, and which sits just offshore as if it were Buck Rogers's space yacht. The Burj Al Arab is well beyond my means, but it's probably best to be looking at it as opposed to sitting in it (or so I tell myself), particularly because the Jumeirah Beach offers nargile served on lounge chairs dotting an improbable lawn, of all things, that stretches from the hotel down to the beach. You can therefore relax in the balmy evening by sucking on a nargile while watching the Burj Al Arab try to blast off, as the waters of the gulf wash up on the white sand, itself dotted with brain coral.

You don't really need to go that far, though. On London's Edgeware Road, there are a number of cafés that offer nargile, and there's also a tobacconist with a wide variety of good tobacco. In Paris, the pickings are slimmer—there's the Baghdad Café, in the 6th, which is no longer run by Iraqis, by the way, but to be quite frank, neither their tobacco nor their coals really hold their own. Better are the one or two Indian places near the Port St. Denis, or the cafés near Belleville or in the Goutte d'Or.

Or you can just buy your own. The best thing to do, of course, is to go to Beirut or Cairo or Istanbul and negotiate for hours with a swarthy man in a cluttered shop, but if this is impossible, you can also buy a nargile in Paris or London without too much trouble. In London, the best place is probably the tobacconist on Edgeware Road, who has a good selection. In Paris, I'd suggest the avenue de Belleville. You can find good ones in the 18th as well, but they don't sell tobacco, whereas there's a small tobacco shop on the avenue de Belleville that sells Tunisian (bad) and Egyptian (acceptable) tobacco. The very best tobacco I've ever found, though, was the "house blend" of a tobacconist in Amman. That sounds exotic, but it must be admitted that the shop in question is in an awful modern shopping mall next to a bowling alley.

You don't need to fly that far, though, for a shopping mall in which you can buy a nargile. There's a perfectly serviceable nargile shop in Broward County, Florida, at the Sawgrass Mills mall. People actually fly in just to go shopping in this mall, although I assume that relatively few of them do so for the nargile selection. I was amazed one day a few months ago when I went to the movies at the Sawgrass Mills mall (yes, sometimes I travel in the United States as well) and I ran across a tobacco shop with nargiles in the window.

It turns out that the shop is run by a Turk, who was pleased to the point of tears to speak with someone who actually smokes a nargile. He said that he hadn't been there too long, but he has sold a few nargiles—although he doesn't think his clients actually smoke them, because no one has bought any nargile tobacco. "They must use them for decoration, or maybe as flower pots." (It should be said that the glass base can make a rather fetching vase.) He planned to keep on trying. I haven't been back to the Sawgrass Mills mall in a while, so I don't know if he managed to survive, but I like to think so.

Apparently, nargile smoke is less detrimental to your health than that of cigarettes or cigars, since the water filters out a lot of the nastiness. On the other hand, you smoke the thing for about an hour. The real pleasure, though, is in sharing a nargile. There's a whole slew of little rituals that surround the passing of the pipe and in lands in which alcohol is theoretically frowned upon, the nargile offers a smokier conversational lubricant. You can pass many an interesting hour debating life, love and politics surrounded by a wreath of apple-scented smoke.

As long as you're not pregnant, of course.

SEX AND DRUGS AND SAMBAL GORENG BUNCIS: AMSTERDAM, NETHERLANDS

Nancy Reagan was right—one drug leads to another. The proof? After allowing myself to write a column featuring tobacco, now comes a column about the Hash, Marihuana & Hemp Museum in Amsterdam. One more step on that slippery slope. . . .

The Dutch sure had a knack for building wonderful cities. There's Bruges (I know, it's in Belgium, but Belgium didn't exist back then) and Utrecht, a beautiful little city that's well worth a visit despite being off the beaten track. But Amsterdam is . . . well, Amsterdam.

First of all, there's all that water. While Bruges and Utrecht have their canals, too, Amsterdam positively lives on the water. For that matter, a lot of the residents actually do live on the canals, in houseboats. The others tend to live in tall skinny houses of four or five stories with pointy roofs and great big windows that have no shutters and, often, no curtains. The Dutch have nothing to hide. The size of a house in Amsterdam, many of which date from the seventeenth century, is related to the size of the canal it lines. Big canals get five- or six-story buildings, three windows wide, while smaller canals tend to get the two-window-wide variety. And if most of the buildings seem kind of crooked, it's not a lingering coffeehouse effect; they really are. A lot of the houses in Amsterdam lean a little one way or another. It's very charming.

Despite its beauty, the first things that come to mind when many people think of Amsterdam are sex and drugs. There's ample reason for this, since Amsterdam does tend to flaunt both. You can't swing a dead cat in Amsterdam without hitting a marihuana-serving coffeehouse (it's amazing how much coffee the Dutch drink) and once the poor dead kitty bounces off the coffeehouse, it may well land in the lap of a prostitute, especially in the red-light district.

It's not as if you could avoid the red-light district either, it's smack dab in the middle of the old part of town. At least these windows have curtains, although they're only drawn when the women who occupy them are busy catering to the fantasies of some man. These fantasies apparently involve heavy older ladies to a much greater degree than one would expect.

In the middle of all this is the Hash, Marihuana & Hemp Museum, at 148 Oudezijdsachterburgwal. It is an interesting little place, a kind of shrine to the hemp plant. There are exhibits that show how hemp was used to make sails, including a fetching wooden model of an old sailing ship; examples of clothes made from hemp fiber; and a wooden duck that displays how waterfowl use hemp to build their nests. This might explain why ducks walk so funny and giggle all the time. There is also ample discussion of the joys of smoking the stuff, including a nice little collection of pipes (and an antique nargile!).

One whole section is devoted to decrying the excesses of the USA's war on drugs. It repeatedly states the claim that smoking hemp in its various forms (hashish, marihuana, etc.) is no worse, or even less problematic, than drinking alcohol and it explains the Dutch government's position—essentially, we would officially legalize it if the other countries of the world would get off our backs, but in the meantime we'll tolerate it (nudge nudge wink wink, and won't you come down to the Bulldog coffee shop and have a puff).

The museum is big enough that one could easily while away

15 minutes or so without getting bored, and it shares a "growing room" full of hemp plants with the store next door: the Sensi Seed Bank.

The Sensi Seed Bank does most of its business selling seeds to entrepreneurial home gardeners who are undoubtedly enamored of the hemp plant because it is really quite pretty, as can be verified by a peek at the growing room. At the Sensi Seed Bank, which has a number of outlets in Amsterdam and a few more in other Dutch cities, one can buy all kinds of hemp seeds, videos explaining how to cultivate the wondrous weed, and various tools of the trade: fertilizers, trowels, bongs . . . your typical gardening implements. According to the young gentleman who was managing the store, they do a thriving business, although they have been hurt by the decrease in American tourism to Europe. It would seem that many of their customers are American, although I don't know what they do with the seeds—they would be crazy to try to bring their purchases home (just read the bit on the American war on drugs in the museum). Maybe they eat them? Roast them up and sprinkle some salt or something?

I must confess that I did make a purchase at the Sensi Seed Bank. I bought a Frisbee. I live in France, and the French consider Frisbees to be toys—they only sell them during the summer, and then they sell you these flimsy little things. I have been looking for a good old 175-gram Ultimate Frisbee Frisbee and lo and behold, they were selling one in the Sensi Seed Bank! OK, so it has the image of a cannabis leaf on it, but it looked good and solid and I snatched it up. Why they were selling a Frisbee is beyond me, maybe they just made an automatic connection between marihuana and Frisbees—something to do with California.

All of this talk of cannabis and such may well end up making you hungry. This is a little problematic for two reasons. First of all, the Dutch tend not to eat out at lunchtime, so many of the better restaurants are closed. Second, Dutch food is resolutely uninteresting.

I know I'm asking for a hail of criticism from people who can't get enough gerookte paling and krabbetjes, but let's face it, it's just not exciting stuff. And it sounds even worse. Of course, everything sounds bad in Dutch. What the hell, since I've already earned the ire of any Dutch readers by insulting their smoked eel, I may as well make fun of the language, which is one of the five ugliest languages on the planet (and I say that out of kindness . . . the other four don't actually come to mind). If you want to approximate Dutch, imagine a German with the flu who has a tongue full of Novocain and is trying to yodel in Swedish. This gives you something vaguely resembling Dutch. Surprisingly, the language does become much prettier when sung—listen to Jacques Brel go on in Flemish in songs like "Marieke" and you may even get used to it. Of course, Brel could make anything sound magnificent and poetic and winsome, even the port of Amsterdam, where the sailors they drink, and they drink and they . . .

But I digress.

Anyway, as I was saying, the Dutch tend to eat sandwiches with milk for lunch (which is one of the reasons the French absolutely detest doing business with them), and if you're wandering around Amsterdam with the munchies around noon then you're going to have some problems. In general, your best bet is to try an ethnic restaurant. There's a Chinatown in Amsterdam along the Zeedijk with some good places (and a large Buddhist temple in case you're in need of peace of mind), but you really should go to an Indonesian place.

Luckily for the Dutch (less luckily for the Indonesians), what is currently Indonesia used to be the Dutch East Indies, and when the locals finally kicked out their colonial occupiers, the latter returned to Amsterdam with a taste for spicy dishes and peanut sauce. There are a lot of good Indonesian restaurants in Amsterdam where you can get among the best satays and sambals this side of Jakarta, often for a good price.

In the end, the best thing to do in Amsterdam—once you've calmed your spirit at the temple, your stomach at an Indonesian restaurant, and your brain at a coffee shop—is to walk around. There are great museums and boat tours and such, and you can look them up in a normal travel guide, but it's the city itself that grabs your attention and just won't let it go. And of course, you should make haste—half of the Netherlands is actually below sea level and the country may well disappear within a couple of hundred years due to global warning. They seem to be stoical about this, though . . . I even saw a coffeehouse named The Greenhouse Effect.

Can hemp be grown underwater?

THE GREAT WALL
OF CHINESE GOLF:
GRAND EPOCH CITY, CHINA

In 1992, the Chinese government built a brand-new walled city for the express purpose of holding meetings with itself. And of playing golf. And of hanging out and participating at banquets and playing tennis and ping-pong and swimming and just generally having a good time. Thus Grand Epoch City was born, about 50 kilometers from Beijing.

Yes, this is another dispatch from a land well outside of Europe, but I've gotten away with it so many times in the past I assume the editors will not give me too much grief and that I no longer need to bother coming up with some lame justification. It just goes to show that you should never give a writer too much leeway. And once again, I'm trouncing on Roy Kesey's remit, but I've bribed him with a fat French dictionary and it must be admitted that China's a damn big country—there's plenty to go around.

Anyway, Grand Epoch City was designed to be roughly a 1/6 model of old Beijing, back when the city still had walls. It contains temples, fountains, winding little hutongs, placid ponds and a myriad of other amenities. And because all work and no play makes the Chinese government a dull boy, it also contains a 27-hole golf course. The entire thing is surrounded by an enormous wall, modeled, of course, on the old Beijing city wall. Although I have not definitively verified this, I assume that Grand Epoch City therefore contains the largest walled golf course in the world.

Grand Epoch City is an amazing place, not least because it's not only big, but also pretty much empty. You have to have seen traditional Chinese architecture to appreciate the phenomenal amount of work that went into building so many copies of traditional buildings. Every roof is adorned with ornate sculpture; every building is graced with hand-painted scenes of battle and hunting and courtly life; the expansive ponds are bordered by exquisitely crafted covered walkways and little gazebo thingies (which assumedly have another name than "gazebo thingies") and bronze statues of mythical monsters with bulging, scaly haunches. Even the sporting facilities boggle the mind: a bowling alley, a swimming pool, table tennis, badminton courts, tennis courts, the biggest climbing wall I've ever seen and more, and all of it indoors. The place cost a fortune, and if it cost no more than that it's only because labor is so cheap in China. For that matter, there's no shortage of labor even now, since Grand Epoch City is crawling with waiters and attendants and people in sundry uniforms who serve no apparent purpose. When the government isn't using it, which is most of the time, all of this opulence is for the benefit of a handful of straggling businesspeople on seminars and city dwellers on larks. The staff seems to outnumber the guests by a magnitude of 10 or so.

In any Western country, and in the United States in particular, anything requiring this level of investment would be swarming with visitors. It never would have been built unless it could provide a reasonable return on investment and that would have required two-hour lines to use the indoor archery range. Profit, though, was not on the list of priorities of those who built Grand Epoch City. It's as though Disneyland were built for the sole benefit of Congress and then opened to the public as an afterthought, yet never actively promoted.

Grand Epoch City boasts a number of hotels, with nice,

spacious rooms and big-screen TVs that carry no English-speaking channels beyond CNN and BBC News. For that matter, there are very few English-speaking staff members. There may be none; in six days, I certainly didn't run across any. You also shouldn't expect to find all the perks you've grown to love in comparable hotels, such as room service. I arrived in Grand Epoch City with a bad cold and somehow explained that I wasn't going out to one of the many restaurants, but would like some soup in my room. This presented a problem for them, but they managed to send by a pleasant young man bearing a bowl of soup big enough to bathe a baby in. I had a little of it, then spent three days trying to explain that there was a bucket of festering noodles in my room and I would greatly appreciate it if someone were to come and take it away. The maid who cleaned my room just ignored it, despite the colony of fungus and the vague stirrings on the surface caused by the rapidly evolving life forms within. Eventually, I got a bilingual Chinese friend to convince them that I had not in fact grown attached to the noodles and that I wanted them destroyed.

Other amenities are likewise lacking. On one memorable morning, for example, there was no water in my room. I was told this was because it was International Water Day. This turned out to be true. However, it would seem that in Grand Epoch City, International Water Day was only observed on the seventh and eighth floors of the main hotel. And only until six o'clock (for which I was grateful).

On the other hand, not even the fanciest hotels in Beijing offer a formal gate-opening ceremony. Every day at 9:00 AM there is a big show outside the main gate of Grand Epoch City. This is meant to reproduce the traditional ceremony during the Qing dynasty by which the Beijing city gates were opened every morning. Apparently, eighteenth century-Beijing greeted the dawn with horsemen, dancers, soldiers and electric golf carts clustering under impressive city gates while a loud sound system blared unsteady music from behind a large sign. But I'm unkind—it is rather impressive, and the costumes are nice.

The gate-opening ceremony is followed by troupes of traditional dancers. Now these are interesting. First, there is a dance that was formerly only performed within the Forbidden City during Qing times, consisting of women in weird shoes (imagine high heels in the middle of the sole) and men wearing martial-looking costumes. The women sway and the men jump around a lot, all accompanied by musicians playing: flute things that sound like complicated kazoos; a really big drum; and two sets of cymbals, one big and one small ("Crash!" and "Ting!"). This is followed by stilt dancers. If the enticement of indoor archery and festering noodles doesn't get you out to Grand Epoch City, it may be worthwhile if only for the stilt dancers. This is a traditional occurrence during the Spring Festival, but in Grand Epoch City they perform every day. I never would have thought it possible to do what they do. Namely, they run around on meter-high stilts and engage in acrobatics that I find impressive even for people who have nothing higher than sneakers on their feet. This includes things like forward flips, handsprings, and human pyramids, all with stilts. This too is accompanied by the kazoo/drum/cymbal corps. There are also traditional Chinese clowns on stilts, wearing green clothes and sporting hideous makeup that makes their grimaces both amusing and vaguely frightening.

There is a museum of Buddhism at Grand Epoch City, although I didn't have time to visit it and it may just have been a garden anyway. There is also a big gray building that looked impressive and different enough for me to ask my bilingual friend about it.

"It's a temple," he replied.

"A temple of what?"

"Karaoke, I think."

I didn't go in the temple of karaoke. I have always shunned karaoke . . . except for one memorable occasion in Kobe, when, after much pleading on his part, I went with a diminutive Japanese friend, but only on the conditions that a) we both get drunk first, b) we get a private room, and c) we pick each other's songs. I knew that what with him being Japanese, he would be very kind to me and give me easy songs to sing, whereas I could give him impossible songs and laugh while he tried to sing them. Hence we started off with me singing "Me and Julio" while he had to sing Led Zeppelin's "Black Dog," which he did with gusto (climbed right up on the table to really belt out the high notes) and no small measure of talent. But that's another story.

Back in Grand Epoch City, another clear difference with real hotels becomes apparent at checkout time. The receptionists make a flurry of phone calls to ask arcane questions about your bill, write everything into a series of ledgers, type it all into a computer that apparently serves no purpose, then give you a handwritten receipt. The entire process takes ages, during which your eye might wander, like mine, to the wall behind the reception desk, where you will find a series of clocks with the time in different cities—as is often the case at hotels. These, though, show the time in Tokyo, Sydney, New York and Saint Paul. Like you, I immediately wondered, "Which St. Paul? St. Paul, Minnesota? Why the hell St. Paul?" One would have thought they would include someplace in Europe: London or Paris, for example. Whichever St. Paul it was, it wasn't in Europe, since it showed the same time as Tokyo. That pretty much ruled out Minnesota, for that matter. Since I had gobs of time on my hands, what with all the phone calls and discussions among the staff about my bill, I had way too much opportunity to ponder this—to the point of it becoming obsessive. One thing to keep in mind in China: never become obsessive about finding the answer to seeming illogical behavior. There's so much of it that you could go crazy. Nevertheless, I tracked down my bilingual Chinese friend over on the other end of the desk. He, too, had time on his hands, since his checkout was going no faster than mine. Through him, I asked one of the myriad employees behind the desk which St. Paul it was. She smiled and looked confused. "St. Paul?" My friend pointed to the clock, which it seems she was only noticing for the first time. This did not help. It was my friend who then pointed out that there is a "St. Paul" in Brazil, and it struck me that the clock referred to São Paolo, which is another mystery. São Paolo before Paris? Really! São Paolo is an awful place in a lonely time zone. Who makes these decisions? I thought of asking the same perplexed desk clerk, but she was double-checking how much water I had taken from the minibar and I thought it best not to disturb her.

Eventually, after three iterations of my bill, I gave up on the relatively minor anomalies that still remained and managed to check out. I can't say that I'll miss Grand Epoch City, but if you plan on a trip to Beijing and you're passionate about archery, rock climbing, tennis, golf, badminton, swimming and bowling, and can't go a day without doing all of them, preferably indoors, and you speak fluent Chinese, then you might give it a try. Otherwise, maybe not.

SWITZERLAND'S LEAST BORING STREET: ZURICH, SWITZERLAND

I expected this column to provoke protests from the Swiss. On the contrary, the emails I received from my Helvetian readers tended to agree with me.

We've already established that, on the whole, Switzerland is not an exciting place. If you were to list the countries in Europe from most exciting to least exciting, Switzerland would be a few pages down. Therefore, it is a definite shot in the arm if while in Switzerland you stumble across an interesting street. There are one or two in Berne, and Lugano can have its moments, but in my book, the least boring street in Switzerland is in Zurich.

The old part of Zurich looks a lot like you've probably imagined German cities if your impression of German cities was formed by the Brothers Grimm. In Zurich's windy little pedestrian streets, cobblestoned and often damp, you almost expect to see Hansel and Gretel skipping along in grubby lederhosen, with cream and jam smeared on their chubby faces. The streets are lined with pleasant old houses, many of which have a kind of little bay built onto one of the windows one or two stories up, generally housing a plant. Tall blocky church towers sport large clocks that chime the hour. All that's missing are lots of rats and a pied piper.

You pretty much have to go to Switzerland to find German cities like this, since just about every German city in what is actually Germany was blasted into oblivion by Allied bombers during the Second World War. Some of them, like Nuremberg, were rebuilt, but you can tell. It's like Warsaw (blasted apart by not only the Allies, but really by just about everyone during the war); the quaint old center of Warsaw was rebuilt, but all they had to go on were photographs taken a few years previously and you get the impression that some of those pictures might have been a little blurry.

Anyway, given the uncanny ability of the Swiss to avoid getting their country overrun, the last time any major violence was inflicted on Zurich was probably done with warriors wielding mammoth bones (that's not strictly true, there were even a couple of "battles of Zurich" during the Napoleonic Wars, but it was really the French and the Russians going at it, with the local Swiss running around trying to keep them from littering between cavalry charges).

So Zurich, or more specifically the old part of Zurich, is resolutely charming, and right through the charming bit runs a street that starts out as the Niederdorfstrasse and then becomes the Munstergasse before it stops being interesting again and turns more typically Swiss. This is the least boring street of any appreciable size in Switzerland.

The whole length of the Niederdorf/Munster street is pedestrian. No cars. That's always nice, now isn't it? But the interesting thing about this street is that it's full of people, generally young people, who are talking and laughing and stopping into the restaurants and the nightclubs and the cabarets that line it and having a pretty good old time in general. This generates a buzz of the kind that is all too rare in Switzerland.

The other thing about the Niederdorf/Munster street is that on it you can find some very interesting shops and stuff. There are those typically European shops carrying trendy, expensive stuff, such as my until-recently-Pregnant-Blonde-Danish-Friend so appreciates. (Please note, for those of you who read the dispatch about Copenhagen, that my blonde Danish friend is no longer pregnant; she gave birth to my new-and-very-short-blonde-Danish-friend, who is even now learning to shop despite her tender age.) It is not these shops that so entice me, however. There are three *other* shops that are definitely worth a visit.

The first is Schwarzenbach's Colonial Goods and Coffee Roasting (*"Kolonialwaren Kaffeerösterei"*). This is a simply wonderful place, at number 19, Munstergasse. The relatively small shop has been there for nearly 100 years and has never been redecorated. (Fear not, it is *cleaned* just about every day. This is Switzerland, all the same.) Schwarzenbeach's is a must and I make a point of going there every time I'm in Zurich. It is filled with treasure, a gastronomical Ali Baba's cave.

Schwarzenbach's roasts its own coffee, importing beans from just about everywhere. All these roasted beans are then put in jars and stacked on shelves, where they look just fine. But Schwarzenbach's also has teas, all kinds of teas, including the elusive smoked teas I love so much. They also have all kinds of dried fruit. I like to get little 100-gram bags of a variety of different kinds: Iranian wild figs, cranberries from Oregon, Thai papaya, pears, Malaysian coconut and many, many more, including, of course, your more typical dates, oranges, apricots, raisins and prunes from all over the world.

Schwarzenbach's also sells spices—dried and ground on the premises—and honey, nuts, exotic rices . . . you name it.

Needless to say, the place smells absolutely wonderful. Really—fly to Switzerland and go to Zurich if only to smell Schwarzenbach's. Do not expect, however, to find anyone who can translate what any of the more exotic fruits are into any language but German. Just guess, point, and take your chances. It will be fine. Trust me.

The next shop along is Barclay's tobacco shop. This is a tiny place with a kind old gentleman behind the counter. He has run it for

33 years. While a surprising number of people in the German-speaking part of Switzerland speak only German, when asked, in German, whether he spoke any language I speak, he responded, in German, that he could speak any language at all. I was not able to test him on *all* languages, but he certainly spoke the ones I can manage. We settled on French, which is, after all, an official Swiss language.

Barclay's has all kinds of tobacco, including, yes, nargile tobacco! Not the very best, elusive nargile tobaccos, but perfectly acceptable ones all the same. Barclay's also has pigeons. While I was chatting with the ancient proprietor, one pigeon came waddling in behind me and began looking at the old man with puppy-dog eyes. That's not true, actually—pigeons have these beady little dots for eyes but you could tell that this pigeon would have really wanted to make puppy-dog eyes if only God had been more kind to him and had graced him with irises. "He's hungry," said the old man, who then reached behind the counter and got a bag of seeds or crumbs or something and tossed a little outside the door. At this point, it became apparent that this pigeon had been elected by his pigeon friends to go in and hit up the old man for a snack while his friends hid behind the statue of the green-armored knight with the black codpiece just outside—they all came flapping out the moment the crumbs hit the cobblestones. When I was a kid and would visit the family in Sicily, my cousins would do the same, sending me to hit up my grandfather for some coins so we could play foosball (*calcetto*) at the café on our tiny town's main square . . . which undoubtedly makes this the only time that Swiss pigeons have been compared to Sicilian boys.

Anyway, fresh from my childhood reminiscences, I continued down the Munstergasse to the Eos bookstore. This is a truly great bookstore. It contains only antique books. The books in it vary according to what the owner manages to dig up at auctions and in attics and such. When I was there last, it was full of old medical texts. *Really* old medical texts, some dating from the sixteenth century.

The windows displayed not only the old books themselves, but also a collection of human bones, including a skull that had a big bandage around it. The bandage was kind of a moot point by now, but gruesomely amusing all the same.

This store, too, has a fantastic smell about it. It immediately reminded me of the library at my university so many years ago (not the one they have now, which is all modern and tidy, but the former one, which had been housed in an old converted church and was full of little passages and wrought-iron ladders). For me, that musty old book smell denotes knowledge; it's heavy with the weight of human understanding. The smell is the only thing musty about Eos, though—it's a lighthearted place, despite the bones. It even has one tiny room that is partly devoted to old children's books, including a pop-up version of Grimm's fairy tales from the '30s, in which a cardboard prince leans forever over Sleeping Beauty, about to bestow his wake-up kiss.

Zurich has a pretty good density of bookstores. I must admit that bookstore density is one of the criteria by which I judge a city, and Zurich comes out well by this standard (Brussels is still tops, though). It also has both a river and a lake, two other criteria on the "pleasant city checklist," as well as streetcars and a number of decent jazz clubs. The only unfortunate thing about Zurich is that it happens to be situated in Switzerland, but if you stay in the vicinity of the Niederdorf/Munster street then you won't get too bored.

Just remember not to litter.

A SLOW BOAT TO JAPAN:
KOBE, JAPAN

There comes a time, perhaps when you're walking through a parking lot in a Japanese city 5,000 kilometers from your wife and children with a jumble of highways crisscrossing over your head, when you become sick of traveling. There comes a time, after you've gone back to your hotel room to drink your way through jet lag in an attempt to fall asleep at a reasonable hour but then begin to sift through your notes to write about it, when you wish your life were somewhat more sedentary.

These things happen. They are temporary, but they do kind of build up, especially in Japan. If you were in a city like Kyoto, then you would go out and walk through the old parts of town, down by the river where the ghosts of glories past would gradually coax your spirit out of its funk. But when you're in Kobe, and the view from just about anyplace, day or night, includes an industrial port and great soaring lanes of traffic, then there's really not much you can do about it but drink.

Kobe has a history of making foreigners feel depressed. It was one of the two great ports of entry after the opening of Japan to the rest of world in the mid-nineteenth century (the other being Yokohama) and it was one of the first cities to include an official "foreign quarter." Even today it has a relatively large proportion of foreigners (a very small relatively large proportion . . . this is Japan, after all). The people in stores and restaurants are slightly more likely to speak English and the street signs are often marked in English as well, which is extremely useful. I once got lost in Kyoto and called a friend to say where I was: "Well, the first character on the street sign is a kind of box thing with a kind of line thing then another line thing that . . . oh never mind." This can be avoided in Kobe—not that there are many places you'll be wanting to go, though.

I have spent a total of three or four weeks in Kobe over the past few years and I never did manage to find an interesting site. Near Kobe there is Himeji, which has an absolutely stupendous castle, but in Kobe itself times are tough for the tourist. I am, however, of the firm belief that *everyplace* has *someplace* that's interesting, and when I recently returned to Kobe after two years' absence, I determined to find it.

Which is how I ended up in a parking lot under an overpass, on my way to the Kobe Maritime Museum.

To get there, I walked from Sannomiya, which is the nerve center of Kobe, in that a lot of the rail lines converge there and it's kind of in the middle. There is also a lot of shopping to be done in the area, an activity dear to the Japanese heart. In fact, just south of Sannomiya Station is Sannomiya Street (or Gallery, or something), which is a long covered pedestrian walkway with all kinds of shops and things of which I take little notice (although it does boast a kick-ass bookstore with a small English section on the top floor). After a while, and a little hook south and then west again, you enter Kobe's Chinatown. Everyone in Kobe tells you to go experience Chinatown, which is vaguely like China except a lot cleaner and with your typical Japanese tangle of overhead electric and phone wires, and not really very Chinese when all is said and done but what the hell else are you going to do in Kobe? They even tell you that you should eat Chinese food from the numerous stalls lining the street, but the Chinese food there tends to be far less than impressive, and there's so much good Japanese food in Kobe that you really have to wonder why you're buying lumps of fried chicken gristle from a Japanese man in a Chinese food stall. If you really want to eat in the street, then you're better off buying octopus balls from one of the ubiquitous little red stands with a smiling octopus painted on a sign. You find these all over in Japan. Why the octopus is smiling when you're about to eat it fried up with egg is a mystery.

Pass through Chinatown and head south and you'll reach the aforementioned parking lot with its coiffure of twisted overhead expressways. This is the gateway to Meriken Park, in which you'll find a couple of hotels and the Kobe Maritime Museum.

First, though, just behind the big gray fish-like sculpture that is marked "café" on its door but "Dance Learning Place" on at least one local city map I've seen, you'll run across a memorial to the 1995 earthquake, a terrible catastrophe that killed 5,000 people in and around Kobe. Meriken Park is on reclaimed land (read: land that was created by throwing rubble into the sea) and was heavily hit. A small stretch of land on the shore has been left untouched since the earthquake and you can get a glimpse of what it must have been like. Large concrete blocks are cracked like crumbled graham crackers and lampposts lean crazily in different directions.

The rest of the city has been entirely rebuilt, and the park is quite peaceful and well arranged, as one would expect in Japan. The park and the museum in it are devoted to Kobe's status as one of Japan's busiest ports.

There are very few major cities that so closely weave a major commercial port into their fabric. Most of the time, the big sweaty port area is off in some maritime ghetto. In Kobe, though, the city and the port mingle. Actually, the port *is* the city in many respects. Part of it may be that the steep wooded hills behind the city never allowed it to spread too far away from the sea, but whatever the reason, if you're in a building of any appreciable height, you're going to see a lot of big cranes and bulky ships.

Depending how you feel about these things, this will be

good or bad news. Well . . . it's not great news either way. You might as well get in the spirit of things, though, and go down to the maritime museum.

Near the museum, in the park, there are already three vessels you can check out, each held up by supports in its own waterless pit. The first of these is a reproduction of a caravel. I assume it's a Portuguese caravel (note: you have to assume much when visiting Meriken Park and the maritime museum, because there is very, very little written in anything but Japanese) because at the time caravels were sailing the ocean blue the Portuguese made contact with Japan and traded with them until the Westerners and their pesky religion were thrown out. Anyway, the caravel is interesting, if you're interested in old ships, which I am. When you're standing next to it (regrettably, you can't go on it), you have to wonder how Columbus ever had the guts to get into one of these things and sail toward the end of the world. It's really small.

Near the caravel is a kind of hydrofoil that looks appropriately fast, and next to that is the *Yamato 1*, a "Superconducting Propulsion Ship." The *Yamato 1* must have been designed by whoever put together the models for the old *Thunderbirds* TV show. It's a big, hulking thing with bulging bits underneath and an ultra-cool glass cockpit that could contain the whole *Thunderbirds* cast, even if they were life-size. I used to have a bunch of *Thunderbirds* toys and none of them were as cool as this thing.

Impatient to get more information on this monster, I entered the maritime museum, much of which is taken up by a rather un-maritime playground. It's a nice indoor playground, though, featuring a psychedelic mushroom-type slide. Why it's there I have no idea. Behind the slide is a nine-meter model of the HMS *Rodney*, flagship of the British fleet that sailed into Yokohama harbor to help the Americans convince the shogun that 200 years of isolation was one year too many and wouldn't you like to open up your market to trade so we don't blow you to hell with all these guns?

The rest of the maritime museum consists essentially of models of cargo ships—models of warships being politically incorrect in the extreme. If, like me, you spent a fair amount of your childhood building models, then you will find this fascinating, despite the fact that cargo ships are probably not what you were building. If, however, you are not enthralled by models of container ships and tankers, then you might be less than captivated, despite the big diorama of the Kobe container port with lights that blink and flash when you press the different buttons.

There is also a display about the *Yamato 1*. Upon recognizing this, I virtually flew to it and watched the little film. The little film is, of course, in Japanese, which means that I only understood when there was a number shown, but I understood enough to learn that the mighty, hulking *Yamato 1*, on display just outside, could manage only a measly eight knots! The films of it moving across Kobe Harbor were pitiful—the thing looked positively anemic despite all the handclapping and shoulder nudging going on in that great glass cockpit. It would seem that while the propulsion system is revolutionary, relying on quantum mechanics or something, the actual performance is paltry. What a waste of bulbous curves!

My disappointment in the *Yamato 1* was somewhat allayed by a very nice evening out with my friend Toshi, who has a favorite restaurant in Kobe to which he has taken me during a number of trips in the past. It's a small, informal, but deceptively expensive place where you eat traditional Japanese food.

I love traditional Japanese food, especially in Japan, where it tends to be far better than it is elsewhere (the absolute worst example being in Warsaw in 1993. I still haven't gotten over that meal). The only thing is, you have to be prepared for your food to squirm. In this same restaurant, I once saw a Japanese woman kindly request that the chef take away the front part of the lobster we were eating. At the time, we were all partaking of its sliced tail, but the front part of it suddenly started waving its legs at her in either anger or supplication and however Japanese she might be, it was too much for her. On my latest evening with Toshi, we had no lobster but we did have, for instance, one large tiger shrimp apiece. These were removed from the tank and began flopping violently as the chef prepared them for us. He cut off their heads (the bit with the legs) and presented us immediately with the flayed tails of the little beasts, which we happily popped into our mouths. Mine immediately did a jig in on my tongue, I assume in some postmortem reflex, which caused me to break out in the kind of expression one assumes when one's food is trying desperately to escape from one's mouth.

"Fresh!" said Toshi.

"Fresh!" I replied, and bit the little bugger in two.

In the end, a friend, good food and copious amounts of sake overcame my initial bout of traveling doldrums and I ended up content enough—but I confess that despite all that I was happy to leave Kobe for the mystical city of Nara.

KNOCKIN' ON HEAVEN'S NOSTRIL:
THE DAIBUTSU,
NARA, JAPAN

In the eighth century, Japan needed a capital. For a few years they futzed around with a couple of locations until they decided to build a capital in what is now the city of Nara. Less than 100 years later, they moved the capital to Kyoto, where it remained until the mid-nineteenth century.

Nara wasn't the capital for all that long, but those 100 years were very important ones in Japan. Notably, they saw the widespread introduction of Buddhism, as well as a series of vicious plagues that decimated the population. These things taken together inspired the rulers of Japan to build great temples in an effort to elicit the favor of God (or The Gods, depending on how you look at it—the intricacies of Japanese religious practice are impenetrable). These temples still exist in Nara, one of the few cities to escape annihilation by American bombers during the Second World War, thanks largely to the effort of Dr. Langdon Warner, an American academic who convinced the U.S. government to spare both Nara and Kyoto for the sake of their cultural treasures.

The biggest of these temples is the Todai-Ji, which contains the Daibutsu—literally, the "Big Buddha." This is a big statue of Buddha. It's really big. In fact, it's the biggest bronze Buddha in the world, at 15 meters. And keep in mind that this Buddha is sitting down. I mean, his *ears* are 2½ meters long. His hand could hold 20 people.

The Todai-Ji is an enormous wooden temple. Both the statue and the temple were built in the eighth century, but the building burned down twice, both times partially melting the Buddha. The current building dates from the seventeenth century, and is only two-thirds the size of the original, but it's damn impressive for all that.

Just outside the temple grounds, and indeed throughout all of Nara's extensive park area, are hundreds of sacred deer. These deer descend from animals first brought here centuries ago and they are so thoroughly tame as to walk up and nudge you for a handout. You can buy little crackers to feed them, which they enthusiastically endorse by showing up in droves and looking at you with those big deer eyes of theirs. One young buck even began nudging me with his antlers. He got a lot of crackers.

Upon entering the temple, I was approached by a pleasant woman who asked if I wanted a free English-speaking guide. I instinctively smiled and said no, hardened by the hordes of more-or-less official guides who assault tourists at so many spots around the globe to try to wheedle money out of you. I then remembered that I was in Japan, after all, and that this does not happen, and that if someone says something is free, it really is free.

I therefore started speaking with one of the guides, and as I was taking notes (yes, I do actually take notes to write these things), a number of others came around and smiled and exercised their variable levels of English.

It turns out that all these guides participate in a program run by the University of Nara. They are volunteers: most of them retired businesspeople, some of them students, one or two professors who just like hanging around the Daibutsu. Two of them were particularly endearing, in a grandfatherly sort of way. They were Tomiyasusan and Nakanosan, both retired and both tickled pink to be hanging out with someone writing about the Daibutsu. Tomiyasusan was especially pleased since he also had a very limited but charming knowledge of French, which he employed with gusto once he learned I live in Paris.

My two new friends gave me all kinds of interesting facts about the place, some of which I actually understood, and then they took me around to the side of the really big Buddha, where we came across a pillar with a hole in it.

The Todai-Ji temple is made of wood, as are almost all traditional buildings in Japan. The structure is held up by great thick impressive wooden pillars, all painted red. One of these pillars had a hole cut in the middle of it, near the floor. The hole is just big enough for a small person to wriggle through, which any number of small people were trying to do as we approached.

"This is the nostril of Buddha," said Nakanosan. "If you can go through it then you have a place in heaven." I remarked that heaven seemed far more attainable for children and skinny people, to which Nakanosan nodded. He suggested I try, but I like to think that my shoulders would stop me before my midriff gave me away. Either way, I'll just have to try being good to get into heaven.

I hung out for some time at Buddha's nostril, behind the towering figure of the Daibutsu. It was quite a show. Most of the supplicants were children, who had no problem at all wriggling into heaven. That being said, there was one Japanese schoolgirl who tried to go through with her backpack still on. What do they teach them at these schools of theirs? Anyway, she ended up taking it off and making her way to paradise.

After a while, though, one little boy begged his father to give it a try. While slight, the man apparently wasn't holy enough, because try as he might and despite the encouragement of the crowd, he couldn't wriggle through. He stood up, dusted himself off, then tried again, this time thrusting his upper body into the hole and managing to get both shoulders in, but that's as far as he got.

After the doomed man came a young woman, who shimmied her way in despite her tight skirt. While it would seem that she is destined for heaven, her right shoe is not, as it dropped off with the final wiggle. Alas, she shall limp her way through eternity.

Finally, a young Belgian guy decided to give it a go. He certainly looked to be the right build for heaven—he probably weighed no more than 130 pounds. He took off his backpack, handed it to a Japanese bystander, and lay down on the floor, initiating a snakelike movement that none of the other contestants had yet tried. Unfortunately, about halfway through he seemed to get stuck. "Pull!" yelled some of the Japanese as a substantial crowd formed. The Belgian finally gave a great shove and was born into the world on the other side of the pillar, to enthusiastic applause from the gathered spectators. I rushed up to interview him.

"Are you pleased about getting into heaven?" I asked.

"Very. It had been a concern of mine."

"How'd you manage?"

"It was Buddha who pulled me through!"

Buddha was less anxious to help an old Japanese man. It's a shame: if I were Buddha, I'd have helped him if for no other reason than his chutzpa. The man must have been nearly 80 years old, but he kneeled down and stuck his head into Buddha's nostril, gave a few valiant but feeble wiggles, then righted himself with surprising dignity, and smiled. I suppose he'll get into heaven anyway.

After observing a number of people trying to take the short road to paradise, I took leave of my friends and left the temple, only to be chased down by Nakanosan, who probably hadn't run so hard in years.

"You . . . should . . . come back," he panted. "We . . . can visit . . . the lotus altar!"

He explained that in their capacity as tour guides they had the right to climb right up onto the dais upon which the Daibutsu sits. They had never done it before, but today was the day! A monk was going to come and explain things to them and the group had decided to invite me along.

"You are lucky!" he said, to which I heartily agreed.

I thanked him profusely for his consideration and his diligence in having run so hard to catch up to me, and we returned to the temple, where all the different volunteers were gathered. I introduced myself to those I had not yet met, asking them whether this were a kind of frog (see my dispatch on useful phrases for an explanation) and then we fell silent as a short monk in a blue robe came to us.

There followed a conversation that seemed to center on me, since my new friends (including the leader of the group, a professor of English literature) kept pointing to me and arguing. After a while, Nakanosan came, shook my hand, and regretfully explained that the monk did not want me to go on the lotus altar. "Don't worry, it's not something racial," he said. "It's not because you're a *gaijin*. It's because you're new." I assured him I was not insulted, but he told me that he was shamed.

The professor of English literature then came to apologize, bowing and shaking my hand while Tomiyasusan tried to negotiate with the monk, despite my assurances that it was all right and that I appreciated their effort and I would be fine. This had become a matter of honor for the guides, though, and the negotiations continued. The monk was intransigent, and just about everyone from the group, even those who knew nothing more of me than that I had apparently lost my frog, came to apologize and express their shame.

Finally, the blue-robed monk left, replaced by a new monk in much nattier black robes. When asked about me, he said, "Sure!" and then told me through a translator that he had a French car, a Peugeot 106, "the one with 16 valves. It really moves!" I made appreciative "*vroom vroom*" sounds and off we went to climb onto the lotus altar, upon which sits the 500-ton bronze Buddha.

If the Daibutsu is impressive from the floor of the temple, it's even more impressive from the dais upon which it sits. It is a beautiful statue and I'm sure the black-robed Buddhist monk said lots of interesting things during the half hour or so that I was up there, but few of my newfound acquaintances really had the English skills to translate with anything approaching efficiency. They managed to point out vague ideas: "the perspective is maintained" or "the lotus carvings are like the sutra" but that's about it. These, though, sufficed—being close to this 1,200-year-old statue, being allowed to touch the bronze, and watching the long, delicate fingers of the monk were fulfilling in and of themselves.

After our jaunt up on the altar, I saw a small stand at which one can donate a roof tile for the preservation of the temple. You make a donation and then are allowed to use a calligraphy brush and ink to mark your name, the date, and your wish, and the tile is eventually incorporated into the roof of the temple. I thought this was a splendid idea, and I can now say that a wish for my sons' happiness helps keep the rain off the Daibutsu.

The volunteer guide company of the Daibutsu strongly encouraged my calligraphic efforts and even insisted I take a picture.

"I have no camera," I said. "I don't like taking pictures."

"No, it's for us," they responded.

Somewhere in Nara is a picture of me, the lucky *gaijin*, holding my roof tile in front of the enormous Buddha, surrounded by a group of genuinely friendly guides.

THE ORIGINAL SINGAPORE SLING

I was once told that Singapore is the country Walt Disney would have liked to create: clean, fun, pleasant, and with hidden security guards lurking behind the façade to lead you away if you step one inch out of line. This is kind of true, but at least the line is a little broader in Singapore than it is in Disneyland.

For one thing, there are all the bars. Singapore is full of bars, ranging from seedy dives to the ultra-classy bar at the Raffles Hotel, where the Singapore Sling was invented.

The Raffles has got to be high on the list of the world's most legendary hotels. It's a great whitewashed symbol of British colonialism, a throwback to the days when, as the Brits would say, the world map was covered in "pink bits" (i.e., countries they owned), and the planet's largest empire was administered by low-key men sporting impeccable white suits, diamond cuff links, stiff upper lips, and snotty accents with which they traded subtle witticisms while being civil to the members of whatever indigenous population were serving them their drink.

In order to remain so civilized, they built places like the Raffles Hotel in Singapore, or the Taj Mahal Palace in Mumbai. Built around the turn of the twentieth century, these places feature lots of white wooden walls, soaring ceilings, slatted shutters, pianos and gin. They have liveried attendants at the door; they have no weeds in the flower beds. These days they are, of course, air conditioned, but they still have thoroughly useless ceiling fans that turn aimlessly way up on those high ceilings because they just wouldn't be the same without ceiling fans. It's a shame, really. Despite 112% humidity in Singapore (the air is roughly as thick as motor oil), these places really should have open windows with languid air flowing through the slats in the shutters, pushed around by overworked ceiling fans. It's like running across the original Rick's in Casablanca and finding that Sam has been replaced with a jukebox. (Note: there never was a Rick's in Casablanca until a couple of years ago, when an enterprising entrepreneur opened one. Last time I was in Casablanca was 1997, so I can't attest to whether or not there is a Sam or a jukebox in the current Rick's . . . maybe I'll go check it out soon.)

Anyway, in the early days of the twentieth century, a legendary bartender named Ngiam Tong Boon worked at the Raffles and he invented the Singapore Sling, evidently because he felt that gin on its own was not appropriate for women. The official recipe is as follows:

> 30 ml gin
> 15 ml cherry brandy
> 120 ml pineapple juice
> 15 ml lime juice
> 7.5 ml Cointreau
> 7.5 ml Dom Benedictine
> 10 ml grenadine

This gives rise to a pink drink, which is inevitably served with a maraschino cherry and a slice of pineapple. It kind of tastes like classy Kool-Aid, but I strongly suggest that you refrain from saying so while at Raffles.

This, of course, begs the question of why you're spending $10 to drink classy Kool-Aid.

If you get tired of dropping your cash for classy Kool-Aid,

you'll want to go someplace both cheaper and livelier. Or so I assume. Chinatown is a good bet. What's more, Chinatown still boasts old-fashioned Singaporean buildings: low three-story affairs with pastel-colored walls and those same tall slatted shutters. Most of the rest of Singapore is given over to skyscrapers; kind of like New York with giant tropical cockroaches. In Chinatown, though, you really do get the impression you're in Asia, especially when you pass a large sign proclaiming: "Cheng Mun Chee Kee Pig's Organ Soup King." Alas, this enticing shop was closed when I went by.

Chinatown is hopping at night, but so is Boat Quay. Boat Quay runs along the Singapore River, until recently a fetid stretch of filth but now quite pleasant, upon which you can find a lot of little tour boats, all low wooden vessels with a small awning of sorts and red Chinese lanterns strung along the sides. They have eyes painted on the bows and they carry tourists and relaxed Singaporeans up and down the river with a low *chug-chug* sound. In the evening this is actually very beautiful; the lanterns make them seem like so many reddish fireflies cruising low on the water.

You can watch them from any of the multitudinous restaurants that line the quay. In fact, if you walk up the quay you'll be assaulted by the waiters, each proffering a menu and offering free beers if you eat their Chinese/Thai/Indian/Malaysian cuisine. No matter which you choose, you'll be able to eat chili crab, which is the Singaporean specialty, and well worth the trip. Be forewarned that you should not attempt chili crab, though, if you're making this a romantic evening, since it is utterly impossible to eat it without making a royal mess of yourself, especially if you've first had a couple of Singapore Slings at Raffles then took up your waiter on his free beer offer (try the local beer, called Tiger).

The restaurants themselves are in the aforementioned old-fashioned buildings set a little back from the water, but they all have outdoor seating under a veranda of one sort or another on the water's edge. This is where you should sit. Or you could go over to

Clark Quay, which is similar but less in-your-face, and where most of the restaurants' riverside seating is in these colored podlike things that really are a bit too Disneyesque for my taste. You feel like you're eating in a decommissioned tilt-a-whirl. The redeeming restaurant at Clark Quay is a Thai place where the food is frankly average but which has a floating dining area moored to the quay with its own Chinese lanterns. Every time a tourist boat goes by, the thing sways a little. I like swaying restaurants.

You will have to go back to Boat Quay for a shisha. There's a little place named Sahara that will serve you a poorly packed shisha by the river. You take what you can get. It didn't seem very Saharan to me, though—everyone who worked there was either Malay or Indian, but they knew about shishas. One night I managed to introduce the pleasure of the shisha to an interesting New Zealander, who once participated in a dragon boat race in Hong Kong Harbor during which his boat sank. I suppose if you have to go down in a dragon boat it's best to do so in a warm-water harbor.

Singaporeans are proud of their multicultural society. The country primarily consists of people of Indian, Chinese and Malay descent and they mix pretty well . . . and all this in a country that's considerably smaller than the city of New York. The extraordinarily convenient thing about Singapore is that this multiculturalism has given rise to linguistic practicality—everyone speaks English, even the cab drivers. This is rare in Asia. This, coupled with the large population of Europeans, means that you can feel pretty much at home. When you've been away from your real home for a while, this can be comforting.

THE LOST CIVILIZATION
OF TORRE:
CORSICA, FRANCE

It's embarassing to point out that it actually didn't occur to me at the time that "Torre" does mean "Tower" in Italian . . . a language I speak. Thus, the passage about why the Torre people are called the Torre people is pretty self-evident: they built towers, of a sort. I'm still just guessing, but it seems obvious to me now. This happens sometimes: you hear a word from language A that just pops up in the middle of a sentence in language B and you don't recognize it, especially if it's not pronounced the same way.

The worst example occurred years ago, when I was spending a drunken evening in the presence of a very good French friend of mine in Dijon. We were racking our memories trying to remember all the artists who played at Woodstock (this was before the days of the Internet, when the answer to everything can be obtained with a click of a mouse). At one point he said, "Canadette." I responded that there were no groups named Canadette at Woodstock. He insisted, I insisted, we argued in slurred tones and he finally stumbled back to his apartment to get the concert album, which he brought back to my place proudly pointing to "Canned Heat."

Roughly 6,000 years ago, someone crawled through a narrow passageway, stood inside a kind of big niche among massive slabs of granite that had formed an impromptu geological pyramid, looked out over the great sprawling bay beneath him and the low mountains on the other side, and decided that a god lived here.

What the person's name was, what the god's name was, in what language these thoughts were expressed . . . no one knows. The person was a member of the Torre civilization, a Bronze-Age people who left traces across the western Mediterranean and then either disappeared or turned into some more literary civilization that then forgot their roots. One thing is certain, the Torre people shared at least one attribute with me—they loved Corsica.

Yes, it's summer again and it's time for my annual Corsican dispatch. Last year I evoked Odysseus, and this year we'll go back further still to the mysterious builders of the Torre. The obvious place to start is in Torre itself, a village from which they may have gotten their name. (Note: this seems like a spooky kind of "we don't know why they called themselves" kind of thing, but it's not that—we don't actually know *what* they called themselves, and I assume there's no mystery as to why archeologists call them the Torre people, it's just that *I* can't figure it out. I've seen conflicting reports, some saying that they are named after the town and others saying that the town is named after them, and if any of you would like to inform me which is true then this particular archeological mystery would be easily solved. But I digress. . . .)

The town is situated just north of Porto-Vecchio. (You *must* go to dinner one or many nights in Porto-Vecchio—go down to the rue de la Porte Génoise and check out one of the restaurants that have been built into the old ramparts and that overlook the bay.) The town of Torre is hardly worthy of the word "town." It consists of maybe eight houses, only three or four of which seem to be inhabited. They are all old, in the way that a big old rock is old. I should mention that while I have been to Torre many times, I have never actually seen anything alive there except a big black dog. It's always the same big black dog, for that matter. It is a very Corsican dog, which means that it doesn't move around much. In fact, pretty much the only reason I'm sure it's alive is that I've seen it several times in the last few years and it hasn't rotted any. I also think it once opened an eye and looked at me, but I may be mistaken.

Anyway, you don't want to go to Torre to see the village itself. What you want to do is go up and see this extraordinary place of Bronze-Age worship, this natural temple to Apollo or Baal, or whomever the Torres worshipped, which consists of a jumble of enormous granite slabs, two of which managed to form a kind of shelter and the whole of which looks out over the bay of Porto-Vecchio.

One would imagine that such an important and physically striking sight would be well marked with all kinds of signs saying, "This way to the really important archeological sight," but no such luck. A few years ago there was one little sign, but someone tore it down, and now you just have to kind of know about it, especially since the townspeople (assuming they really exist and that the big black dog doesn't do these things on his own) put up a "No Entry" sign on the road so that you can't even drive into the town anymore but have to park in the middle of the tiny road that leads up to it then hoof your way up to the top. Once you get there, this is what you do: bear left, then walk between the inhabited house on your left and the apparently uninhabited house on your right, pass the sleeping black dog and you'll see a rusty metal gate. Go around this and on your right you'll see a path going up with brambles and things only slightly barring your way. Push through them, climb some crude stone stairs (which may or may not be natural, I've never worked that out) and you'll reach a kind of passageway/cave-type thing on your left. Walk through there and you'll suddenly find yourself in this granite enclosure with a precipitous drop in front of you and the Mediterranean spread out far below. You will immediately feel the urge to worship a heathen god.

On top of all this is a dolmen, a stone structure in which Neolithic people in Europe buried their dead . . . or at least the most important of their dead. You need only exit the shrine and climb a little further up to examine this and its eerie chambers.

Near Torre is the town of Arraghju, where the Torre civilization built what can really only be described as a castle, or at least a fortress. It is known as the Castle of Arraghju and it is far better marked than is the site of Torre. In Arraghju, there really are a lot of signs marking the way, and at the bottom of the trail leading up to the structure (it is high above the town), there is even a little café-type thing where you can buy ice cream and sandwiches and beer (among other liquids . . . incidentally, Corsicans make a beer out of chestnuts, a traditional island staple, that I can't stand but that may tickle your fancy).

The hike up the mountain to the castle is not as easy as one might expect for a place that has a café at the bottom. Bring lots of water and wear good shoes. When last we went up, we passed a family that included a number of young children, all wearing flip-flops, and they did not seem to be having a fun vacation experience. For that matter, years ago I climbed up to Arraghju with a two-year-old who simply couldn't handle it and whom I had to carry on my shoulders. Neither did I have a fun vacation experience that day.

In the end, though, you will arrive at the castle and you will be impressed. Really. I mean, the structure is seriously old, yet it is clearly a formidable defensive redoubt. It was built entirely out of rocks piled on top of each other—ranging from small to very large one-ton rocks. However, for a jumble of rocks it has a clear structure. There is a big gateway as the only entrance, formed by topping the rock walls with a few very large flat rocks. The outside wall of the circular castle is topped by what was obviously a guard walk and in one area in particular you can climb a stairway into a kind of guardroom: by standing in it you can just see over the top of the wall, allowing you to hurl nastiness down on any assailants with minimal exposure of your own vulnerable bits. True, it's not Château Gaillard or Krak des Chevaliers (ah, I should write about them one day) but then they aren't 6,000 years old.

   Something happens when I stand in places like that. You look around and wonder: What wars took place here? What sort of men were these, and who were their assailants? Did they believe that their deeds would go down in history? Would they be disappointed if they knew that they have not? Who were the gods they worshipped in their shrine and who was the chieftain they buried in the dolmen? You can sit on a mountain in the sun and look at the sea and wonder about these kinds of things in Corsica. Pondering is better in the sun.

CITIES IN THE SAND:
RIO DE JANEIRO, BRAZIL

Rogean Rodriguez was born and raised in a favella in Rio. As a child, he would go downtown and shine shoes. One day, when he was 13, he came across Alonso Dias, who had built a city in the sand. Alonso had learned how to make sandcastles back in his native Colombia, where he perfected his art to the point that people would give him money to look at his sandcastles.

After a while, Alonso's sandcastles attracted enough attention that he began to get commissions from hotels and even shopping malls to build big sandcastles for them as a promotional stunt. It was then that he decided to start traveling around Latin America, both for a change of scenery and for a chance to ply his trade in other places. One can hardly travel around Latin America without coming to Rio, and it was there, on the Copacabana Beach, that young Rogean saw the Colombian's sandcastles and was so mesmerized that he forgot all about shining shoes and would just come and stare at the cities in the sand.

Eventually, Alonso started showing the boy how to make sandcastles, too. Rogean had no family, and neither did Alonso, so after a while they decided to make their way together. Rogean became the adopted son of Alonso.

I ran across them on the same beach upon which they had met, and like Rogean, 10 years before, I was fascinated by what they had built in the sand. There were towers and spires and windows and staircases and statues and belfries and flying buttresses and architectural wonders that I would have found impressive enough in stone, let alone sand. Alonso was proud of his creation, and he was proud of his adopted son. "He will take over when I'm gone," he said. "And then his own son will take over." Rogean beamed at me. "I have a wife," he said, "and we just had a little boy."

"Maybe one day, together, we will build my dream," Alonso said. He then took out a book of drawings and photos and press clippings to show me a sketch he had made. "It's a theme park, all built out of sand!" The theme park featured statues and castles and little booths to buy ice cream, plus a big banner over the entrance that said something I couldn't read.

If I found it difficult to squint at Alonso's drawing in the glare of the Brazilian sun, it was at least partly because my head was still pounding after the previous evening's excesses. It's so damn easy to exceed in Rio. I had been out all night in the company of a bunch of mostly Brazilian friends, sprinkled liberally with other Latin Americans, a couple of French and a South African whose lack of samba skills was compensated by his unbounded enthusiasm and near fatal blood alcohol levels. My own lack of samba skills was so complete that no amount of alcohol could make up for them, though Lord knows I tried.

We had spent most of the evening at Scenarium, a club in the old part of town where you can buy the paintings, baubles and books that lie around while the entire crowd pulsates to the rhythms produced by a band of old-time samba musicians who appear to have developed a kind of symbiotic telepathy with the people swaying and shimmying in front of them. I spent most of the evening either watching the band or expounding on philosophy and international affairs in that kind of slurred, fevered enthusiasm one can only express when one is very drunk. I have no doubt that everything I said was seriously stupid, but then I imagine no one remembered it anymore than I remember their own incomprehensible replies. These conversations inevitably end up in flurries of giggles or with someone grabbing your hand to drag you onto the dance floor for an unsuccessful but enjoyable samba lesson.

An evening like that is hardly a proper precursor to a day of exploring a city, but if you plan to go to Rio just to spend your nights lounging in your hotel and then going to bed early, you might as well stay home in Podunk. Anyway, the next morning I dragged myself out of bed and went out to visit *Christ the Redeemer*.

It's true that I usually try to avoid describing the patently touristy destinations when writing these things, but you just have to go visit *Christ the Redeemer* in Rio. The statue stands at the pinnacle of the Corcovado, one of many towering spires of rock that jut up in the middle of the city. To get there you can either drive or take the train. You should take the train. It is a small three-car affair that runs on a track with the kind of gradient one expects from a ski slope, not a railroad. It was built by the Swiss, who know about steep railways, and you can catch it way down below then sit and look out the window as it winds its way through the tropical forest that makes up a surprising proportion of the land area in Rio. Once at the top, you can walk up a series of steps to the great big statue itself, where you can observe myriads of people standing in front of it with their arms stretched out so that their friends, lovers or spouses can squat a few feet in front of them and take pictures of them superimposed on the 30-meter statue of Jesus behind them. All together, they kind of look like the final scene in *The Life of Brian*.

The thing you need to do up there on "hunchback" mountain is to get in front of the statue of *Christ the Redeemer* and look the *other* way, down on the city 700 meters below. When I was there, clouds were skidding along below me, allowing peeks here and there and then occasionally parting to afford a brief, spectacular view of the whole city.

In my book, Rio may well be the most beautiful major city

in the world. It's all mountains and forest, the buildings like a glittering layer of rock candy sprinkled over the folds of the terrain. In the middle is a big lagoon and all along the edges are the beaches, with the wide gray Atlantic stretching away to the horizon.

No other big city so revolves around beaches. No other city has so many *songs* about its beaches, come to think of it. It's not a rare sight to see businessmen in jackets and ties sharing the sidewalks with people wearing bathing suits and carrying surfboards. For that matter, the people with surfboards may wear ties some other time during the day—who can tell?

On those beaches you just might run into an old Colombian and a young Brazilian making cities of their own in the sand. If you do, then stop, gawk, and give them a few coins . . . they're saving up to build a world of sand.

THE STREET PERFORMERS OF BARCELONA, SPAIN

I have meant to write about Barcelona for a while now. I've even mentioned it from time to time and one impatient reader went so far as to write to me to ask if I had any suggestions for her before she left. (I'm ashamed to say that I never did respond, and for this I apologize profusely. Hopefully she's not too upset with me and is still reading this column and can glean some small use from it. Now that she's probably back home.)

The thing is, it had been some two or three years since last I had the opportunity to visit Barcelona, which is two or three years too many. It's not the kind of city that you want to avoid for that long. Conscious of my duty, I therefore decided to go back, accompanied for once by my wife, for a romantic long weekend. This was purely in a spirit of professional conscientiousness.

There's a hotel near the Plaça de Catalunya that will arrange things for you so that once you come back from dinner you'll find a bottle of champagne on the mantelpiece next to a bowl of strawberries with cream (two spoons), a hot bubble bath already drawn, little candles all over, and your bed strewn with rose petals. That sounds irremediably syrupy, but it's not, really, and the hotel itself is very slick and modern, and when it comes down to it, it's just romantic. I'd tell you which hotel it is, but these things are doubly worthwhile if you track them down on your own. Anyway, it's a good base for a romantic weekend.

Which raises the point that Barcelona is a romantic city, but in a young way (Venice being a romantic city in an old way . . . which reminds me that I have never written about Venice either). Barcelona moves, it lives, it throbs, and in no place does it throb harder and faster than along Las Ramblas.

Las Ramblas is a long road, running from the Plaça de Catalunya to the harbor. It's really more of a promenade than a road, the cars being restricted to two narrow strips of asphalt on either side of a wide pedestrian walkway. It's this central median that provides the entertainment, as it is perpetually filled with strolling people and a myriad of street entertainers.

Most of whom, in fact, don't actually *do* anything. Las Ramblas, you see, is particularly well known for its human statues. You can find human statues in most major cities—in many cases, being a human statue is the last refuge of the talentless street performer: "I can't sing or dance, but I can paint myself green and pretend to be a tree." There are certainly plenty of these types of human statues along Las Ramblas (including one who pretends to be a tree), but you can also find those who take human-statuing to unexpected heights.

For example, there is the guy who is painted all in black with specks of gold, wearing wings. I assume he's some kind of ambiguous angel, but whatever he is, it's just beautiful. Really. And then there's the guy who has built an ornate structure out of rubbish, all painted a kind of copper color, and who paints himself the same kind of copper color then melts into his own sculpture. My favorite, though, is a skinny guy with a little Leninesque beard and glasses, all painted gun-metal gray and sitting on the rail of a subway station. He's very metallic.

He also doesn't move, whereas the less artistic human statues tend to ham it up for picture-snapping tourists. While this is certainly in character for the human statue Elvis, it seems distinctly out of place for the human statue tree, for instance.

Besides those already noted, a brief catalogue of Las Ramblas's human statues on a weekend in August (admittedly the height of human statue season) includes:

Julius Caesar
The devil
A very white guy
Mickey Mouse
Che Guevara
2 Korean soldiers
A cowboy
A cowgirl
Several Indians
A guy in an electric chair
A guy manning the wheel on a ship

. . . and, of course, lots of Egyptian statues and the like.

If you're looking for performing artists who actually *perform*, then you're better off checking the streets of the Barri Gotic, the section of the old town just to the east of Las Ramblas. This is a fantastic warren of tiny, winding streets that contains the nicest square in Barcelona, the Plaça Real. This is actually not as old as it looks (nor as old as the surrounding streets) but it fits right in. It consists of a large open space bordered by arcaded sidewalks. It also has palm trees planted in it. That's nice.

Around the edges are a number of trendy cafés and restaurants, all of which have seating that extends out into the central plaza. On a summer's evening, all manner of performing artists come to dance and prance and sing and play. Most of them, it must be said, are pretty bad.

The worst of them must be the Romanian belly dancer. I hesitate writing about her, because it's a pretty sorry sight, but she has an act wherein she wheels her wheelchair-bound husband in front of a café, he then presses a button on a cheap boom box and she wiggles and jiggles in a thoroughly un-artistic impersonation of a belly dance while wearing the kind of belly-dancer costume the Disney store sells to little girls who want to pretend to be the princess in *Aladdin*.

Nearby, though, I did run across one of the most striking street performers I've ever seen. He was a remarkably tall and thin German guy on enormous stilts, wearing only a very, very long pair of black trousers and black and white body paint on his chest and face. He swirled and twirled to flute music, dancing his heart out and bounding around a small square in the Barri Gotic.

All of this, though, was nothing compared to a man who calls himself Mu. As the Barri Gotic stretches toward the Plaça de Catalunya, you run across the remnants of the Roman wall that used to surround the city in ancient times (visit this—Roman walls are always good). Near there is an old church, and sitting next to the church was Mu, flanked by a stoned percussionist and a young guy playing the trumpet. Mu was playing a kalimba, an African instrument that's kind of like a lyre in a tortoise shell, and singing improvised lyrics into the midnight air.

Mu's lyrics were sung in a mix of English, French and Brahme (an African language). Those that I understood dealt with life, love, injustice, the breeze . . . whatever. He sang into his kalimba, or sometimes raised his face to the night, eyes closed. Four or five of us sat, mesmerized, for near an hour while others wandered by, hesitating but continuing on their way. A dog sat watching, head on paws.

Mu is from Guinea-Bissau, and has been in Barcelona this past year or so, making a record with a group he formed called Qbamba. The people he was playing with are not his regular musicians. "They just showed up, you know, man? They play well, though."

And they did.

Barcelona is a magnet for singers and lovers and dreamers and poets and sculptures. I don't know why . . . or rather I do know why: you can feel why, you can wander through its streets and feel it in the breeze on a summer's evening and then it's obvious, but what I can't do is explain it . . . so I'll just stop trying.

FORTUNE-TELLING RABBITS: ISTANBUL, TURKEY

W hy do you want to get your fortune told by a rabbit?" asked my Beautiful Turkish Friend.

"Because it's cool, and they're cute, and despite all the times I've been to Istanbul, I never had a rabbit tell my fortune."

She made a kind of puffing noise that Turkish women are wont to make, and we headed off to Ortakoy, not so much because the rabbits there are anymore prescient than anywhere else in Istanbul, but rather because it's a simply wonderful place to go for dinner.

Ortakoy is a small neighborhood on the Bosphorus, not far from the whopping continent-spanning bridge, which has an unfortunate tendency to tower over it in its whopping way. Even with the bridge, Ortakoy has retained its inimitable charm: small wooden buildings lining cobblestoned streets lead to the central square, which is on the water and usually has tiny fishing boats bobbing up and down next to it (plus enormous freighters gliding by not too far away on their way to or from the Black Sea). On this square are a number of restaurants, most of them specializing in fish. Ortakoy is a great neighborhood to go to if you're in the mood for fish.

People from Istanbul eat a lot of fish and almost inevitably it ends up being some special kind of fish that you can't find anyplace else. On this particular occasion, my Beautiful Turkish Friend informed me that it was palamut season, an eagerly awaited occurrence during which the palamut swim back to the Black Sea. Apparently, once a year they swim from the Black Sea to the Mediterranean, but very deep, so you can't catch them, but then later they swim back, at which time they swim near the surface and are snatched and gobbled up by hungry Turks. (Note: my Beautiful Turkish Friend cautioned me that she might actually be mistaken about which direction is deep and which is shallow, and promised to look it up, but I think I know my readers well enough to bet that you won't really care and probably don't plan on fishing for palamut in the Bosphorus in the coming weeks anyway.)

So we strolled around Ortakoy for a while looking for fortune-telling rabbits before dinner, but there were none. Not a one. It was probably too late in the evening.

"To cheer you up," she said, "I'll buy you a lollipop. Lollipops are better than fortune-telling rabbits anyway."

It wasn't exactly a lollipop. It was macun. Macun is a cross between chewing gum and taffy, and is served by street vendors who have brass trays divided into sections, each containing a different flavor of macun. They twirl a stick in the flavor or flavors you request and serve it up to you. We had a choice of banana, strawberry, kiwi, orange and cherry. At the insistence of my Beautiful Turkish Friend, I tried a mix of them. She had strawberry.

It was good. And sticky.

As it turns out, my Beautiful Turkish Friend's aversion to fortune-telling rabbits and her preference for lollipops is the result of deep-seated childhood memories. It would seem, so she explained over our palamut, that when she was a girl, fortune-telling rabbits and macun were offered by the same man in her neighborhood of Istanbul.

"At the same time? Didn't the rabbits eat the macun?"

"No, you silly man. (*Puffing noise.*) Sometimes he had rabbits and sometimes he had lollipops. He never had them both at the same time."

Which means, of course, that the presence of rabbits *precluded* the presence of lollipops, and my Beautiful Turkish Friend does like her lollipops.

"It's not just that," she said, when I offered this as a subconscious root cause of her aversion to fortune-telling rabbits, "it's also that whenever he had his rabbits, I would worry to myself that if I paid the rabbits to tell my fortune, maybe the rabbits, which are not very intelligent creatures, would smell one of my *friends* and pick out *her* fortune instead, in which case I'd be stuck with a bad fortune and I would have wasted my money. Much better to spend my money on ice cream."

"Not lollipops?"

"Aren't you listening? (*Puffing noise.*) When there were rabbits in my neighborhood there were no lollipops, so I had to settle for ice cream."

Which made sense.

I should here mention that my Beautiful Turkish Friend has a beautiful name, which means, when translated, something like "feeling" or "sense." It should also be said that I tend to find many Turkish women beautiful, and they exacerbate this by sporting names such as these. For instance, my Beautiful Turkish Friend has beautiful friends of her own with names like "Love," "Happiness," and "Mystery."

Beats "Cindy"—let alone "Gertrude"—any day.

Anyway, the lack of fortune-telling rabbits in Ortakoy did mean that if I wanted to get my fortune told then it was going to have to be elsewhere.

A couple of days later, I therefore set out for Sultanahmet. I had been staying near Taksim Square, which is the heart of Istanbul in a lively/shopping/business sort of way, but not in an historic sort of way. Sultanahmet is the historic center, where you'll find the great tourist sights that you really, really, must see (including Topkapi and, one assumes, John-with-a-c, who works there as a guide). Since fortune-telling rabbits tend to hang out either near relaxing Turks (hence Ortakoy) or tourists, you have a good chance of finding them in Sultanahmet.

I decided to walk. I love walking from Taksim to Sultanahmet (not to mention that the ungodly traffic in Istanbul means that walking from any point A to any point B, except during the dead of night, is probably faster). You walk down the Istiklal Caddesi, which is one of the liveliest streets on the planet. It's entirely pedestrian, really long, very wide and bursting with life. What's more, once the Istiklal Caddesi turns right a little, you can continue straight on, down the Galip Dede Caddesi, which is Istanbul's music street.

Most cities have music streets—places where musicians go to buy instruments and equipment. In Paris, it's the rue Victor Massé, behind Pigalle (I should write about that one day); in New York there are a few, but West 38th has a strong bid; in Cairo, it's Mohammed Ali Street, near the bazaar (great place too) . . . etc. The Galip Dede Caddesi is particularly developed, with literally dozens of stores selling guitars, pianos, traditional Turkish instruments, and the kind of cymbals one can only find in Turkey and that are greatly valued by drummers the world over.

This will bring you down to Galata Bridge, over the Golden Horn, where you'll pass scores of people fishing (for little silver fish that probably only swim sideways every other month and it's the season right now and we should go eat some) and then, on the other side, to the Spice Market.

This is definitely the right way to approach Sultanahmet. The Spice Market is a little bit like the Grand Bazaar (which we'll get to shortly) in the way that Philadelphia is a little like New York—not as big, not as impressive, but with a charm and an important history all its own. Its construction was initiated in the sixteenth century by the mother of a sultan and completed many years later by the mother of another (mothers of sultans were often the real power behind the throne during the Ottoman Empire).

The Spice Market, or "Egyptian Bazaar" to the locals, smells real nice. You enter it's 400-year-old doors and are immediately hit with a wave of smell that you'll find nowhere else. It's the smell of the Orient, the most vivid remaining vestige of the exoticism that was once Istanbul. I had never smelled anything even vaguely like the Spice Market until . . . well, until I first went to the Spice Market. This is why it's the perfect way to enter Sultanahmet: it gets you primed for the history of the place in a way that no guide ever could.

After the Spice Market, you really should go up to the Grand Bazaar.

Too many tourists approach the Grand Bazaar as a kind of ancient shopping mall. They go there to *shop*. Don't do that, especially not the first time. Expect to spend money, yes, but think of it more as a money-sucking village, or even as an entire money-sucking subculture. This is, in fact, not far from the truth. Years ago I once found myself in the bazaar in the company of an American friend who wanted to buy a Turkish rug (and who was more or less an expert in such things); a Turkish man from whom I had just bought a leather jacket (which I still wear regularly); and the leather salesman's sister, who sold carpets and was in deep negotiation with my American friend about one or two pieces from her stock. As neither the young leather-man nor myself were even remotely involved in this particular transaction, we got to talking over on the side, and he told me about his family history. He said that while they had always been merchants, they weren't really part of the old guard in the bazaar—they had originally been from the Turkish community in the Crimea and had only moved to Istanbul, and the bazaar, recently.

"When was that?" I asked.

"About 200 years ago."

The bazaar is a city in a city—a covered city, with arches and columns and a many-vaulted ceiling running along the wide thoroughfares and the narrow alleys. In its center is the "Old Bazaar," from the fifteenth century, which is built quite differently. Instead of the vibrant blues, yellows, reds and whites of the rest of the world that is the bazaar, the Old Bazaar is built of red brick; its ceilings are much higher and the merchants there primarily sell jewelry and antiques—weapons, etchings, magnificent carvings of ivory and meerschaum.

All that's very well, but you'll never come across a fortune-telling rabbit in the bazaar; street space is too precious. I therefore left the bazaar and set out on foot toward the epicenter of Sultanah-met: the space between the Hagia Sophia and the Blue Mosque.

I would normally go on about both of these, but the editors are already probably nervous about the length of this dispatch and they can easily be looked up. Suffice it to say that the Hagia Sophia is truly one of the wonders of the world, second in my book only to the Eyptian pyramids (which I suppose I should write about one day as well—I had a nasty run-in with a camel there once). What is more precisely to the point is that across from the entrance to the magnificent underground Byzantine cistern, I found a young man with fortune-telling rabbits! My quest was over!

Sahan has been plying the fortune-telling rabbit trade for 14 years now (although he might have misunderstood, he looked to be too young) and he was very glad to introduce me to Bonçuk, Siri and Pamuk, his three rabbits.

"Tell the rabbit your name," he said, which seemed only fair since I already knew theirs. Upon learning my name, Bonçuk wiggled his nose the way rabbits do and then chose among the dozens of folded up pieces of paper in front of him. He drew one with his little teeth and Sahan took it, handing it to me. The other rabbits did nothing but observe. I assume they were in training. I, of course, understood not a word of the little piece of paper, but lo and behold, the fortune-telling rabbit trade has apparently modernized itself these past few years, because Sahan looked at the slip of paper, punched a number into a kind of portable voice thing he had, and proffered it to me. It explained, in English, that according to Bonçuk, I would be successful if I could overcome one last obstacle. In the typically optimistic mood one feels after having one's fortune told by a rodent, I assumed this means you'll soon be seeing a novel of mine on the *New York Times* best-seller list.

Happy with my fortune, I went off to dinner at Yesil Ev, then for a nargile and tea at the Dervish Café, which is pretty much a perfect evening, despite the fact that I was unfortunately alone.

As I sat puffing my apple-flavored smoke under trees bathed in ethereal green light, with the minarets of the Blue Mosque all lit up behind me, it struck me that this would be a good time to write something about Istanbul, so I took out my notes and wrote . . . well, this, and as I did so it struck me that often, life is good.

FLYING OVER
(AND STOPPING IN)
BANGKOK, THAILAND

Out my window, I see the tops of clouds and a sunrise. It's kind of weird watching the sun rise through an airplane window while you fly east; it's as though someone hit the fast-forward button on your life. Life is short enough without a fast-forward button.

This, coupled with the fact that I'm flying directly over it, has led me to the chilling realization that I have not yet written about Bangkok, despite the fact that I returned from my last trip there over two months ago. I have therefore taken out a crumpled pile of little scribbled-upon slips of hotel paper, a few canceled tickets to Thai sites, and my computer and am trying to finish this dispatch before I arrive in Vietnam (just a stopover on my way to Manila. Too bad.)

I figure there must be only one company that provides those little slips of hotel paper, because they always have pretty much the same format: roughly 12x9 cm, with some kind of bogus coat of arms on the top and the hotel's name underneath, then the address and phone number on the bottom. You'll find a thin pad of these things near the telephone, and sometimes another one in that kind of stationery kit on the desk (or in the top drawer), the one that also includes bigger versions of the same paper, a postcard or two, and a couple of envelopes.

I never use the big paper or the envelopes, but the little sheets are really useful for taking notes to write these dispatches. I actually save the little pieces of paper afterwards. I have a drawer full of them. I suppose it's partly because I'm such a hopeless photographer. I never, ever take any pictures of anything and these little slips of paper and the dispatches serve as a photographic substitute.

Talk about an auto-analytical digression. Anyway, back to Bangkok (which, according to the image of the little plane on my seat's screen, is rapidly slipping behind us).

Bangkok is like the drain in the world's bathtub: not particularly appealing, but an inevitable destination. People naturally flow to it, like water, sometimes despite themselves, and if you're not careful I suppose you could get sucked into the whirlpool at its rim and lose yourself.

But enough quasi-mystical apocalyptic crap has already been written about Bangkok (or sung by Murray Head). Bangkok is also just an interesting place to go. There are many high points: genuinely beautiful temples, the palace, the barge museum (where you can see stunning royal barges and their frontispieces that poke their way out of Thai mythology. Even from a purely literal point of view there are highs.)—I went to dinner at one place perched on the top of a 60-story building. The restaurant is the roof of the skyscraper, and the diners sit outside, choosing their proximity to the railing on the basis of how afraid they are of heights. While I was there, a thunderstorm came up and we watched bolts of lightning approach until the waiters finally shooed us downstairs, where every table has its unoccupied double so that in such occasions the diners can be effortlessly relocated. I protested; the lightning was mesmerizing and I wanted to stay and watch. The idiocy of this only struck me later. I suppose that's why bugs fly into those blue zappy things—maybe they know about the danger but they can't help it.

Come to think of it, those blue zappy things might be a good metaphor for Bangkok too, along with the drain thing.

And then there are the low points. While Patpong is well known, there are numerous other areas of ill repute, and all of them tend to resemble each other. You walk down streets pulsing with neon while women try to entice you into bars with American names (lots of Old West motifs). Inside, there is an inevitable stage festooned with inevitable poles upon which bored-looking young women do something that is supposed to be dancing while other young women (or maybe not—it can be disturbingly hard to tell) make the rounds of the bar's patrons, sitting next to them and proposing various personalized services.

You generally don't get propositioned if you're a woman yourself, or if you're a man accompanied by a woman. In that case, they leave you alone. When last in Bangkok, I spent one evening exploring a particularly seedy street with a couple of colleagues: a curious lady from New Zealand and a South African man. Of the three of us, the New Zealander actually felt the least awkward . . . but then again it could be a cultural thing; I've never known a New Zealander to feel awkward about anything. Anyway, thanks to the presence of a woman in our little group, we avoided any direct propositions while checking out the bars.

Which raises the point that men, when in strip joints with women, act like . . . well . . . dorks. This is based only on this one occasion, and is further limited to my examination of only two males (myself and my South African friend), but I'd be surprised if it weren't a universal phenomenon. I mean, on one hand, we had gone into these places only to check them out, and for my part, out of a spirit of journalistic inquisitiveness (please don't snicker) so you want to *look* a little, but you don't want to *look* with a female friend sitting next to you. You need to pretend that you're not interested at all while you're looking. Just a little. She, on the other hand, had no such qualms and provided a running commentary.

Then again, it's such a sad sight that it's not really that difficult to turn your head away. Nobody who isn't drunk really seems to be enjoying themselves, least of all the performers who are gyrating around the poles.

There are tales of more unusual entertainment, places where women not only pretend to have sex with a pole, but where they engage in all kinds of genital gymnastics (usually involving props, sometimes involving fire). This, we managed to avoid, abandoning the tawdry regions of the city to go to the night market, where merchants sell their wares from thousands of tiny stalls and where it is impossible to find anything to drink that isn't beer.

My plane is well past Bangkok by now and is descending towards Ho Chi Minh City, so I'd better wrap this up—cut to the quick, so to say, and tell you about the silk weavers.

On our last day in Bangkok, my New Zealand and South African friends and I managed to spend a full day going around the city in a boat with a very pleasant guide, who was herself the friend of a Thai friend (you with me, here?). She took us to a place that is definitely worth a mention.

There used to be a thriving silk-weaving trade in Bangkok itself. Now, though, this has moved outside the city and only one place remains in Bangkok where women still weave Thai silk on traditional wooden looms. One would assume that a place such as this would have tour busses parked outside and camera-toting Japanese parked inside, but this is not the case. For one thing, it can only be entered through a narrow alleyway off of the Sansub Klung, one of the many canals that cut through Bangkok. For another thing, it would be physically impossible to put more than a dozen or so people in the room anyway.

Inside, you'll find a very old gentleman with a very long name that I unfortunately did not catch and two or three women working old wooden looms that go *click-clack, click-clack* when they do something with their feet. Scattered around the walls are photos, clippings from newspapers, pictures of Thai royalty and a calendar. A small TV plays for the benefit of the workers and books of ledgers are scattered on plastic furniture. Three or four electric fans make a vain effort to cool things down.

You can buy silk directly from the old man with the long name (note: the best clothing purchase I ever made was 12 years ago when I bought three Thai silk shirts on the street in Bangkok for $2. I still wear them.), but he seems not to care overmuch about selling anything to you and I have to imagine that if you don't have some way of communicating in Thai (interpreter, actually being fluent yourself, Babel Fish, etc.) then it would be impossible. But hopefully you'll be encouraged by the news that this place exists, even if I haven't given you enough information to actually find it (it's near Jim Thomson's house, which is a landmark of sorts that actually has something to do with silk, off the canal, near the flowers [actually, there are flowers all along the canal, but what the hell], near a caged toucan and behind a broken blue bicycle).

We're pretty low now and they're going to make me turn off my computer in a moment, which means I don't have enough time to tell you about Thai massages, where deceitfully delicate little Thai women push and pull on your limbs and walk on your pajama-ed back, nor about feeding the fish who hang out in the canal near the Buddhist temples because they know no one will kill them there, or . . .

Too late, Vietnam approaches.

BOILED DUCK EMBRYOS: MANILA, PHILIPPINES

A Filipino reader kindly informed me that the truck-like things are called "jeepneys." According to him: "Jeepney drivers are good at knowing who paid when and where he is going. Fare is passed on from passenger to passenger until it reaches the driver and change is passed the same way back to the passenger." He also informed me that balut is best eaten hot and that my Filipino friends probably fooled me into eating it cold just to make it more gross.

Manila probably has all kinds of things to recommend it—I've heard tell of the world's smallest volcano not too far from the city; of striking gorges; of a nice seawall; of an old town that retains some charm. I have never seen these things, so I can't report on them. I have, however, eaten boiled duck embryos in Manila, so I'll tell you about them.

I suppose you're thoroughly disgusted by now, but it's not really as bad as it sounds. I mean, after all, I've eaten insects, sea slugs, fruit that smells like rotting excrement, and living creatures that have tried to crawl away, and compared to all that, boiled duck embryos are no big deal. Or at least, they shouldn't be.

Nevertheless, I do confess that I hesitated when it came time to shell my first boiled duck embryo—known as balut in the Philippines. It should first be said that you can't find them in restaurants, or at least not in most restaurants. The way to acquire balut is to buy it from vendors in the street. This is, of course, well nigh impossible, or at least unadvisable, if you're not Filipino, which means that you're going to need to rely on a friendly Filipino. Happily, this is easy, since Filipinos are resolutely friendly people and they will be thrilled and not a little impressed that you want to try balut.

It was my Filipino hosts who procured some balut for themselves, my colleagues, and me. They took out their plastic bag full of balut while we were sitting in a traditional restaurant eating things like grilled squid, a couple of kinds of pork, and tilapia—a very good freshwater fish that could save the world according to environmentalist aquaculture specialists (long story). All of this was eaten without knives, since Filipinos don't use knives. They cut with their spoons. Now, I always try to maintain a strictly neutral, nonjudgmental view on local cultural traits, but this no-knife thing does seem kind of pointless to me (no pun intended). One Filipino told me that it was because the Spanish hadn't allowed Filipinos to own knives when they were the colonial overlords of the Philippines (the Spanish always got along swimmingly with their subject populations). Anyway, at the end of our knifeless meal we were presented with the balut.

Balut is made by taking a fertilized duck egg that's been incubating for 17 or 18 days, and quickly boiling it. The result is a cross between a hard-boiled egg and . . . well . . . a baby duck. They are eaten cold. There's a right way to eat balut and a wrong way to eat balut. The right way to eat it is this:

1. Break the egg on its large end. This already is difficult, because duck eggs are dismayingly symmetrical. If you break it on its big end then you have a nice little cup that prepares you for step two. If you break it on the small end, you get a rather pitiful tiny beak or something.
2. Using the egg as a kind of cup, tip it up to your mouth and

drink the "juice." It actually tastes like very nice chicken soup, although personally I'd much prefer it if they didn't call it "juice."

3. Eat the yellow bits. This tastes like hard-boiled egg poached in chicken soup. Or perhaps like the red bits inside a crab. Or maybe a mix of them. Or something.

4. Eat the white bits, which will hopefully mask the feathery bits inside. This is crunchy. Don't think about why.

5. Drink some beer.

The wrong way to eat balut is any other way.

Objectively speaking, balut is good, and, for that matter, you eat a lot of babies in France anyway: duckling is a delicacy and suckling pigs are all the rage in Corsica. And, of course, you don't have to be French to eat veal or lamb. Still.

That's about it, really. To a degree, I'm cheating by writing about Manila, since I haven't really had a chance to explore and my recent trip there was my first. I wasn't even planning to write about the city, but it was difficult to pass up telling you about embryonic ducks. Since, though, this is pretty light, I did make some notes during my three-day visit about a few other specificities.

Small personal transportation devices. Cities throughout Asia abound with small taxi-type vehicles. (Please note that I in no way include Japan in the word Asia—Japan is Japan.) In Thailand, they are called "tuk-tuks"; in India, they are called "autos" (short for "auto-rickshaw"), etc. These are three-wheeled devices with two-stroke engines, open sides, and a small bench in the back where you can squeeze three people as long as they have relatively small asses. In Manila, these do not exist. Instead, you find vehicles that are kind of like bicycles with sidecars, some with the same rickety motors, others just with pedals. The passenger compartment is covered on top and open on the sides. This is the only city I know with these things.

Larger transportation devices. The streets of Manila are full of very funky car-truck-van things that are kind of a cross between covered stretch pickups and pygmy busses. They all have pretty much the same design, which looks like it was based on a small American truck of the 1930s. The rear of these vehicles, where the passengers sit, have roofs, but are open on the sides, and passengers can jump on and off the back then squeeze in to sit on one of the two long benches lining the sides. The vehicles are either shiny aluminum, or gaily painted, or have pictures on them, or are some combination of the above. They have spare tires bolted onto the side, near the driver. I have no idea how the drivers make money, since I didn't see anyone paying to get on or off them, and neither do I have the slightest idea how the riders know where they're going, since I can't imagine these things follow set routes. I suppose I could look this up on the Internet, but some mysteries are best left mysterious.

Don't believe the taxi drivers. Assuming you don't want to take the Filipino version of a tuk-tuk (they are pretty dangerous, in fact), then you're going to end up in a taxi. While as a whole I find Filipinos honest, pleasant and helpful, this does not necessarily apply to the taxi drivers. Your taxi driver is very likely to flatter you by telling you you look like some improbable movie star, and then explain that he needs 10,000 pesos to get his mother/wife/child/brother into/out of the hospital/army/navy before Christmas/Easter/it's too late. This gives you 36 different possible stories (ranging from "I have to get my child into the hospital before it's too late" to the less common "I have to get my mother out of the navy before Easter"). Filipino taxi drivers are not alone in this, but since they all speak perfect English you may be somewhat more subject to intricate bullshit than would otherwise be the case.

OK, so I'm no expert on Manila, I admit it, but there are a few quick observations for you in case you find yourself in that part of the world. And, of course, you now know the right way to eat boiled duck embryos.

THE NESTING HABITS
OF ROMAN CARS:
ROME, ITALY

A ll roads lead to Rome. Once they enter Rome they become streets—little winding streets packed with traffic. Eventually, the cars that make up the traffic stop in some semblance of what is generally known as parking. In Rome, however, the entire concept of parking is somewhat different than it is on the rest of the planet.

When you walk around in Rome, you get the nagging impression it's the cars themselves that determine where they go to roost. The drivers are like little parasitic organisms—gut bacteria or something—residing in their innards, expelled from time to time so the cars can get on with their lives. As such, when walking around a piazza you can easily believe that the cars have not *been parked*, that instead, they are *nesting*.

There is no neighborhood in Rome in which this is more the case than in Trastevere. This is on the other side of the Tiber (Tevere, in Italian), across from the ancient magnificence of the Forum, the Coliseum, etc. For many years, Trastevere has been one of the best places to spend the evening if you happen to be in Rome. For that matter, even if you don't happen to be in Rome, it might well be worthwhile to go there just to spend the evening in Trastevere.

The neighborhood is traversed by Viale Trastevere, a broad

boulevard, but you don't want to go there. You're much better off wandering around the tiny streets and the little *piazze* that seem to be almost accidents; existing only because a street decided to widen a little, or because two or three happen to have come together at some point.

That's one of the things about Rome: some cities are obviously planned, other cities are more chaotic yet bear the marks of their various creators, but Rome seems to have built itself. There's a warmth in the place that isn't generated by the inhabitants, but rather by the cobblestones and the buildings themselves. The inhabitants just bask in it. You can't really enjoy Rome to the fullest unless you learn to bask in it as well, but the process of learning this particularly Roman skill is one of the most enjoyable educational experiences you'll ever undertake. Once you master it, you can easily spend entire evenings just strolling around in Trastevere, stopping in a trattoria here, a pastry shop there, or just sitting on the steps of the fountain in the Piazza di Santa Maria in Trastevere watching couples stroll by.

Anyway, back to the cars. There tend to be relatively few in the Piazza di Santa Maria in Trastevere, which is really more or less the center of the neighborhood. I'm not sure why this is the case; the square does represent the largest expanse of potential parking space around. I assume that either the police actually enforce parking laws in this piazza (in stark contrast to their behavior in the rest of the city) or perhaps it just doesn't present the right nesting environment for the cars. If, however, you head down any of the streets leading out of the piazza, then you'll soon come across ample examples of automobile nesting behavior.

The cars tend to congregate in *piazze* as opposed to parking in the streets themselves. This can be explained by simple evolutionary theory: if even a single car were to stop in one of the streets, which are barely wide enough to drive through in the first place, then this would effectively block the street, therefore cutting down on potential mating opportunities. The *piazze* are the only places they can come to rest while still leaving some semblance of passage.

For instance, at the Piazza Tavani Arquati, I recently observed the automobile equivalent of an orgy. In the center of the piazza were 14 cars, all parked in a big cluster, most facing each other. A further 25 were parked along the edges. These had the appearance of waiting until they could jump into the fun in the middle. There was just enough room for other cars to creep through this stationary mass in a vain attempt to find some empty spot, but, of course, empty spots don't exist.

It should be said that I have seen someone actually park. This was in the Piazza S. Calisto, where another jumble of 16 cars squatted in the center, and one of those large, hideous family Fiats had just come across that rarest of things—an empty space. I stopped to watch the maneuvers, which were delicate and involved. Two men stood outside the car, making violent hand motions to the driver, a young woman, who was attempting to squeeze the Fiat into a space that was just barely wide enough for it. This operation was observed by myself and a bored-looking dog sitting in the car next to the wiggling Fiat. I was making notes so as better to write this whole thing up, and after a few moments the two men waving their arms noticed me standing there scribbling on a piece of paper. This made them very apprehensive. They kept shooting poisoned glances at me, and I realized that they might think I was some kind of parking spy reporting back to the carabinieri. Not that this deterred them, of course. After a few more wiggles, during which I stopped writing and tried to smile innocently, the young woman actually succeeded in inserting her car into the space, and then somehow managed to open the door and with much effort squeeze herself out. Once they left, the dog went back to daydreaming about whatever dogs daydream about (other dogs, I guess) and the car sat contentedly in its group of peers, scoping out the Audi in front of it.

This general pattern, a cluster of cars in the middle of the piazza, usually with outrigger cars lining the edges, is the norm in Trastevere. You'll find it in almost all the larger *piazze* (which are neither all that numerous nor all that large). The smaller *piazze* often don't have the sheer space for a good cluster, but they'll still have as many cars as possible lining the sides. In the Piazza di San Rufino, for instance (total of 18 cars, most nose-in, some lining the edge), I came across a real gem—the ultimate Roman car. It was a tiny old Autobianchi, maybe from some time in the '60s, untouched by the polluting effects of car washes or repair shops, the roof held on by prodigious quantities of brown tape, the seats worn to the point of having white fluff poking through what remained of their covering. In front of this car sat a disinterested dog, on a leash that appeared simply to be draped over a little handrail on the building behind it, probably in nominal deference to some little-enforced leash law. He looked as friendly as did the Autobianchi and vaguely wagged his tail when patted on the head.

The cars are, of course, supplemented by legions of scooters. Italians love scooters. Once when traveling to Milan for an important business meeting, I was picked up at the train station by a distinguished elderly Italian colleague in an impeccable suit, who had proposed to take me to the meeting himself. To my surprise, instead of going by car or by cab, he handed me a little skullcap helmet and invited me to get behind him on his Vespa, after which we went zipping through the traffic for a good half hour, our briefcases lodged in front of his feet. "Only way to travel in this country," he shouted through the slipstream. Needless to say, in Rome every spot that isn't occupied by a nesting car is occupied by a resting scooter. I recently saw a young couple waiting at a red light on a beaten scooter, both with those little helmets, the woman clutching his waist with one hand and a rose in the other. I can't imagine anything that better illustrates Rome—traffic and romance.

AIRPORT KISSES

There I was, in Paris's Charles de Gaulle Airport, a place in which I spend far, far too much time. For once, I was early. It was one of France's occasional "everyone goes on strike" days. Part of the fun of these kinds of days is that you're never exactly sure to what degree the call for a nationwide strike will be heeded. You might come to the conclusion that the issue in question is trivial and no one will actually strike, only to find that absolutely every scrap of infrastructure is paralyzed. On the other hand, having been so deceived the last time, you might take myriad precautions only to discover that everything is working almost normally. It's these uncertainties that make life in France so exciting.

I had decided to leave for the airport a couple of hours earlier than I would normally have left, to allow for strike traffic (once, during a particularly difficult strike that happened to occur during a snowstorm, it took me over five hours to cover what was normally a 40-minute drive). This time, though, the strike traffic was far lighter than I had expected, so I found myself just hanging around in Terminal 2F.

Terminal 2F is a great big soaring concrete cathedral to the god of airplanes. It's a pretty impressive place, assuming you really, really like concrete. It's younger sister, Terminal 2E, was designed to be an even greater concrete cathedral, but a chunk of it collapsed upon itself (and a couple of travelers) two years ago and it doesn't quite generate the same aesthetic effect anymore.

Anyway, having nothing to do while waiting for my plane, I just started wandering around observing things. My attention was drawn to a young couple who were wound around each other in a passionate embrace, and this got me thinking about airport kisses.

When you travel a lot, you end up witnessing many airport kisses. These are not the same as street kisses or bedroom kisses or hospital kisses. They're not even the same as train-station kisses (I think it's because of the lines and the security in airports, or something). Airport kisses are a class unto themselves.

The couple that first grabbed my attention consisted of a slight young man and a young, rather plain woman with a mole on her cheek. Their kiss was of the lingering kind, a kiss that stops from time to time so that you can look into each other's eyes. It was a kiss that said they would be apart for a while. He said something to her, her lips formed "OK" and they kissed again, him holding her face in his hands.

This is a typical kind of airport kiss, and I suddenly realized that this would make a good topic for a dispatch, so I decided to spend the rest of the time before my departure checking out kisses on that Tuesday morning in Terminal 2F. Besides, to be frank, I had nothing else to do.

The next one I saw was an entirely different type of airport kiss—it was a woman kissing a toddler who was sucking on a bottle. They were obviously traveling together, probably waiting between flights. The toddler bore the signs of fatigue that could only be produced by that awful period between connections, but he was bearing it like a real little trooper, and his mother seemed proud.

Which raises the point that there are really three broad categories of airport kisses: arrival kisses, departure kisses, and co-traveler kisses.

Departure kisses are the ones you probably immediately

started imagining when I first raised the whole point about airport kisses (not to mention that it was a departure kiss that got me going on the topic in the first place). Those are the passionate ones, those are the lingering ones. People don't want departure kisses to stop, because after they do, one of them departs. This applies whether they are amorous departure kisses, like the young couple I saw, or parental departure kisses, like the ones I've planted on my own children from time to time, the kind where you squeeze your child and smoosh your lips against his cheek until he starts getting embarrassed and tries to wiggle away.

Departure kisses are usually followed by the non-departure half of the kiss standing around looking like a fool after hearing those terrible words: "I'm sorry, you're not allowed past this point." The departing half of the kiss then gets in some line while the non-departing half stands and waits until the departee is definitely out of sight, which these days, with all those slow security lines, might take a hell of a long time. Recently, I was at another terminal at the same airport standing in a security line with a man who kept waving back to the non-departing half of his departure kiss while taking off his shoes, his belt, his jacket, etc. Off came an article of clothing, up went a wave. Far behind us, a short woman in a red jacket was waving back from behind a metal barrier. Even after he had gone through and was out of sight she stood looking at the metal detector.

But departure kisses aren't the only kind, and they're certainly not the best kind, so I went downstairs to the arrival hall to observe arrival kisses. Arrival kisses are always shorter than departure kisses, because there's so much to say and so much more time to say it. Arrival kisses tend to be more forceful, less tender, and surprisingly, often more tearful. This is a thing I've noticed. While it has never bothered me that no one comes with me to say goodbye when I leave from an airport, I confess a twang of regret that no one is ever waiting to pick me up, because arrival kisses can be so very nice. Alas, if anybody is waiting for me it tends to be a taxi driver. None of them has ever kissed me, let alone jumped into my arms, as sometimes occurs with arrival kisses.

Arrival kisses cause more of a traffic jam than departure kisses, because they often immobilize someone who's pushing a great big cart full of luggage, thereby blocking the passage of everyone behind. Some airports are particularly prone to this kind of thing—it's a function both of airport layout and local culture. For instance, you can take hours to get out of the airport in Madras, where entire extended families come to throw themselves into the arms of just about everyone getting off the plane and the entire airport becomes clogged with arrival kisses.

The last kind of airport kiss is the co-traveler kiss. These are actually the best. I mean, you write poems and songs about departure kisses, and arrival kisses give you that wild adrenaline burst, but co-traveler kisses are still the best in the long run. These occur between two people who have set off on a journey together. Either they're kissing because they're happy to be leaving together, happy to be arriving together, or happy to be on their way, but there's always a shared complicity and a shared excitement in co-traveler kisses that you just don't find in other kinds of kisses. You're kissing in a setting that's different, you're kissing in the midst of a journey, and a journey shared with someone you want to kiss is usually a journey worth taking.

LES FRITES DE LA LIBERTÉ:
BRUGES, BELGIUM

French fries are probably not French, as the French Embassy was quick to point out during the whole "freedom fries" silliness. For the French, the things are quintessentially Belgian, and for the Belgians, it's downright heresy to imagine that anyone else could have conceived of their beloved national dish.

This, of course, raises the question of why Americans call them "French" fries. After all, no one else does: for the French they're simply *frites* ("fries"), which is short for *pommes frites* ("fried apples," actually), which is also what the Germans surprisingly call them in those quaint little accents of theirs, and which is itself short for *pommes de terre frites* ("fried potatoes," keeping in mind that potatoes are actually called "earth apples" in French). You still with me here? Anyway, the Brits call them "chips," not to be confused with "potato chips," which they call "crisps."

I'm sure you're duly fascinated by now, but the whole point of this is to bring us back to Belgium, and the passion that Belgians have for fries. (We shall heretofore refer to them simply as "fries," to avoid any political overtones, and I can't help but note that my beloved homeland has attained a frenzied level of inanity when fried potatoes can have political overtones.) So what the hell was I saying? Ah yes, we were discussing the Belgians and their fries (or *frietjes*, for the Flemish-speaking half of Belgium, where linguistic political overtones are rife).

You can't swing a dead potato in Belgium without hitting a fries stand. These can be wagons, booths, vans, just about anything, really. They usually have one or two people inside frying up fries. I remember once driving from some tiny part of Luxembourg to some other tiny part of Luxembourg, which is a very tiny country, and in so doing crossing an even tinier finger of Belgium that sticks into Luxembourg. When we crossed the border (as evidenced by a tiny sign mentioning that we were now in Belgium), we immediately saw two fries stands. About five minutes later, we crossed the border back into Luxembourg and saw no more.

Belgian fries are to McDonald's fries as fries are to worms (remember that if you ever retake your SAT, it's a rare but telling trick question), and the best place to sample them is Bruges, in the Market Square.

It's not really that the fries in Bruges are better than the fries anyplace else in the country, it's simply that if you're going to go to Belgium you really should go to Bruges, and if you go to Bruges you'll undoubtedly find yourself in Market Square, staring up at the enormous belfry, in which case you may as well sample the fries from one of the two little green stands there.

Stands that sell fries are, as I just pointed out, legion in Belgium, and these two hold what may be the most sought-after location in the country, right in front of Bruges's most visited attraction, in the city's biggest open space. The stands are painted a dark green, the kind of green you see on fountains and poster pillars in Paris. (Come to think of it, that same green is also used on fences and little buildings in Parisian public parks, as well as just about anything relating to the municipality in Paris. I never thought about that before. I wonder where that green came from.) The shacks are made of wood, and in either of them you'll find two people taking orders from the vast crowd in front, while simultaneously frying up a storm. The stands also have vestigial wheels, which are far too small and frail to support the shacks themselves and are apparently purely for show.

The stands have a surprisingly large menu considering that they are designed to sell only fries. Upon examination, though, it becomes evident that over half of the menu space is taken up with the choice of sauces.

Americans tend to put ketchup on fries, and indeed ketchup is available. In Belgium, though, the standard thing to put on fries is a creamy type of mayonnaise. However, when Belgians want some variety in their lives they go out on a limb and put all kinds of funky things on fries, so many different funky things that the menu of a simple fry shack inevitably sports a hefty list of sauces, such as ...

Peppersaus
Provençal
Curry
Americain
Andalouse
Pickels
Samourai
Tartaar
Stoofvlessaus
Looksaus
Mammoetsaus
Gele Bickysaus

... and I've left out both the more mundane and the difficult-to-spell (i.e., those sauces with such a wealth of Flemish consonants, sprinkled with *o*'s and *u*'s, that I don't trust my hastily scribbled notes and fear that if I guess at what I've written I'll bring down upon myself a torrent of hate mail from irate Flemish/Dutch speakers who already don't like me because of my comments about their language in the Amsterdam column).

And that's not all, because the two stands sell more than just fried potatoes. They also serve hot dogs and bratwurst. Unfortunately, these too are deep fried. I only discovered this when I ordered a bratwurst (to tell the truth, I don't really like fries all that much) and found, to my profound disappointment, that it was crispy and slick. I then understood why no other patrons were walking away from the fries stands with anything else but neat little plastic containers of fries, covered with samurai sauce or whatever.

Once you have your little plastic container of fries, you can walk around Bruges like a real Belgian and feast your eyes on one of the most beautiful little cities in northern Europe. Look up Bruges to get a handle on all the sites, but make sure you don't miss the spot where the Rozenhoedkaai becomes the Braambergstraat (incidentally, it's always best to try to pronounce Flemish names with a mouth full of fries—helps the pronunciation). Here, you have a fantastic perspective on a big central canal that makes a sharp turn, with medieval houses hovering over it and a big old willow tree apparently growing out of the canal, its long branches brushing the dark water. Splendid.

You should also take a carriage ride in Bruges. I agree, carriage rides are often pretty lame and you feel kind of silly, but if you're ever going to take one then you should take one in Bruges. For one thing, the Flemish are notoriously tidy, as is evident in the overall level of cleanliness in the city, and the carriages in Bruges are without a doubt the neatest, cleanest, shiniest carriages this side of Versailles. They even have impeccable poop chutes. For those of you who are unfamiliar with poop chutes, these are leather devices one attaches to the butt of a horse. The horse poops into them and the poop slides down into a container, avoiding horseshit-strewn streets (such as the one on which I live, but that's another matter). The carriages in New York also have these devices, which of course accounts for the pristine nature of Manhattan streets, but in New York they live up (or down) to the hygienic expectations one might have for equipment such as this, whereas in Bruges they're actually *beautiful*. Can you imagine just how fastidious a culture has to be to boast impeccable equine poop chutes?

So there you have it: fried potatoes, beautiful canals and shiny black poop chutes. If that doesn't get you to Bruges, I don't know what will.

THE CURSE OF THE MUMMIES: CAIRO, EGYPT

I'm not a superstitious man, but it seems that I am suffering from the curse of the mummies. Consider these mysterious "coincidences":

Twice, in the space of four months, I have found myself in the presence of mummies.

Both times, they were exactly the same mummies!

On both occasions, I wanted to take notes about these mummies so that I could tell you about them . . . but . . .

Both times, no notes survived. The first time, I did indeed take the notes, but then they mysteriously disappeared. The second time, I didn't even get that far—the curse of the mummy struck before I even left the hotel, causing me to forget to bring paper or pen. And I'm usually so organized.

It's that last point that can shake your faith in rational empiricism and cause you to go edging toward superstitious, mystical hogswallop. I mean, I never forget anything. Usually. Sometimes. Except for underwear.

Come to think of it, the second-to-last time I was in Egypt I forgot to bring any underwear whatsoever, and this for a weeklong stay. This kind of thing does, admittedly, happen on rare occasions, in which case I'm forced to wash my shorts (or socks—I forget socks more often than shorts) every night in the sink, with hand soap, then leave them to dry on a towel rack. This can work in Egypt, where the ambient humidity is on the lower side of low, but in more humid settings this often lead to harried work with the hair dryer upon waking and a vaguely damp tush all through the morning. Even in Egypt, though, it's a pain to have to wash your undies every night, so on my second day there I went to a nice spanking-new shopping mall to look for an underwear shop. I found one rather quickly, much to my surprise, and it was stocked with sensible undies of all types, made from nice soft, cheap Egyptian cotton. It was also staffed by four veiled women who spoke nothing but Arabic and to whom I had to explain in pantomime that I needed to buy shorts for myself and I didn't know my size in Egypt and what did they think? I firmly believe that if, when he was my age, Donald Rumsfeld had been obliged to go through an experience like that while trying to retain his dignity and not offend anyone else, the world would be a safer place today.

But I digress. This is not about Egyptian undies, it's about the curse the mummies laid on me, the curse that destroyed or preempted all the notes I was planning on using to write this dispatch. Since I have no notes at all, this will all have to be from memory, which means that my normal astoundingly detailed level of research will be somewhat compromised. (Speaking of which: for those who continue to tell me that I misspelled the Swedish phrase about rats and cookies . . . I know, I lapsed, I apologize.)

The Egyptian Museum is in the middle of Cairo, which is hardly surprising. It contains all kinds of extremely interesting stuff, all of which is carefully labeled with tiny yellowing scraps of paper containing very little information, marked in Arabic and then a random European language if you're lucky. It is, therefore, an extremely confusing place, which is a good thing in my opinion. After all, the twentieth century was the era of demystification, a *fin de millénaire* effort to make everything easily understandable and accessible to all, culminating in the Internet, where the world's great mysteries throw themselves open like whores to anyone with a computer and a password. It used to be that it was impressive to know some obscure fact. Today, if you let drop the fact that the modern brassiere was not invented by Otto Titzlinger but by Mary Phelps Jacob (in 1913), you're prone to a remark along the lines of "Like, get a life!" inferring that you spend your time on the Net harvesting useless arcana.

OK, you'll have to excuse that bit. I actually love having all the world's more plebeian libraries at my fingertips. It does, though, make my point . . . which I've entirely forgotten by now.

As I was saying, the Egyptian Museum is a very confusing place with all kinds of wonderful things that you can learn about in any good guidebook, or even better, with any good guide, who will lead you around the museum and recite exactly the same sentences as every other guide in front of exactly the same pieces. The guides call themselves Egyptologists, which in this context means "tour guide," and they know all the right sentences very well, but tend to be extremely iffy when you stray into historical domains outside their pre-established routines. (One insisted to me that the Romans arrived in Egypt before Alexander the Great, while another was unaware that Cleopatra had borne children for both Caesar and Mark Anthony. All they need to do is to look this stuff up on the Net, after all.) So the rest of the museum is worth a good day of rummaging around and I'll leave it to you to discover it all. I will, though, tell you about the Royal Mummy Room.

Guides can't enter. This is a very, very good thing, since it means that you don't have bulging groups of jostling tourists being shouted at in a smorgasbord of languages. The mummy room couldn't hold any bulging groups anyway; it's very small. In it are 11 of Egypt's most illustrious pharaohs.

If the mummies' curse hadn't doomed my notes, I would have been able to tell you exactly which 11 mummies are there, but alas, I can't. Each of these mummies, the names of all but one lost to the memory-rotting curse, are striking. By striking, I mean that you look at them and you are stricken—*whap!* On all but two, the wrapping has been removed from their faces and I dare you to look into the mummified face of a 3,500-year-old king without suffering a moment's pause. If you can do that—if you can look at the blackened faces of these mummies then crack a joke and pop out for a quick bag of Fritos and a whiz with none the wiser and not a second thought then . . . well, then you're a shallow jerk and you'd best face up to the fact and live with it. They're just lying there, sometimes with outstretched hands, their lips drawn back in deathly grins and their noses shriveled into their faces, wrappings hanging from their fragile fingers. Their teeth are white. They have toenails. They ruled one of the greatest nations on Earth 1,000 years before Rome was even imagined, hundreds of years before Helen caused such a ruckus with her pretty face and her thousand ships, and here they are, lying under glass reaching up at you.

Of them all, though, the most impressive must be Ramses II; the great builder, the founder of the temple of Abu Simbel, the pharaoh to whom Moses sang, "Let my people go" . . . The Man, in a nutshell. He's lying in the Royal Mummy Room with his henna-died hair, his arm lifted in apparent supplication. He has a lingering look of determination on his face, despite the frogs and the locusts and the red, red blood flowing in the Nile.

You should save Ramses II for last, though. The way to do the mummy room is to turn right once you've entered, on the outside lane, check out the mummies along the edges, all of whom are impressive, all of whom shall remain by necessity nameless. Make your way in a counterclockwise rotation around the room, examining one king after the other. If there are a lot of people in the museum that day, then there will inevitably be a hum of conversation that rises, rises, rises until a uniformed guard shouts, "Hush!" in an attempt to retain some semblance of respect for all the dead kings. This causes the hum to subside (takes a few moments, as people realize he's an official and he's hushing *them*), but then the hum rises again until he shouts again . . . and so on. Kind of like waves on a beach.

I can tell you that the first mummy is appropriately hideous. If memory serves, he was killed violently, and it shows: agonizing look on his face and holes in his head. The next couple are fully wrapped, with dried plants adorning them yet. Then comes a series of other mummies, each with its own ghastly personality, and this brings you full circuit around the room. In the center, then, are two mummies, the second of which is our beloved Ramses II, his hand stretched out and his neck craning, wisps of light colored hair around his head and a 3,000-year-old expression on his face. Be forewarned, though—show the utmost respect to these ancient kings, or you may find yourself cursed, forgetting your notes and struck with the insurmountable urge to write long, pointless, even aimless paragraphs that only end when an editor finally takes pity on you (much like a veterinarian kneeling next to a wounded horse) and cuts off your dispatch before you can. . . .

THE CHÂTEAU D'IF:
MARSEILLE, FRANCE

A number of readers wrote to tell me that they had read The Count of Monte Christo *after having seen this column and that Edmond Dantès was indeed the coolest. I'm very, very happy to think that I contributed to anyone's discovery of Dumas.*

It is a fact that by far—and by "by far" I mean by millions of miles—the absolutely coolest character ever to grace the pages of any book ever written was Edmond Dantès, the famous Count of Monte Cristo. Even James Bond is an uncultured buffoon compared to the magnificent count. When I first read that book I was immediately overcome with a deep, unshakable regret that I was not and never would be the Count of Monte Cristo. The thought still saddens me.

Although Edmond Dantès only ever existed in Dumas's imagination, a character possessing such an extreme degree of coolness leaves a trace on the world, or so I think, kind of like a powerful personality leaves a ghostly presence. This, coupled with the fact that it's a pretty cool place in its own right, led me to the Château d'If.

In the first volume of *The Count of Monte Cristo*, Dantès is wrongly accused of treachery and is sentenced to life imprisonment on the dreaded Château d'If, a place from which escape is impossible. There, he meets the Abbé Faria and becomes the learned man's disciple, communicating with him via a tunnel dug between their two cells. It is then that he learns the skills that begin to turn him into the ultra-cool, quasi-superhero he later becomes and it is there that he learns the location of the vast treasure that will make him a very *rich* quasi-superhero (and you thought Bruce Wayne was the first . . . believe me, Batman doesn't come up to Dantès's toenail when it comes either to riches or coolness). It is also thanks to Faria that Dantès is able to escape the dreaded island, although I won't tell you how just in case there's a great gaping hole in your literary culture and you haven't yet read the book (in which case, stop now, buy it, then come back).

Anyway, the castle certainly does exist. It was built, or at least begun, in the sixteenth century, both to protect the approaches to the port of Marseille and to watch over the sometimes unruly and recently acquired city. The castle takes up the entire island of If, which is pretty small, and the keep itself has three towers, which is kind of weird. The reason is simply that the construction was intentionally carried out at a somewhat leisurely pace, one tower being built at the time of the keep's construction, and then other towers being built at roughly 50-year intervals. They simply never got around to building the fourth. Life is kind of leisurely in Marseille.

You can visit If by taking a boat from the port of Marseille (wonderful place, Marseille—visit the city too, spend some time there, walk around the old city, eat some bouillabaisse). The boat only takes about 15 minutes to get out to the castle, where it pulls up to a small dock, from which you climb a fortified passageway up to the main gate. From there, you can pretty much walk around as you like. There's a small fee to get into the keep.

The castle did indeed serve as a prison, and a number of famous prisoners were interned there, both fictional and real. You can visit these cells once you're inside the keep. Some of them are very claustrophobic, but some seem not so bad, with a window or two and even a nice fireplace. It seems that the more aristocratic "guests" were given better accommodations.

There are also two cells that have been labeled as those of Dantès and Faria. There's even a little tunnel between them (nowhere near as long as that described in the book). I asked one of the attendants why they had labeled these cells as having held people who never existed, and he explained that these were the cells that had inspired Dumas when he visited the castle in the 1830s.

"You're sure about that, huh?"

He hesitated a little. "So I'm told," he replied.

The keep itself is pretty small, but in my book this makes it charming. Some castles are more like towns, and while this can be damn impressive, the Château d'If is more approachable—kind of a Castle McNugget. Furthermore, since it was a prison, after all, one doesn't expect it to be all big and airy, now does one?

One thing it does have is a lot of little passageways, especially those leading to the towers. I like that—castles should have passageways.

Of all the nonfictional inhabitants of If , the most unusual and perhaps the most famous was the rhinoceros. In 1513, the king of Gujarat decided to offer an Asian rhinoceros to Emmanuel the Fortunate, king of Portugal. Emmanuel, always anxious to gain a few brownie points with the pope, decided to send the animal to Rome, by ship, as a gift to his Holiness, Pope Something. The ship wanted to put into Marseille, but apparently it was decided that this wasn't prudent and instead it stopped off at If, where it stayed for a few weeks (this was before the castle was built).

No one in Europe could ever remember having seen a rhinoceros (the Romans were familiar with the animals, but they had apparently been forgotten in the interim), and there was a steady stream of admirers who came to the island from the mainland to ooh and aah and ogle the thing, including François I, soon-to-be king of France.

The rhino then took ship again and sailed off to be delivered to the pope, but the ship slammed against the rocks off of Genoa during a violent storm and sank. The rhino's carcass washed up on the Italian coast some time later, much worse for the wear.

Albrecht Dürer, the great German engraver, was asked to make an engraving of the animal for posterity's sake. The fact that he hadn't actually *seen* it was deemed less important than the fact that he was one mean engraver, so he just worked off of a sketch by Valentin Ferdinand. This engraving was, for many years, the only extant image of a rhinoceros in Europe. Today, you can find copies of it all over, and you can buy a T-shirt sporting the engraving in the castle's gift shop. It's a pretty cool engraving, when all is said and done.

Not as cool as Edmond Dantès, of course, but then *nothing* and *no one* will ever be as cool as Edmond Dantès. Did I already mention that?

THE (OR AT LEAST A)
TEMPLE OF SPANISH SOCCER:
MADRID, SPAIN

It is now over. As I write this, we all know what happened during the World Cup—we know about the wins and the losses and that head butt. Ah, that head butt; the butt that France will never forget.

Before it all, though, I had the rather unique and unexpected opportunity to visit that shrine to Spanish soccer, the stadium of Real Madrid.

I can already hear the Catalans wincing—did I say shrine to Spanish soccer? But what about their beloved Barcelona? Fear not. In order to balance things out, I visited the Real stadium in the company of a man born and raised in Barcelona, a loyal Barça fan from the depths of his dark eyes to the tips of his Catalan toes. It was he who translated the running commentary provided by the attractive young lady who was our tour guide, all the while adding a number of comments of his own.

He began by giving me an overview of the Real team: "Beckham sells shirts. They all sell shirts. In fact, the whole team consists of famous men who are too old to play football, but who are very good at selling shirts."

"Ronaldo isn't that old, is he?"

"No, he's just fat."

This introduction was delivered as we walked down to the pitch to visit the players' bench. This consisted of a nifty little roofy-thingy, under which were rows of seats in which we were allowed to sit. I, for one, thought the seats were very nice, kind of like the seats in a Jaguar. They were heated, too, although they didn't turn on the heat for us.

The stadium was empty except for us and a couple of other groups of tourists. The field looks a lot bigger in person than it does on the television. A man drove a riding mower back and forth and back and forth over the enormous pitch and I couldn't help but wonder how long it takes one person to cut all that grass. The smell of mowed grass filled the air.

As we wiggled our butts (Did I say butt? Alas.) on the Jaguar seats, I listened to the truly awful song that leaked from speakers over our heads.

"What the hell is that music?" I asked my Catalan friend.

"Terrible, isn't it? It's the Real song."

"They have a song?"

"Yes, they do. It's horrible."

I tried to make out a few words, but my Spanish is nonexistent. My friend leaned over again: "The Barça song is much better," he said.

We were led by the tour guide down the tunnel through which the players enter. It's very nice, all blue and white—Real's colors. We then proceeded into the visiting players' locker room.

The one thing that immediately struck me in the locker room was the smell. The locker room smelled exactly of nothing. There was no smell. I, for one, associate locker rooms with a smell that is far from nothing, that instead reeks of people who have just engaged in a lot of unrestrained sweating, but this locker room didn't smell at all. And it was clean. Not just clean as in "hygienic" but clean as in your mother's kitchen. Amazing. I'm still not entirely convinced that this particular locker room has ever really been used by actual sweaty men. Maybe it's a mock-up, a reproduction of the *real* locker room that's preserved someplace else, not open to the public so that the flash of cameras doesn't degrade the artwork or something. I'm not even sure that any of the conveniences really function, since the shower rooms, Jacuzzis and toilets were all cordoned off by blue-and-white security ropes.

After the locker room we made our way through a series of staircases and passages to the trophy room.

If I ran Real then I would make sure that before every game, the opposing players were forced to go through the trophy room to get to their locker room (wherever the real one might be). The trophy room is more of a trophy-room complex, where different rooms succeed each other, each filled with wall-to-ceiling trophies. In front of the entrance is a little plaque declaring that Real Madrid is the most winning sporting club in history.

I'm not quite sure how you could calculate this, when it really comes down to it. For one thing, as is the case with many sports clubs in Europe, Real is not only a soccer team, but a basketball/handball/and God-knows-what-else team. I have no doubt that the sum total of all their various wins from all their various teams comes to something quite impressive—for that matter, I've seen the trophies—but how do you really compare? That being said, even my Catalan friend admitted that they are, indeed, a team that has won a lot of trophies.

"But then, they were founded in 1902," he pointed out. "It's true, they *used* to be very good. That was before Barça became so dominant."

Just behind him was a small plaque commemorating Real's victory over Barça in the 1943 semifinals of the Spanish league, 11 to 1.

"Come on, that's really bad."

My friend looked at the plaque. "Yeah, that's really bad."

The trophies are more interesting than you would think. For

one thing, they are very varied. For instance, there are . . . a lot (OK, so I didn't have time to count them) of Spanish-league trophies, but for some strange reason, those from 1960, 1978, 1982 and 1988 are all bigger. Through my friend, I asked the attractive tour guide why, but she just looked at me strangely.

"Are you sure you're translating properly?" I asked my friend.

"He's translating properly," she replied in English. "I just don't know what you mean."

"The ones from those years are larger. Why? There doesn't seem to be a pattern to it. Were the crops particularly good that year or something?"

She looked at her watch and said, "Oops, got to be moving on."

The most impressive trophies, though, are not the league trophies or the championship-league trophies, nor any of the trophies you'd ever have heard of—no, the most interesting trophies are the really weird ones, trophies from little summer excursions to out-of-the-way places like Taiwan. ("They take summer trips so they can sell more shirts," explained my Catalan friend.) One of them looked like a medieval oven and another one looked like . . . well, I can't really describe it. Let's just say a big weird metal thing.

"How did they get these trophies?" I asked my friend.

"They probably beat the local high school team with their third-tier players, then sold them lots of shirts."

Which explains a lot.

At the end of the trophy exhibition was a large panel with the pictures of last season's Real players. I was surprised to see the great Portuguese player, Luis Figo.

"I didn't know Figo played for Madrid," I said.

My friend clenched his teeth. "You're kidding? They bought him from us in 2000. We call him Figo Iscariot."

The trophy room was the last stop on the tour. After that, we were led into the inevitable gift shop, where we could have bought all kinds of horribly kitsch things and where, of course, we found rack after rack after rack of shirts.

During the World Cup, most of the "old men" of Real ended up proving that they can still play football as well as sell shirts . . . and, of course, one of them showed that he can still throw a head butt. Alas.

OF ROMANS AND PUSSYCATS:
PROVENCE, FRANCE

T he French province of Provence is named after the Latin word for province, which is *provincia,* and not because it's a French province, because, after all, *all* French provinces are provinces. This useless and confusing piece of information is meant as an introduction to the fact that Provence was dear to the ancient Romans.

Of course, after the Battle of Alesia[1] all of Gaul came definitively under Roman rule, but Provence had already been firmly Roman, and the Romans always held a warm spot in their hearts for the area, which is brimming with all kinds of cool aqueducts, arenas, theatres and the like.

The above has undoubtedly made it clear that I'm a bit of a Roman history nerd. I even collect ancient Roman coins and can spend hours poring over some lump of greenish bronze just because it has the faintly visible outline of a galley's prow, three pellets and an ear of corn. Imagine, therefore, how excited I get in Provence, where you can't kick a stone without uncovering a new arch and where the

---

1 Alesia was Caesar's greatest victory, during which he defeated the great Gallic chieftain Vercingetorix and definitively conquered Gaul, and if you had paid attention in history class you would know that, which reminds me that I really should go back and visit the battleground again and then write about it, which itself only reinforces the point I'm about to make in the next paragraph up in the main text.

very dirt remembers the passage not only of Caesar, but of Hannibal before him.

It's easy to understand why the Romans loved Provence—it's a great place. The cities are wonderful, the villages are wonderful, there are rivers and gorges and olives and fruit trees and all kinds of niceties. The edge of Provence is the shore, which English-speakers call the French Riviera and the French call the Côte d'Azur, or "Azure Coast," because the water is blue. Really blue. The Mediterranean is bluer, somehow, than other large bodies of water. Maybe the Romans put dye in it or something.

Anyway, in Provence you can, and should, visit Nimes, with its arena, and Arles, with an arena of its own that's just as nice (according to the inhabitants) and a theatre to boot—not to mention its very cool ancient cemetery. You should also definitely visit the Pont du Gard, which is an immense Roman aqueduct that has been spanning the valley of the Gardon River for over 2,000 years and is truly one of the wonders of the world (if you have, in your mind, a picture of a Roman aqueduct from some long-forgotten source, then it is probably an image of the Pont du Gard). When recently I visited the Pont du Gard, I proudly wore my "Et Tu, Brute?" T-shirt, sporting an image of the famous Eid Mar coin, minted by Brutus in . . . oh, you don't care.

All of these things are wonderful and you should go to Provence and stay a long time and read about them, then check them out and then decide to stay even longer and go to one of the many summer arts festivals. There. Now, let's go to Lançon, which you'll never visit.

Lançon is a relatively small town of 7,000 people, not too far from Salon-de-Provence, which itself boasts, primarily, an air force base. Lançon, sadly, does not contain any Roman vestiges, since it is a relatively new village, only having been founded in the seventh or eighth century AD. For all its modernity, it is a striking place. It winds up a steep hill topped with an impressive, though small, circular castle. The town traditionally had three concentric defensive walls, although most of the outermost wall and parts of the second wall have been dismantled over the centuries.

The town has all kinds of tiny winding streets and if you've read any of these dispatches you must know by now that I love tiny winding streets, particularly if they are lined with stone houses hundreds of years old, and doubly so if they are the lived-in, what's-so-special-about-us kind of houses that wear their centuries with easy grace. This is very much the case in Lançon (and is not a rare trait in Provence in general).

In order to get the most out of Lançon, I visited it with a few friends, some of whom have the great good fortune to live there, and with Stéphanie, who runs the tourism bureau (which consists, pretty much, of Stéphanie). We arranged a private tour, which is possible and can be done by calling up Stéphanie.

Anyway, Stéphanie began by giving us a few hard-to-believe facts:

1. Lançon was the only village that was granted permission, some eight or nine hundred years ago, to use as its coat of arms a modification of the coat of arms of the celebrated Seigneurs de Baux. No other village was ever granted this honor.
2. Lançon contains the only place in France that produces *both* wine and olive oil!
3. Lançon contains two archeological excavations, and one of them has just unearthed a clove of garlic from 500 BCE, which might be the oldest found in France.

Needless to say, we were very impressed by all this. After expressing our amazement in appropriately awed tones, we set out on a very, very thorough visit of the town.

I won't give you a street-by-street history of Lançon, though

Lord knows I now could, but I will linger for a moment over a street named Pavé d'Amour, which loosely translates as "Hunk of Love" Street. I, for one, think this is one hell of a street name. It turns out that it is due to the town's one nationally recognized landmark, an ancient building known variously as the Hotel de Luxembourg and as the Maison des Templiers, because apparently it was once inhabited by the Templar knights.

"Why 'Hunk of Love' Street, though?"

Stéphanie seemed a little shy about the question. "In the sixteenth century, there were a lot of . . . parties in it."

"Parties?"

"And ladies who were very open to . . ."

"It was a bordello!"

"In a way."

In a way my eye.

Just below the second rampart of the town is the church, which was begun in the fourteenth century (taking over main churchly duties from the chapel of St. Cyr, farther down the hill) and expanded in the seventeenth. In front of the church lives M. Deluy, who apparently serves as the town's living font of history. His house is built into the second rampart and is filled with bric-a-brac, as he used to be an antiques dealer before he retired. He spends a lot of his time sitting outside his house, in front of the church door, which is where we found him, in the company of several cats and an ancient Citroën Ami 6.

"Looks like a 1970 model," said one of my friends, when I asked about the car.

"Seventy-one," said M. Deluy, as he stroked a gray cat.

The church, like many French village churches, looks larger from the inside than from the outside. It is a strange church, made stranger by a little side chapel containing kitsch plaster statues of the Virgin Mary talking to a pair of children. Mary wears a golden chain with a hammer and a pair of tongs, which seemed really strange to us.

"I have no idea," said Stéphanie, when asked about the symbolism. I therefore decided to go ask M. Deluy. Truth be told, I was kind of looking for an excuse to talk to M. Deluy.

M. Deluy said, "The statues?" then got up to lead me into the church once again, leaving my friends and Stéphanie to chat on the church steps.

"Did you see Moses in there?" he asked as we entered the church, to which I replied in the surprised-negative tense (remember your French grammar?).

"Moses the cat," he specified, which reassured me somewhat, but we hadn't seen any cats in there either.

"You like cats?" M. Deluy asked, with a look in his eye that made it clear that much depended on my response to this question. Thankfully, I was able to respond with utmost sincerity that I do, indeed, like cats very much. M. Deluy grunted and then we went over to the statues.

"Notre Dame de la Salette," he said. I had never heard of that particular Notre Dame.

"But what about the hammer and the tongs?" I asked.

"How should I know?" he responded. "It's not like I believe in that hogwash. It's a shame Moses isn't here, though. He loves the church, that's why I named him Moses. He's usually in here. I know, let's go get him." At that, he hurried out of the church to look for Moses.

"You seen Moses?" he asked another old man walking by.

"Isn't he in the church?" the old man responded.

M. Deluy then went around the back of his house (through a gateway in the rampart). "There he is!" he shouted. I only saw a gray blur as the cat ran into the open door of the house. M. Deluy blocked the doorway with a roofing tile and then rushed past me to go back around the house. "We'll get him from the front," he said.

This tactic worked, and soon M. Deluy had a handsome

young black and white cat in his arms. I went over to scratch the cat's head, and he started purring. "Come on," said M. Deluy, as he carried the cat into the church.

When we went through the doorway, he dropped the cat, which immediately ran to the front of the church and jumped onto the altar, where he paraded back and forth, his tail high in the air.

"See," said M. Deluy.

I went over to pet Moses again and I noticed that the white cloth over the altar was covered in cat hair.

"The altar used to be farther back, but that was when the priest used to turn his back on the parishioners. Then the pope turned the priests around. You know, that pope, the one who's dead."

"John XXIII?" I asked.

"Yeah, that one. Damn, I forgot about my mother!" . . . which was not at all what I expected M. Deluy to say. "Might as well leave Moses on the altar, he likes it here and can jump out the hole in the back."

He said this as he scurried out the door and got in the 1971 Ami 6 to drive across town and pick up his mother, who was supposed to come over for dinner and who must have been older than can safely be imagined. We waved goodbye and offered heartfelt thanks to him, then hung out a little more on the church steps because it's a nice place to hang out.

By that time it was getting late. We took a little walk around the castle, which can't be entered because it's private (people actually live in it, which is very cool). It was then time for an aperitif. We convinced Stéphanie to join us and headed off for a long evening of talking and laughing and hanging out on a wide terrace overlooking the hills of Provence, where people have drunk and eaten and laughed and talked since the time of Caesar.

ERBALUNGA:
CORSICA, FRANCE

My father-in-law's mother was named Diane Erbalunga. Erbalunga is a very unusual name for a Corsican, and doubly so for a Corsican hailing from the south of the island. Erbalunga is, in fact, the name of a village in the very *north* of the island.

My father-in-law once explained to me the reason for this unusual moniker. One of his ancestors had gone into hiding (a common thing in Corsica) and had left the south to go underground in the north, in the village of Erbalunga. After a few years he was overcome with homesickness, especially since northern Corsicans were so different from normal people—i.e., southern Corsicans. He therefore decided to return. Still being on the lam, he couldn't very well use his own name (the respectable Pietri), so he adopted the name of the town in which he had hid. This was a great disguise, since no one would ever expect a southern Corsican to take a northern Corsican name. So did he go undiscovered until his dying day (except to the entire population of southern Corsica, who knew damn well who he was but would never spill the *fagioli*).

The details of the story had remained somewhat fuzzy to me, but one thing I did know was that the town itself was rumored to be magnificent. I had also seen pictures of it, since it graces many a Corsican postcard. As such, this year's Corsican dispatch concerns the storied town of Erbalunga.

I should point out that not only is Erbalunga in northern Corsica, it is situated on that little nub of a peninsula that sticks out of Corsica on its northern tip, and that adds so much to the island's distinctive shape: Cap Corse. And it's true that the culture on Cap Corse is very different to that on the rest of the island. For one thing, they fish there.

It would surprise many to learn that, on the whole, Corsicans don't fish much. Or at least, traditionally they didn't fish much. For that matter, they were never too hot on boats in general. In fact, Corsicans didn't even like the idea of the shore for most of their history. The shore was the home of roughly two gazillion malaria-bearing mosquitoes and a favorite pillaging destination for Moorish pirates (hence, ironically, the Moor's head on the Corsican flag). Except for the major cities (Bastia, Ajaccio, Calvi, Bonifacio and Porto-Vecchio), the population traditionally spent the summers up in the mountains and then would only come down to the shore during the winter, with their animals (cows and goats, mostly). This is why so many Corsican villages actually have a strange kind of dual-village arrangement, the main village perched on some mountain deep in the interior and a kind of secondary village of lesser importance down by the coast. Of course, these days the secondary villages have become far more important, since they are popular tourist destinations (the U.S. Army took care of the malaria in 1944, when they doused everything with DDT: no more malaria—or birds, for that matter).

Anyway, the one exception to this rule was on Cap Corse, where many of the villages came right down to the sea and where people have always fished. One of these fishing villages is Erbalunga.

There's only one road that leads to Erbalunga; it's the coast road that goes up from Bastia toward the tip of Cap Corse and it's one of the most stunning roads you'll ever find. The village bursts into sight as you swing around one of the innumerable curves: there's a stretch of brilliant blue sea and a series of ancient houses that seem to be wading out into the water like a group of stone bathers, led by a round Genoese tower perched on a pile of rock.

The town is bordered on three sides by the sea. You approach it from the fourth, on foot (no cars are allowed in the town center). You are greeted by a grand old house that seems abandoned, fronting a small square. The house has one balcony in the front. It seems inevitable that at least once (at *least* once) some lovelorn and swarthy young Corsican man must have stood under that balcony and pleaded his case to a dark-haired beauty above. I'd like to think so, anyway. (Although it's quite possible that this used to be the town hall, in which case I assume that no one ever dared sing a love song to the mayor.) To the right of this building, a narrow passageway winds between low houses down to the water, a shallow stair every few feet, an archway overhead from time to time. Once you reach the water, you can explore the rocks on its edge and appreciate how they continue in patterns under the surface as far out as you can see.

Back in the town's center, other passages with other archways can eventually carry you roaming past cats and drying laundry to the tower at the town's end. This is one of Corsica's network of 150 watchtowers, built by the Genoese in the sixteenth century to help warn of attacks by the aforementioned Moorish pirates. The tower is crumbling, but somehow this only adds to its charm. Wasps tend to the flowers growing out of the cracks in the stone.

The third side of the village holds the tiny fishing port, where small boats bob around behind a low breakwater and where seabirds perch on posts.

Erbalunga seems like a great place to hide out for a few years. Upon returning to my father-in-law's house in the south of the island, I asked again about his ancestor. It turns out it was his own grandfather, and it wasn't some dark murderous issue—he had simply wanted to avoid the trenches of the First World War. He was a deserter.

"He didn't kill anybody?"

"No. You must be thinking of 'the Turk.'"

"Who's 'the Turk'?"

"He was a distant cousin. He shot a continental [note that Corsicans consider anyone who is not from Corsica a 'continental'] about 30 years ago then went into hiding for a while. For a few days he even slept in the room where you sleep when you're here."

Which was news to me. "He wasn't really Turkish, was he?"

"Of course not. We called him that because . . . well, I don't remember, but he shot some lawyer from Lyon because he was looking at his daughter. He was acquitted."

"Doesn't seem like circumstances for acquittal."

"Well, he ran a nudist colony, after all, and the lawyer kept ogling his *naked* daughter. The Turk told him to stay away, said that if he came back he'd kill him."

"And he came back."

"Right. So the Turk killed him. When a Corsican tells you that he'll kill you if you do something, it's usually best to believe him. Especially the Turk. He was mean. I remember he had a dog. I used to like that dog. One day, no more dog. 'He was bothering me,' the Turk said, 'so I shot him.'"

"Pleasant guy."

"Mean. He gave himself up after a few weeks and was tried and acquitted. I mean for killing the lawyer, not the dog. Self-defense, they said. But the Turk never hid in Erbalunga. Probably never went there at all."

Which is a shame for the Turk, but probably not such a bad thing for Erbalunga.

ALEXANDER
THE NAVAL TROMBONE PLAYER:
ST. PETERSBURG, RUSSIA

In 1991, I lived in the 17th arrondissement in Paris, near the rue Leningrad. One day, some municipal workers came along and crossed out the name on the street signs with crosses made of masking tape, and put up new street signs underneath: rue St. Petersburg. In true French tradition, the people in the neighborhood formally protested, saying that this was a royal pain in the ass, and that the name shouldn't change. After all, Place Stalingrad hadn't become Place Volgagrad. The response of the municipality was that Place Stalingrad was named after the *battle*, whereas the rue Leningrad was named after the city, which was obvious by looking at the streets around it, which are all named after European cities (rue de Turin, rue Madrid, etc.). The fight went on for about as long as the battle itself had lasted, but in this case, the local inhabitants lost. The street was renamed.

I remember at the time thinking how easy it was to change history, and wanting to go to St. Petersburg before it changed yet again.

St. Petersburg was built by the will of a strange man, Peter the Great, who decided that Russia should become more "European." I finally got to visit the city recently, where I had the good fortune to be shown around by a local lady named Ana.

"When Peter came here, the weather was nice. He was very lucky. But he didn't know what the weather is usually like."

"The weather's nice today."

"You are lucky, too. He saw an eagle fly overhead; this was good sign. He decided to build the city here."

Personally, I think he made a good choice. But, of course, I don't have to live there in the winter.

St. Petersburg is a magnificent place, the broad Neva River flows through it and it is graced by delightful little canals. On the major streets, the buildings are beautiful: shades of green and yellow, with white trim. According to a number of people I spoke to, the city didn't look quite so stunning a few years ago, but Putin cleaned it up to prepare for the G8 summit that took place there in July 2006. I suppose you couldn't very well allow old Peter the Great's ghost to contemplate a meeting of the world's economic powers in his very own city while paint peeled off the walls. I couldn't help but notice that once you went down some of the more out-of-the way streets, the greens and yellows of the building façades tended to give way to a uniform gray-brown grime, and the streets boasted potholes that would put Manhattan to shame, where crumbling old Ladas are parked next to obscenely expensive Bentleys . . . all in all, more typically Russian.

If you stick to the more touristy areas, though, you won't be disappointed. There is, of course, the Hermitage, the contents of which can be amply studied in more informative travelogues. Take a gander, though, at the enormous square on the south side of the Hermitage, Dvortsovaya Place. Russians are good at making whoppingly big central squares—witness Red Square in Moscow. Dvortsovaya is in a league of its own, though, and is actually prettier (albeit it doesn't boast St. Basil's Cathedral). In the center is Peter's column, with all kinds of Roman imagery that I won't get into, and around it are people rollerblading. Russians don't allow cars on their whopping squares (except for official-looking black cars, that go wherever they damn well please).

On the other side of the Hermitage is the river, upon which I had the good fortune of taking a dinner cruise with a whole bunch of Russians. Caviar with blinis and vodka on the Neva . . . life can get worse than that.

You'll probably do all that anyway, but I also strongly suggest that you hang out some in the park near the Admiralty, culminating in Dekabristov Place, where there is a great bronze statue. The statue itself is worth a look—Pushkin wrote about it (you'll hear a lot about Pushkin in St. Petersburg). It depicts Peter the Great on a rearing horse, dominating a pinnacle of stone. It is supposed to be the only equestrian statue in the world with a horse supported only by two legs, but you should be warned that Russians have a tendency to tell you that whatever Russian thing you're looking at is the only one of its kind.

Anyway, the thing about the park is not only the statue, it's the weddings, and the four-piece horn band that lingers near the statue. Local couples come to this park after their wedding to have pictures taken. On any given day, even during the week, when the weather (which is, effectively, lousy most of the time) is OK, the park is pretty much flooded with wedding parties. You'll find white-clad brides, milling drunken guests, and one formally dressed man with a blue sash. There's one in every wedding party. He is the best man, and his job is apparently to pour champagne for anyone who shows up with anything that can contain liquid. Take a cup with you.

Near the statue is the horn band, which zeroes in on passing wedding parties and plays pretty much anything they want in return for a few rubles. Their versatility was astounding—in fact, it was more impressive than their actual talent, and I simply had to get to know them.

The leader of the band is named Alexander, and I was thrilled to learn that he speaks English. Or rather, that he can communicate more or less in something that sounds like English.

"American! You are American! And you are French, too, yes? Friendship with Russia, France, America is *big!*" And he threw his arms widely to the side to demonstrate just how big. As one of his arms was equipped with a trombone, this nearly killed one of the smaller members of a passing wedding party, but nothing phases Russians.

"And you are musician, too, you say? What music?"

When I explained that I had previously been in a rock band, and that we had made an album, he immediately brought his trombone to his lips and played . . . get ready . . . "Smoke on the Water." Deep Purple was wise not to include a trombone in the band.

"And listen this, too!" after which, he played "La Marseillaise," which sounded a little better than "Smoke on the Water," but not quite as stirring as the scene in *Casablanca.*

It turns out that Alexander is only a part-time musician. "Rest of time, I am officer in Russian navy," at which point he snapped to attention, trombone at the ready, and gave me a crisp salute, which I did not return, since I was too busy laughing. He immediately laughed, too, and slapped me on the back. Still hurts.

"Listen, you can help me with green card, yes?" I explained that I really didn't think I could help him with a green card, but he asked for my telephone number anyway. Now, I've always made it a policy not to give out my phone number to Russian sailors, so I took his instead. I must confess that I haven't given him a call yet.

St. Petersburg is beautiful, but it's the conversations that make the visit. Aside from my conversation with Alexander the Naval Trombone Player, there was the conversation with Ana about leaders. I have always been surprised at the general Russian attitude toward Gorbachev (hate him) as compared to Putin (like him), which is so very different from the attitude in the West.

"Russians want strong leaders. Putin is strong leader, Gorbachev was weak."

"And so Putin is loved?"

"No, he is hated. Pushkin said Russians will always hate those who rule them, but we want to be ruled. No one can be an effective leader and be loved."

I cited Jefferson, one of the most beloved rulers of the United States, who was, and still is, deeply loved.

"How long did he rule?"

"Eight years."

"Pfffff! This is nothing."

All this discussed on the wide banks of the Neva, with Peter and Paul's fortress low on the other side.

And then there was my discussion with Peter, who was also in St. Petersburg while I was there. Peter is a Slovakian friend with whom I've had the pleasure of sharing many a long discussion in many a city. In 2004, I watched the Czech Republic lose to Greece in the European Football Championship while in a sports bar in Moscow with Peter, who was the only person there supporting the Czechs. Interesting evening.

In St. Petersburg, Peter and I took a long, leisurely walk along the Nevsky Prospekt, St. Petersburg's equivalent to the Champs Élysées. The street is a broad avenue; a river of light, enticing and entrancing. As we strolled through the milling crowd (there is always a crowd), our conversation drifted back to the '80s, when he was a university student in Bratislava. Throughout the '80s, I remember watching events in Eastern Europe, wondering what would happen. When student protests began in Prague, and then in Bratislava in '89, so many of us waited with bated breath. Peter was in the midst of them, afraid but excited at the idea of change. We talked about our lives *before*: what he had learned as a child about *us*, and what I had learned as a child about *them*, although, of course, his "us" had been my "them," and vice versa. These are fascinating conversations to have in Eastern Europe. I remember a discussion like this in Budapest in 1992, talking with a Czech and a Pole about the early '80s, and the Solidarity movement. The Pole explained that he had been in the army then, stationed in the south, and that in his unit they discussed what they would do if ever they were ordered to march on Gdansk . . . or what they would do if the Czech army came over the border. The Czech looked at him wide-eyed and said that at the time, he had been in the Czech army, and they had had the same conversations . . . what would they do if they were ordered to cross into Poland? The two men looked at each other, across a barroom table this time instead of a border, and then smiled and ordered something more to drink.

Forgive me a moment's reflection here, but this is what traveling can do for you: it can break down the "us" and the "them," it can cut through all the bullshit we learn secondhand from those we respect but who themselves don't really know what they're talking about. Traveling can open windows to a wide world, because once you start swimming around in it, you realize that the world is both far more vast and far smaller than you thought. It can even throw a few trombone-playing sailors across your path, and from time to time, a Pushkin, or a czar, or better—a friend.

A TO ZAGREB,
CROATIA

With respect to the prevalence of petting in public parks, I came across a study from Bradley University some time after having written this dispatch that measured the degree of promiscuity in different countries (talk about field research). Along with Latvia and Serbia, Croatia scored highest in Europe on their "promiscuity index."

There are a number of different ways to organize a systematic exploration of European capitals. You could do it geographically: west to east, for instance, in which case I suppose you'd start in Lisbon (Have I never written about Lisbon? Forgive me if I haven't, it's a great city.) and end in Istanbul (OK, Moscow is farther east, but it doesn't touch Asia). Or you could do it chronologically, starting in Athens and ending in Minsk, perhaps (founded only in the eleventh century). Or, you could do it alphabetically, starting in Amsterdam and ending in Zagreb.

If you choose the latter course then it might occur to you, as you walk around the little streets near the cathedral in Zagreb, that the game's up . . . you're in Zagreb . . . end of the line, at least from an alphabetical perspective.

And to a degree, it is kind of the end of the line. I'm not saying that Zagreb isn't a nice city—it is, very much so. It's just that after a while you get the impression that if you've seen one Eastern European city . . . well, maybe you haven't seen them all, but except for the really impressive ones, you've probably seen scaled up or scaled down versions of most everything someplace else, and this might lead you to the conclusion that you may actually have been traveling just a bit too much.

In Zagreb, things tend to be scaled down with respect to other cities: the cathedral is nice, but small; the streets are charming, but small; the parks are wonderful, and small. It's true that the parks boast some impressively massive trees, but everything else is kind of, well, dinky.

Dinky can be refreshing sometimes. I mean, you don't necessarily want to feel overwhelmed everyplace you go. Zagreb is a manageable city, with all the basic city things you'd expect: streets and buildings and the like. It also has the requisite train station with taxis in front and bus stops in front of them. It even has a king-on-a-horse statue. Most Eastern European cities have a king-on-a-horse statue, consisting of a bronze medieval king looking very stern in his armor, sitting on a stern-looking horse while he stares down a McDonald's or something. Croatia was usually part of someone else's kingdom, but they have a king-on-a-horse statue anyway. Their version consists of King Tomislav holding a scepter and looking appropriately mustachioed. When I was there he wasn't overlooking a McDonald's, but it did seem like he was checking out a poster for an upcoming Pearl Jam concert. Judging from his expression, he is not enthusiastic about Pearl Jam.

Up from Tomislav Square runs a series of parks, which is in fact part of the "Zagreb Horseshoe," a broad U of parkland that makes its way across the city. That's nice. What's also charming is that these parks are full of couples making out.

Just about any city park is bound to have its share of couples sitting on benches or lying in the grass making out, but I'm convinced Zagreb holds some kind of record when it comes to lip wrestling. This is particularly evident once the sun goes down. If the weather's nice, then every bench holds at least one couple either sitting side by side or with the woman straddling the man, both concentrating intensely, soft smacking sounds floating on the breeze.

Why is it that people from Zagreb seem to engage in public-park petting more than people in other cultures? I asked this question of an acquaintance there, who seemed perplexed. "Don't they do that in France, too?" he asked. They do, but not to the same degree. He shrugged his shoulders. "We are passionate people," he replied. "And maybe we have fewer hotels than Paris."

Both statements are true. Regarding the passion of the Croats, another friend from the city told me that Zagreb is "a German city populated by Italians who speak Russian." I couldn't help but note how appropriate that description is. The city itself is distinctly Germanic in feel—more Austrian, or even Swiss, in its architecture than anything else. However, the atmosphere in the restaurants, the streets, and certainly on the park benches, is far more Italian than Germanic. And Croatian does sound a hell of a lot like Russian when you come to think of it (but I confess that most Slavic languages sound more-or-less like Russian to me).

In my book, this adds a certain cool unpredictability to Zagreb. This whole German/Mediterranean thing sometimes works very well, but sometimes it goes horribly awry. An example of the latter case is a restaurant near the cathedral that will go un-named but which contains a lot of tourists and serves what is purported to be traditional Croatian food (although I can personally attest to the fact that its wares resemble traditional Croatian food in the way that the plastic facsimiles outside of Japanese restaurants resemble the food served inside). It's not the food, though, that wins the prize for ickiness—it's the ambiance. As is often the case with touristy restaurants that purport to give you a real "local" experience, you will be served by staff uncomfortably wearing whatever garb will strike foreigners as seeming the most authentic. In Russia, this involves fur and strange hats; in Germany, it may require lederhosen. In Croatia, it involves bright colors and neckties. (Croatians invented the necktie, which takes its French name, *cravate*, from a mispronunciation of *Hrvat*, which means Croatian in Croatian. You with me?) But hell, they could wear whatever they want in these restaurants and I wouldn't complain, as long as they could get the damn music right.

There are two possibilities, music-wise, in places like this. Possibility number one, which is usually the lesser of two evils, consists of a folk band playing gypsy music. It's always gypsy music (at least east of the Oder River). Apparently, gypsies ruled Eastern Europe in the past. Possibility number two consists of a younger guy with a complicated keyboard (the kind that includes a rhythm machine) doing a mix of Western and local pop songs. May the gods spare you from possibility number two. In this particular Zagreb restaurant, I was subjected to possibility number two, while sipping my strange soup. (Did I also mention that these restaurants always serve at least one kind of strange soup, often served in a bowl made out of stale bread?)

Enough, though—here I am berating one bad Croatian restaurant in what is, after all, a lovely and manageable city. Let's move on to something more pleasant, therefore . . . the wax-scrapers.

I'm not really sure that Zagreb's wax-scrapers are any different from other cities' wax-scrapers. It might just be that I never really noticed wax-scrapers before, and during my recent stay in Zagreb I was particularly sensitive to their presence. But on reflection, I think not—I think Zagreb really does have a thing about wax-scraping.

Just to clarify things a little: by wax-scrapers, I don't mean just anybody who goes around randomly scraping wax; I mean people who clean the melted wax from those big metal votive-candle racks.

You know those things, right? You go into a church and you find a big metal rack where you can usually drop in a donation and then light yourself a votive candle, stick it in a holder, say a prayer, and leave it to burn. There are many reasons to leave burning votive candles, whether they be in remembrance of a departed loved one or in supplication for some coveted item. (I confess that the last votive candle I lit was probably a pitiful celestial bribe for a new bike, but it must be said that I haven't lit any votive candles in quite a long time.) Anyway, needless to say, these things get covered in melted wax as the wishes and memories burn away, and someone has to clean all that melted hope off the black metal.

I wouldn't be surprised if you never gave a moment's thought to who actually scrapes off the waxy detritus of divine supplication. Certainly, I had never asked myself that question, and if I had, I would have imagined that it's done by short, hooded monks wearing frayed ropes as belts. In Zagreb, though, I ran into wax-scrapers all over, and they didn't look anything like monks. I even found them outside the churches. There's this really nifty city-gate-like affair when you enter the old walls (up near St. Mark's, with its very cool roof), and this gate has its own rack of votive candles. Well, there was a wax-scraper there, too, and she was scraping wax with the fervent energy of a true believer . . . or of someone with an obsessive-compulsive cleaning fixation.

The wax-scrapers hover around votive candle racks like wasps tending their nests. They remove excess wax with nondescript metal implements and they tidy up the candles, both those that are burning and those that are there for the offering. I assume they also collect the coins in the offering boxes, but perhaps this is outside their domain of responsibility. The wax-scrapers I saw were invariably older people, dressed in normal (as opposed to ecclesiastic) clothes. I don't know whether wax-scraping is their full-time occupation, or whether they're volunteers. They had a kind of volunteer air to them, but I might have been mistaken.

As a rule, it seems Croatian wax-scrapers don't speak English. Or at least the ones I tried to talk to don't. I wanted to get some insight into this whole wax-scraping thing, and I tried to strike up a couple of conversations, but it was always in vain. They either ignored me entirely, lost in their duties, or shrugged at my queries. Wax-scraping remained and will remain a mystery to me.

As for the other particularly Zagreban activity—making out on a park bench in the cool evening breeze—well, I didn't bother trying to interview any of its practitioners, but then I hardly needed to ask about that. New York has a couple of parks as well, and I was young once, too.

KAFKA'S EROTIC DREAM: PRAGUE, CZECH REPUBLIC

Ah, Prague. Many European cities have their "historic quarter," where beautiful old buildings overlook sinuous streets that run their cobblestoned length into squares featuring statues and churches and clocks and towers. Lord knows I've written about enough of these places. In many cities, though, the historic section feels like a museum; carefully preserved, but vaguely irrelevant. The historic part of Prague, though, *is* Prague. You never walk your way into a modern, hulking concrete part of Prague, the nice part just goes on and on.

I imagine there is some awful functional zone in Prague, and I'm sure that there are those of you who could tell me about it, but I beg mercy—let me go on thinking that the entire city is just like the city I know, a city that invites and pets and coos at you, a city that seems to want you in the worst way.

I don't really know Prague. I've been there a few times, I've wandered its streets with wonder, but this is a city you can't really *know* with so perfunctory a relationship as that. It's a city with a lot of secrets . . . it's no wonder Kafka built his tortuous worlds here, and it's no wonder that the castle of his nightmares bore so many rooms.

Nor is it any wonder that he came up with the idea of the book *The Castle* in the first place. You'll probably be on the right bank of the river, in which case the castle will be looming at you from across the water. The castle in Prague was built to loom, perched up on that hill. If you want a real Kafkaesque experience, then hang around until it's foggy, preferably at night, then walk down to the riverbank to get loomed at by the castle. You'll immediately feel as though someone's out to get you.

Not that Prague is a gloomy place. For example, there's the Charles Bridge. Built in the fifteenth century, it stretches across the river, bearing only pedestrians and statues of religious figures, many of whom sport shiny brass halos. The bridge is always full of people who seem to be strolling along it for the sake of walking on the bridge itself, as opposed to wanting to get to the other side. There are artists and lovers and sellers of trinkets, as well as tourists and Czechs engaged in friendly debate. There are also seagulls. Now Prague is really far from the sea, so I can only assume that some bohemian seagull couple flew up the river at some point in time (I have no idea where the Vltava River flows, but all rivers eventually reach the sea, don't they?) and fell so thoroughly in love with the city that they decided to make their avian lives there, thus engendering generations of landlocked seabirds. Or so I like to think.

The bridge is bracketed by impressive medieval towers, and near the one on the right bank is a statue of King Charles, who gave his name to the bridge. This statue is worth a look, because it represents the archetype of a medieval king. Charles stands there with a kingly robe, the kind of crown you used to draw on kings when you were in grade school, and a really whopping sword; his full beard jutting out under a kingly chin. And through all that royal paraphernalia, he's smiling! I'll have to look up the history of Charles to find out why he seems so happy. It may just be because he lived in Prague.

Anyway, keep on strolling. You have to stroll in Prague. Check out the red street signs with white letters. How many cities have red street signs with white letters? Eventually, of course, you'll end up in Old Town Square, which is genuinely beautiful, and if it's before 9:00 PM you'll probably find a crowd hanging out in front of the astronomical clock (*Prazsky orloj* in Czech, minus the squiggles). They will be waiting for it to chime. You should wait, too. The clock was built in 1410, and refined in 1490 by Jan Ruze. Legend says that Ruze's eyes were put out after he finished so that he could never build a clock that would rival it. No one else ever did.

Every hour, when the circles in the circles line up on the face of the clock, a little skeleton appears, ringing a bell (ask not for whom this bell tolls . . .), then a succession of apostles parade by a couple of little open windows. The skeleton keeps ringing his bell and the people below take pictures while they consider their mortality. Well, at least I considered mine.

After that, you'll probably need a bit of a pick-me-up, a reminder of the joys of life. You may consider stopping by the nearby Sex Machines Museum, on Melantichova 18. The official description of this place is: "an exposition of mechanical erotic appliances, the purpose of which is to bring pleasure and allow extraordinary and unusual positions during intercourse." I have the impression that the "pleasure" element is largely subservient to the "extraordinary and unusual" element. I must confess that I hesitated before entering—a lone man wandering into such a place, particularly a lone man wearing a trench coat, could seem somewhat unhealthy. I therefore made sure to have out my pen and little bits of paper so as to make it clear that I was only entering out of journalistic professionalism. I'm not sure this was entirely convincing.

The Sex Machines Museum is spread over three floors, with a steady increase in intensity as you go up. On the lower floors you can find things like nightgowns with strategically placed holes in them and "God wishes it" embroidered on the front. Apparently, there used to be people who needed such reminders in order to steel up the courage to undertake the act of intercourse. There is also a small screening room showing antique porn, including a 1925 Spanish film, *The Confessor, or the Friar's Blessing*, featuring a man dressed (partially) as a priest and a very fat lady who is confessing something to his nether regions. One can assume that God wouldn't wish this at all.

God would probably also have serious reservations about the practices of those who invented the objects on the top floor, which contains whips and chains and masks and outfits that can get your skin crawling. In between, you'll find all kinds of frankly perplexing things. The pieces of furniture are particularly incomprehensible, and I found myself staring at one or two of them for quite some time, trying to figure out how the hell they are supposed to be used.

There are also, of course, a myriad of plastic and glass prostheses, mostly representing male genitalia, but some representing those of the fairer sex. One consisted of all the more blatantly erogenous zones of a woman in one portable plastic mishmash, about the size of a basketball. It looked like the twisted experiment of a mad, sexist geneticist.

You also have to check out the patent applications posted on the walls throughout the museum. These are real applications, taken from the U.S. Patent Office. My favorite was a 1995 patent (#5,385,154) for a "couple's intimacy reciprocating and pivoting two-seat assembly." There's a diagram, but it looked like a mechanic's manual for a helicopter, and the rationale for this device remains a mystery.

There was also an old "erotic bench" found in the Italian countryside, a very naughty seesaw, a boy's "anti-masturbation device," and a robotic machine that boasted an "interchangeable member." I shudder to imagine what one interchanges the member *with*.

Come to think of it, the Sex Machines Museum might not be the best way to cheer yourself up after considering your mortality. Sex is apparently not a very cheerful activity for some. In that case, I suggest you go back outside and stroll some more—try not to peer at the castle on a foggy night, but instead sit in a café at a table made all wobbly by the cobblestones and enjoy the sheer beauty of the place. Who knows, maybe you'll take a lesson from the seagulls and end up nesting there.

SHAKEN, NOT STIRRED: MONACO

Y

It must be admitted—no matter how down-to-earth, no matter how sensitive and caring and cuddly he is, every man has at one time or another dreamed of being James Bond. These dreams can take many forms, depending on your favorite scenes, but the phenomenon is probably universal. OK, maybe the Dalai Lama has never felt a need to say, "My name is Lama, Dalai Lama," but the rest of us just can't resist the idea.

As for myself, Mr. Bond is at his coolest and most Bond-ish when he is in a casino, his bow tie either impeccably circling his neck, or perhaps later in the evening, hanging in two weird-looking squiggly black lines down his dickey. Scratch that, I don't suppose Bond wears a dickey. Anyway, that's one of the reasons I've always insisted on tying my own bow tie—a pitiful play for Bondness. Often, I can be seen at formal events, just before they end, with a vodka martini in hand and my bow tie hanging down my shirt (nor do I wear a dickey). This invariably doesn't work at all. I have yet to be approached by Ursula Andress.

But then, what was missing, you see, was the casino. Since I was recently in Monaco, I figured this was the perfect place to try out the James Bond thing (although sadly, I didn't have my tuxedo with me—I had to make do with a dark suit).

Monaco is Europe's second smallest country (after the Vatican City). It also boasts, by far, the highest per capita rate of million-aires of any country in the world.

Monaco used to be just a geopolitical oddity in nineteenth-century Europe, a crumb left behind after the festivities of the Napoleonic Wars. Then, in 1856, Prince Charles III decided that a casino would be a great way to raise some cash. After futzing around with some less-than-spectacular buildings in the old town, he decided to use an empty hilltop. (Empty hilltops are rare in countries that measure roughly one square mile, but he found one.) He named the hill after himself: "Monte Carlo," or "Mount Charles." He then asked the great French architect Charles Garnier to work some baroque magic, and the casino was built in 1878.

Like Garnier's greatest creation, Paris's Opéra Garnier, the casino is breathtaking. Even the entry hall is overwhelming, with its towering volume and its intricately carved walls and ceiling. In order to enter the casino itself, you have to tear your eyes away from the architecture, show your ID and pay 10 euros, after which they stamp your hand with a UV stamp and give you a free plastic cup full of Budweiser . . . or so they would if my old college friend Bob were running it. Luckily, he is not.

You are then allowed to proceed into the main hall, which is a hymn in wood and velvet. A number of roulette and baccarat tables dot the room, where well-dressed rich people circulate discreetly.

The only other casinos I've ever been in were in the United States, and they were largely populated by overweight AARP members in fluorescent jogging suits, toting buckets of quarters. James Bond would have looked distinctly out of place in them. In Monte Carlo, however, he would fit right in. Even the Italians in jeans and T-shirts looked good. (It should be noted, however, that rich Italian men, and all Italian women, have some kind of super-natural ability to dress far better than you could ever dress, even if they're wearing rags.)

The tables range from those with a 10-euro minimum to

those with a minimum that looked pretty maximum to me. The baccarat tables showed sums that could have more easily been posted in scientific notation. There were some blackjack tables farther back, and, yes, a room with slot machines (and angels carved into the ceiling), which was populated by four Japanese tourists and an old man with a long white ponytail. There are also the private gaming rooms, where spies get together to stare into each other's eyes and gamble away the world's security. At least, I suppose so. They wouldn't let me in to check.

Since I take my obligations to my readers very seriously, it was clear that I couldn't make a foray into the casino without participating in the gaming experience. Otherwise, my report would hardly be complete, now would it? As I had come with a friend, I convinced him that we both needed to lose some money. We therefore went to get chips. You can only get chips with cash, but you can get cash next to the guy who gives you chips. The logic of this escapes me, but I assumed James Bond would know, and so just went with the flow and got my chips.

We decided on roulette as the least complicated way to lose our money, and headed over to the small-stakes table (10-euro minimum). There were a few people around it, and four different croupiers. Three of these men sat around the table and wielded long polished wood sticks with plastic things on the end—kind of like classy pooper-scoopers. They manipulated chips all over the table with these things, moving with a fluidity one usually only observes in martial arts films and ferrets. The chips flew all over, apparently as a result of barely whispered instructions by the more worldly people sitting near us. Since I didn't know how to talk to the croupiers using this subtle language, I just put my bets on the one part of the table I could reach on my own.

The fourth croupier sat in this chair at the head of the table, up near the roulette wheel itself, which seemed to be made of a sort of tawny gold. The wheel spun surprisingly slowly, while one of the croupiers sent the ball whizzing around in the opposite direction. As soon as he did this, the chips accelerated their dance around the table and the pooper-scoopers flashed like wooden lightning bolts. The croupiers spoke in curt, polite sentences, switching effortlessly between French and Italian, the occasional smile flashing on their thin lips.

Since the only part of the table I could reach without having to stretch or converse with a croupier was the bit where one bets on the color red, I kept betting on red. Of course, this meant that black came up . . . again and again and again. As I watched my pitiful pile of chips dwindle into nothing (very pretty chips, by the way), one of those disgustingly fashionable Italian men came up and threw a couple of 500-euro bills on the table. One of the croupiers immediately changed them into chips. (I thought you had to go to the desk at the back to do this, but apparently if you can flip a thousand in cash on the table, you're allowed to take some shortcuts.) He issued a terse set of instructions to the croupier, who flicked the chips onto the relevent places then verified their position with his pooper-scooper. All of his numbers lost (he should have just played black), so he threw another grand onto the table and tried again. He lost that too, shrugged, and went to try another table.

Some people have a lot of money.

My friend and I were both down to our last chips, and I decided that I'd kick myself forever if I were to switch from my astute strategy ("RED!") and then lose, so I plonked down my last chips on red, while he put his on the number two.

Of course, two (which is black) came up, and he won 750 euros.

"I'll buy you a drink," he said.

"Damn straight you will," I replied, and we left.

Monaco is more than the casino. There are a lot of interesting things to do there, such as the aquarium and a museum with dolls and automatons, but you'll end up losing all your money before you can do anything else, then you'll have to make your way back to some less surrealistic place, inhabited by normal people. As an example, there's a billboard—an entire billboard, mind you—on one of the main streets in Monaco that asks, "Need insurance for your super-yacht?" Where else in the world would it be worthwhile to put up a *billboard* for super-yacht insurance? You might slip an add into "Rich Bastard Living" magazine, but a billboard? This leaves you standing in the street near all the Bentleys and Rolls-Royces, contemplating the fact that you most definitely *don't* need insurance for your super-yacht, that in fact you don't even have enough cash in your pocket for cab fare back to the hotel, and that it's about time to go home.

That's when you'll most regret not wearing a tuxedo, because if you were wearing one, you could untie your bow tie and let it hang down your dickey-less front and practice drawing your Walther PPK in front of your hotel mirror.

LYON AND LIGHTSABERS:
LYON, FRANCE

France is a very centralized country. Just about everything revolves around Paris. The French even have a tendency to split the country into two parts: Paris and Province. Province is simply anything that isn't Paris, or at least in the Paris area (not to be confused with Provence, which is a specific region in the south). Province can mean Pau, near the Spanish border, or it can mean Gisors, only an hour away by car. Neither are Paris, therefore they are Province.

French places in Province often suffer from a stigma of being kind of slow, laid-back, a bit outmoded . . . provincial, in a nutshell. And it must be said that there's a bit of truth in this. Paris leads a harried life, and Parisians get all caught up in it, whereas if you head out to Dijon, for instance (I must write about Dijon soon) then there's a hell of a lot more strolling as opposed to running, and while perhaps they don't actually drink more wine than the Parisians, they do seem to enjoy it more. Come to think of it, they probably do drink more wine.

France's second largest city, Marseille, doesn't really fit with the idea of Province. It's a bustling, noisy, growing place in its own right, and the culture in the south of France (not to mention the accent) is so very different from that in Paris that if one were to say to a Frenchman, "I'm going to Province this weekend," he wouldn't imagine that you mean Marseille.

France's *third* largest city, though, could lay a pretty good claim to being the archetypical Province city. What's more, Lyon (like Marseille) has a history much longer than that of Paris, as it was one of the largest cities in Gaul at the time of the Roman conquest, and became a thriving Roman town (by the name of Lugudnum).

Lyon is wrapped around the confluence of two rivers: the Rhone and the Saône. Both are big and fast and powerful, and when they meet, it's a sight to see. Particularly since the city itself is enticing. It's easy to become infatuated with Paris, what with her flashy clothes and her beguiling ways, but after she's worn you down, it may behoove you to take a look at her little sister. You might realize that she has a hell of a lot of charm as well, even if she is more discrete.

A lot of that charm is over in the "old city," which has its requisite windy cobblestone streets, centuries-old buildings, and red-tile roofs with eaves that hang overhead. It also has a great big hill that sports a striking white cathedral and some appealing Roman ruins. The cathedral was built by the Lyonnais when they promised the Virgin Mary they would do something nice for her if she were to keep the Prussians from invading the city in 1871. She held up her side of the bargain, so a few years later, she got a cathedral. I don't know if they tried something similar in 1940. If so, maybe they didn't ask nicely enough. Anyway, I strongly suggest walking up one of the streets with the preface "montée," such as the Montée Nicolas de Lange. This street includes one of the longest stairways I've ever seen. It's pretty, though—lots of plants hanging over the walls on either side of the stairs, and numerous twists and such.

Back down in the old city, head over to the Palais de la Miniature. It must be said that this is a relatively obscure place, but look for it. It consists of lots of little worlds, most of which were created by Daniel Ohlmann.

Dan Ohlmann started out as a sculptor, then became an interior designer. He did a lot of work in theatre, and realized that the scale models he was building of proposed sets were more fun to make than the sets themselves. For the past 20 years or so, he has therefore devoted himself to the creation of miniatures—originally, he worked primarily for the movie industry (he collaborated on many films, including, for instance, Luc Besson's *The Fifth Element*), but for the last few years he's been building miniatures mostly for their own sake.

Ohlmann calls these dioramas "realities," and it's hard to argue with the appellation. They tend to be about the size of a two large breadboxes (Why on earth do we use the "larger than a breadbox" question? How many people are familiar with breadboxes? I remember we used to have one, but it's quite possible that you don't have a clue what I'm talking about.), and they consist of three-dimensional representations of real places. The museum he's created on the rue Juiverie in Lyon contains a number of them, and they can wreak havoc with your brain. For Ohlmann, they are like three-dimensional photos; he wants the viewer to enter them in his mind. This is why he never includes images of people.

The "realities" range from the dining room of Maxim's, in Paris (2,700 hours of work), in which every tiny glass, every fork, every rose on every table, as well as the stained glass in the walls, is rendered in perfect detail . . . to a highway tunnel. There seems to be little rhyme or reason in his choice of subjects, but Ohlmann is an artist, and who's to question an artist's whims? It certainly does make for a varied experience.

The museum, which is relatively new and very under-visited, is expanding as well. Through his contacts in the world of cinema, Dan Ohlmann has acquired a number of props used in various films, and is setting up a new exhibition in which he's going to display the props and show films explaining how they were used. These range from a gruesomely lifelike foot, transpierced with a nail, to . . . are you ready . . . a lightsaber.

Yes, a real lightsaber (well, except for the glowing part that slices through bad guys). Now, since I have a valid excuse for passing myself off as something of a journalist, not only did I get to interview Dan Ohlmann, but he even gave me a tour of this new, unopened part of the museum, where he showed me the lightsaber and he let me hold it.

As is often the case with men, I was once a boy, and I really wanted a lightsaber. Not a toy, mind you, but a real one, and there I was, with a lightsaber that had been used during the filming of the original *Star Wars* movies. Of course, I waved it around a little, and discovered that it's really heavy. Apparently, Lucas didn't want his actors to feel like they could just wiggle the thing in some sissified little way, so he made sure the lightsabers had some heft to them. I'm very glad he did. I would have been desperately disappointed if the thing had felt like it came in a cereal box.

And that wasn't all—Ohlmann also has that little golden head they used in the filming of *Raiders of the Lost Ark*. You know, the one at the beginning, where Indy swipes it off an altar and replaces it with a bag of sand, then gets chased by a giant marble? That's the one. I touched that, too, although I did manage to resist the considerable urge to try and swipe it, replacing it with a shoe or something.

All that in itself would be worth the visit to the museum, but let's not forget the miniatures, which are also worth a visit, which means that you should just visit the damn place.

And, of course, there is the city, with its aforementioned little-sister charm, and its fantastic food, and its big rivers and its Roman amphitheater (where you can attend concerts or ballets) and its not-quite-so-harried lifestyle.

CRATER LAKE, OREGON

I feel as though I should write some kind of commentary on this column, but I really don't want to. Sorry.

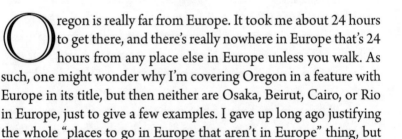

Oregon is really far from Europe. It took me about 24 hours to get there, and there's really nowhere in Europe that's 24 hours from any place else in Europe unless you walk. As such, one might wonder why I'm covering Oregon in a feature with Europe in its title, but then neither are Osaka, Beirut, Cairo, or Rio in Europe, just to give a few examples. I gave up long ago justifying the whole "places to go in Europe that aren't in Europe" thing, but since the majority of you are in the United States, Oregon might be so far outside of the domain of exoticism that it may raise eyebrows, whereas Manila does not.

On the other hand, North America and Australia are the only inhabited continents that have not yet appeared in this feature, and while Australia (which is even farther from Europe than is Oregon) might be an understandable omission, there are those who have wondered why I have not yet written about the United States. I am, after all, American. Or rather, from New York.

But why Oregon? Why not my hometown, for instance? Particularly as I go to New York at least once or twice a year, and I've never been to Oregon before in my life. Well, part of it is that from a European perspective at least, Oregon is very exotic. Many Europeans think you sprinkle it on pizza, if they've heard of it at all. Another reason is more prosaic—as I write this, I've just spent a week alone in Medford, Oregon, sorting out details both sordid and mundane and struggling with three distinct types of loneliness, not all of which are my own. Writing about Crater Lake will help.

The other reason is that there's actually a narrative arc to this dispatch. Most of my dispatches don't have a narrative arc; they instead have a distinct tendency to wander a bit. Wandering might not be entirely inappropriate for a travel column, but when you have an arc crying out to be narrated, it's not something to ignore.

The narrative arc centers around my white box, because after four days in Medford it became clear that I had to bring a white box to Crater Lake. This, then, is the story of the white box.

The four days in Medford are worth a story of their own. In fact, they're worth a book, but it would be a book full of pathos and the aforementioned variations on loneliness, and that, coupled with the length of it all, means I can't really tell that story here. Suffice it to say that they produced the white box, and then I'll skip directly to the evening before the trip to Crater Lake.

I took my box and drove in the stupendously large SUV the rental company had given me (I had asked for the smallest car they have. God knows what they would have given me if I had asked for a large car, but I assume it would have had tracks and a cannon.) to Ashland to attend a performance of *The Tempest*. I left the white box in the car during the performance itself. I assumed there wasn't a lot of theft in Ashland, Oregon, and, for that matter, the thief would have had one hell of a shock upon opening the box.

One of the best things about the United States is that you can be in the middle of (let's face it) nowhere, and it turns out that the place has a world-renowned Shakespeare festival, where people of all walks of life show up in all manner of attire to watch Shakespeare . . . and they know the play. You figure you'll be in some backwater where the only entertainment is swatting flies and eating deep-fried, sugarcoated batter nuggets, and it turns out that the drivers of those pickups are sitting next to you commenting on the actor playing Caliban by saying things like, "Damn, but he was good as Mercutio last year." You feel doubly the dolt, first because you had entirely forgotten about Caliban's *existence*, and second, because you had prejudged just about everyone around you on the basis of their being from the middle of (let's face it) nowhere.

It was a great performance, an extraordinary evening, and a good way to prepare for the trip to Crater Lake.

Crater Lake is in a caldera (the crater of an extinct volcano). It's a *very* big caldera and it came from one hell of a volcano. Mount Mazama exploded almost 8,000 years ago, leaving a seven-mile-wide hole on top, which has since filled with water, creating the deepest lake in the United States. The lake is known for being very big, very deep, very blue, and just generally impressive. It's the kind of place you remember, and that you'll end up seeing pictures of even if you aren't trying to find pictures of it. It was the ideal place to bring my white box, and a welcome close to what had been a trying week.

The trip didn't start out being impressive. As I drove out of Medford on a sunny Saturday morning, I couldn't help but notice a string of Abby's Legendary Pizza shops. There were at least three, one every mile or so. My grandfather was a pizza man, and he never told me any legends about Abby. For that matter, it's a relatively rare name in Italy (roughly on par with Jedidiah). Lastly, how much pizza do they eat on that particular strip of Route 62 to warrant three identical pizza places in as many miles? These questions nagged at me.

Very quickly, though, the route became scenic enough to distract me from thoughts about Abby's pizza or the white box in the back. In fact, as I drove the 60 or so miles to Crater Lake, the road got more and more beautiful, and my thoughts more and more empty and somewhat melancholy.

Beauty will sometimes do that to me, bring on this kind of melancholy.

The road runs along the Rogue River for a while, which splashes over black rocks among big pine trees. After that, the pine trees just take over—enormous trees with rugged bark. These are trees that have lived. In Europe, most forests have a kind of managed look to them; they're very inviting, very friendly. Here, you have the impression of intruding in a world that would much rather you left, a world that is alive in a different way.

As the miles ticked by, the road got curvier, the trees got bigger, and my melancholy deepened with the passing beauty. The stereo didn't help, since I had Pink Floyd on. I couldn't help it, I had to listen to it. As I drove up to Crater Lake itself, I actually felt a tear come to my eye, but it was a very intense passage in the music ("... you wore out your welcome with random precision, rode on the steel breeze ..."). Also, I have sensitive eyes.

You don't see the lake until you get to the top of the rim. I decided not to look. I didn't want to see it from the car, I wanted to see it on my feet. I turned off the music and drove along Rim Drive to the west until I came to an overlook, where a number of cars were parked. At least 30 people were hanging out on a paved lookout spot, enjoying the view. I decided once again to avoid it, trying only to see it with peripheral vision. I needed to be alone with my box. That was the whole point.

I knew there was a hiking trail off to the left, and I took the box and started walking. There was no one else. The trail ran along the outside of the rim, well above Rim Drive, but well below the actual edge. As such, I couldn't see the lake from the trail, but Oregon's Cascade Range spread its woods to the distant horizon. It was a magnificent sight.

After about a half hour, still having come across no one, I decided to try to climb up to the rim itself. I picked a spot that didn't look too steep—after all, I was carrying the box—and left the trail, heading up.

It wasn't an easy climb. Although there was some sparse vegetation, the ground was all volcanic ash; it was more like sand, or dust. It was gray and it got in my shoes, and made it difficult to climb. Furthermore, I was over 7,000 feet high and the air was thin. I had to stop once to catch my breath—I didn't put the box down, but I drew great lungfuls of air and looked at the view again. The box had proven to be deceptively heavy, and the slope deceptively steep.

After a few moments, I set out again, and with a final effort, managed to crest the rim, where the earth suddenly opened up before me.

I found myself teetering on the edge of a 1,000-foot-high cliff, a vast circle of blue far below, broken only by a small pyramid of rock that looked like it had been dropped in as an afterthought. There was a slight breeze blowing from the south. I just stood there and looked. My eyes weren't big enough to see it all.

I've seen a lot, and I've described a lot, but I'm powerless to describe this. Sometimes when I write these things, I wonder if it isn't just *words*—if it's not all a waste of time, because how can such things be described? I can write "blue," but that's not it. The lake isn't one color, for that matter; the water paints itself onto sheer gray walls a thousand feet high and it all stretches in a circle larger than any circle I could have imagined. It looks like a god made this, and if this is all that he made, then he was a great god indeed. The sky, and the water . . . and then words fail me.

Words don't usually fail me.

I sat down on a rock at the cliff's edge and tried to take a few notes, tried to think about how to put all this, but I found I was too distracted, and realized that my note-taking was just an excuse not to do what I had come here to do. So I stood up and looked again, drank in the image of the lake and the cliffs and the dust at my feet, considered the fact that I was alone, all alone, facing all of this.

Finally, I picked up the box and opened it . . . then I scattered my father's ashes to the wind.

A TREE OR NOT A TREE?:
CHENNAI, INDIA

I must confess from the start: it's been many years since I was in Chennai. I've been meaning to get back, if for no other reason than to write about it (as well as to see some old friends), but Chennai has remained off the paths I've been beating these last few years, so I'm going to have to rely on memory.

Chennai (formerly known as Madras) lies on India's east coast, firmly in the south of the country. The city is not a big tourist magnet, and there are damn good reasons for that. Like just about every Indian city (with the possible exception of parts of Bombay/ Mumbai), its roads are clogged with a perpetual traffic jam, caused less by the quantity of cars than by the masses of scooters, mopeds, bicycles, livestock, pedestrians, and just *stuff* that is continually circulating on them. I could never drive in India—it's not dangerous for the driver, but I can't fathom how anyone can actually propel a motor vehicle through such mayhem without leaving a swath of flattened people and animals behind.

Once, a business contact from Chennai came to spend a week with me in Paris. The poor man had never left the south of India in his life. I went to pick him up at the airport, and he spent the next half an hour clinging terrified to the dashboard. He had never gone faster than about 50 km/h in his life (it's just not possible on Indian roads . . . too crowded). Once I had slowed down to a crawl, he loosened up a little and started looking around at Paris. I was proud to show him my adopted city, but his only question was, "Are there no cows in the street?" Yes, Indian roads are very different from European or American roads.

But I digress. I didn't want to write about Chennai's roads, not about her tourist attractions (for aside from a few temples, there really are none), I wanted to write about the banyan tree.

There was a time, some years back, when I spent a number of weeks in Chennai, spread over a few different visits. Despite its lack of historical attractions, Madras does boast great, cheap food, as well as a plethora of Indian music and dance to appreciate. But still, a body wants to get out and wander from time to time.

One place I quickly decided to wander to was the beach. The beach is about 12 kilometers long, and probably about 500 meters wide at most points. It is sandy and flat and easy to walk on. The beach is festooned with merchants selling all kinds of things. There are very few people in the water: a few young men in bathing suits showing their prowess in the waves, fully clothed women who wade in to their knees and laugh as their saris spread across the water's surface. Most people just walk along the beach. I was once approached there by a boy on horseback, who galloped up to me and reined the horse to a stop to ask if I wanted to take him for a spin. I have to confess that I've never been on a horse's back. The closest I came was a donkey named Luigi in Sicily when I was 12, as well as the various camels that have plagued my life, so I said no and the boy galloped off again.

The beach is also home to many fishermen, who cast off into the Bay of Bengal in skinny little boats that look like they were made by lashing a couple of pieces of driftwood together. At least, it used to be home to the fishermen—the 2004 tsunami swept death up onto this beach, and many of the poor who lived there perished. But when I was there last, this particular tragedy lay hidden in the unknowable future.

The beach was definitely worth a visit, so I decided there must be more to the city. I asked around and was pointed to the grounds of the Theosophical Society to discover the great old banyan tree.

Banyan trees are sacred to Hindus, to whom they represent eternal life. The banyan tree at the Theosophical Society in Chennai was represented to me as the world's largest (which isn't really true, but you have to make allowances for local biases) and I made my way over to check it out.

But first, I wanted to find out what the hell the "Theosophical Society" was. Or is. I therefore researched it as best I could and learned pretty much nothing. As best I can tell, it was one of those quasi-mystical nineteenth-century pseudo religions that were so attractive to overfed and underskeptical British and American aristocrats. A couple of them created this philosophy/religion thing and for some reason decided that its headquarters would be in Madras (for Madras was still Madras then, before linguistic sensitivities converted it to Chennai). The tree was already on the grounds when they purchased the land, and had been for some 300 years.

The grounds of the Theosophical Society are pleasing and peaceful, which is a welcome respite from the rather smelly tension of Chennai itself. The tree, though, is not at all what I expected. I was escorted around by a kind, older gentleman who was some kind of security guard, although what he was guarding is a mystery. I suppose he was guarding the tree itself. He explained that the main trunk had been destroyed a few years ago by a storm, which left only the secondary trunks. This means that the tree doesn't look anything like a big old tree. Instead, it looks like a thicket of small young trees.

This confused me, since I didn't know anything about banyans at the time. He explained. Banyan trees are a kind of fig tree: they generally have a central trunk, and then as the years go by, they drop "aerial roots" that descend into the ground and basically serve as the starting point for new trees. This means that old ones can pretty much create their own little grove.

This begged the point that if the original, central trunk had been blown down by a storm, was this still *a* tree, or was it the *descendants* of the original tree? I asked this of the security guard, who said he didn't rightly know. It depended on whether I meant in a *philosophical* sense, or whether I wanted to know if the roots are connected, or what. I said that all aspects of the question merited a response, and he stopped and began to think about it.

He never really finished thinking about it. He said he would look it up, or talk to some friends about the question, and that I should come back and ask him.

Now here's the thing—I never did go back, and I can't help but wonder if he found the answer, whether botanical or philosophical, and whether he was disappointed that I didn't come to find out. I'm kind of disappointed myself.

TUCK & PATTI
AND JEFF AND STARLIGHT:
CORSICA, FRANCE

My readers quickly informed me that the name of the bassist who played with Jeff Beck is Tal Wilkenfeld, an Australian prodigy whose star continues to rise. Unfortunately, she is six years older than my son (not that that would stop him).

Patrimonio is a small village in the north of Corsica, which is known for two things—its wine and the "Nights of the Guitar," a festival that lasts for about two weeks in July and that regularly features some of the best guitarists in the world.

Depending on when we come and who's playing, I try to get up to Patrimonio (a good 2 ½ hours by car from where we stay) for at least one concert during the festival, but these last couple of years have been unlucky for me. This is extremely unfortunate, because the concert venue for the Patrimonio festival might well lay claim to being the best imaginable place to see a concert.

A major factor here is that Patrimonio is in Corsica, which is, as we established years ago, the most beautiful place in the world. The village itself is located on one of Corsica's typical windy mountain roads, with your standard Corsican stunning scenery and hairpin turns. The concerts take place in a kind of natural amphitheater, centered on the village's monument to its war dead. (All French villages, no matter how small, have a monument to their war dead, primarily from the First and Second World Wars, that is mind-boggling—the village might look like it holds 100 inhabitants and some chickens, and yet there will be endless lists of the fallen inscribed in stone. But I digress.) For the festival, this monument is hidden by the stage, which is open, and the stone arch that tops the monument serves as a backdrop.

The stage is flanked by trees. In fact, there are trees all over. The natural bowl has been carefully terraced, and about 1,500 plastic chairs are set up on the little grass terraces, in 10 rows. Fifteen hundred sounds like a lot, but looks like very little, and there's really no place that's more than 30 meters or so from the stage. Behind the stage, the land falls off sharply, with low mountains rising a few miles off, and through a cut in the mountains, you can see an inlet of the sea far below.

The last time I was at Patrimonio I saw Popa Chubby, who loves playing there. If you don't know him, Popa Chubby is a large man who plays hard, electric, New York blues. He's so large that his guitar looks like a ukulele when he's onstage. I've seen him a few times, and he's always remarkable, but something happens to musicians at Patrimonio . . . they play even better. When I saw him, he rocked the place to the ground for three hours. I was there in the company of a Corsican friend, who took great pleasure announcing to the other spectators, in Corsican, that I, too, was a New York guitarist—as though I was Popa Chubby's less voluminous brother.

Needless to say, as soon as we arrive in Corsica, I check out the lineup, and this year we arrived early enough to make a trip to Patrimonio a possibility. What's more, it turned out that on one blessed night, both Tuck & Patti and Jeff Beck were going to be playing.

I'll assume you know who Jeff Beck is, and I further assume you'll understand why no guitarist of my generation could possibly not want to go see Jeff Beck play. You may not know who Tuck &

Patti are, though, and that's a shame. Personally, I consider Tuck Andress to be one of the best guitarists in the world, and the duo he forms with his wife, Patti Catchcart, who has the voice of an alto angel, is beauty incarnate.

What's more, my two sons are now at the age where they have started to appreciate real music. (As opposed to the crap my wife listens to [and I'll allow myself nested parentheses here to point out that my wife doesn't like reading in English and therefore I won't get in trouble for having written that, but either way, she knows my views about the commercial drivel with which she floods the car when she's driving].) Where was I? Ah, yes, my sons.

At 12 and 14, both my sons are musicians: the younger one is turning into a kick-ass drummer and the older one plays keyboards. Both of them wanted to come see the concert, despite the five hours of travel and the late, late night, so we went traipsing across Corsica to Patrimonio.

The town itself is probably worth the detour. Most Corsican towns are, particularly those that produce so much wine. Patrimonio also boasts a weird menhir from the Torre civilization, one that's about 5,000 years old, and looks something like a large dagger, about two meters tall, topped with a scary-looking human face of unspecific gender. Like most things dealing with the Torre civilization, no one knows much about it or what it represents. The menhir has its own little stone shelter near the stage, and copies of the menhir flank the stone arch behind the musicians.

We arrived early for the concert and took seats near the front. The spectators are a varied lot, and as can be expected in a place that sees its population increase by roughly tenfold during the summer, there are many tourists: Italians, Germans, and, of course, continental French. However, there are also a lot of Corsican natives. Corsicans tend to have a deep-rooted affinity for music. Traditional Corsican music consists largely of harmonic male vocal groups singing haunting and very complex polyphonic pieces, but music of all kinds is greatly appreciated. Until a few years ago, even a city as small as Porto-Vecchio boasted a top-rate blues club. The audience at the festival is always varied, attentive, and very happy to be there. They are dressed in shorts and T-shirts, and as we wait for the musicians, people are eating ice cream and Corsican pastries sold from little stands over near the menhir. A few people with guitars are playing *jazz manouche*, à la Django Reinhardt, on a small side stage nearby. No one is jostling for position, no one is stamping steel-toed boots in anticipation of pogoing on their neighbors feet. They are licking fig-flavored ice cream instead.

The concerts always start just before 10 PM. At that time, the sun has just set behind the mountains that can be seen in the distance behind the stage, and the sea, far below, has taken a metallic gray hue. The sky has turned my very favorite color—white on the edges, dipping to a darker and darker blue as you look up, until it's black overhead, with the more robust stars already shining through. The Corsican maquis, that thick tangle of sweet-smelling vegetation that lines the slopes behind the spectators, is buzzing with crickets and *cigales*, those loud Mediterranean insects that sing to distant mates.

Tuck and Patti came on to enthusiastic applause, and wielded magic for over an hour. Tuck explained that they had wanted to play Patrimonio for some time, and they were very happy to be there— and it was obvious that they were, indeed, very happy to be there. Every song produced frenzied appreciation, as Tuck did things on his Gibson that really shouldn't be possible, his guitar sounding like an orchestra. Patti sang with her soul on her lips, actually managing to get the entire crowd to sing in harmony for their encore rendition of "Time After Time." I can't even get my bassist to sing harmony, and she managed three-part harmony with 1,500 people. Despite the promise of the legendary Jeff Beck, the crowd didn't want them to leave.

Once they did, though, Jeff Beck lived up to his legend, playing his fusion with a vengeance. The band was fantastic, and included a female bassist who looked to be no older than about sixteen, but who played like she's been doing this for 50 years.

It was then that my older son yelled into my ear, "I'm in love."

I informed him that I would not be at all averse to him marrying Jeff Beck's bassist. It sounds kind of weird, but what the hell. Unfortunately, despite my best Net-based research, I can't find out who the girl was. If anyone has a clue, I'd be most grateful for the information—as would my son.

After a number of encores, Jeff Beck came to the mike and thanked us: "You're wonderful, and it's great to be back in this place—it's so beautiful," he waved his arm over the mountains and the sky and the trees and the sea in the distance. "Make sure you keep it that way."

I can now safely affirm that Jeff Beck and I share certain important opinions.

ZVOUROS,
THE CLAWED GUARDIAN
OF THE ACROPOLIS:
ATHENS, GREECE

I've been traveling quite a bit these last 15 years or so, as some of you may have noticed, and yet there always remained a long list of places to which I haven't been. Of course, one could argue that the number of places I have not visited is infinite. (That's not actually true: if we limit ourselves to the planet Earth, and to the landmass of the planet Earth [since visiting every bit of ocean would be tedious to say the least] then we are dealing with roughly 148 million square kilometers of land. If a "place" is assumed to take up at least 10 square meters, that means that there are roughly 14 billion places on the planet, which when it comes down to it is close enough to infinite for our purposes.) I have, all the same, visited a good number of the more widely acknowledged "interesting" places on the planet. In a nutshell, there aren't all that many places left that provoke the reaction, "You mean you've *never* been to _____!" I call these my YMYNBT places for short.

I had a YMYNBT list. Not a formal one, mind you—I'd hate to be one of those people who visit places just to say they've been there—but after a while, you do kind of keep track. The one big, enormous, whopping place on the top of that list was Greece.

Yes, I had never been to Greece.

Furthermore, as may also have been noticed by the more attentive of my readers, I am rather (passionately) interested in history, including the history of ancient civilizations, and let's face it, a hell of a lot of European history starts with Greece. So when I recently had the opportunity to go to Athens, I jumped at it.

Once in Athens, you shouldn't go to the Acropolis right away. You should make your way towards it, engage in some historical foreplay before the main event. First, you should go to the Temple of Zeus, which unfortunately now consists only of the temple's base and 15 stupendous columns, each 17 meters high. One other column was blown down by a gale in the nineteenth century and lies like a giant sliced hot dog across what would have been the temple's interior. I suppose it could be a disappointment, but think of it as that first kiss after dinner.

Then you head to the agora, the Greek equivalent of the Roman Forum. The classical agora of Athens dates pretty much to the foundation of the city. It was here that Athenians voted, it was here they discussed, it was here that Socrates corrupted the youth of Athens, here that Plato bothered everyone with the inconvenient truths of 2,400 years ago. You need some imagination to see beyond what might look like a dusty space full of crumbled rocks, but my imagination has been running rampant with images of the ancient world for quite some time and needed little prodding to imagine men and women in white chitons strolling arm in arm, fearfully discussing the evil empire to the east (it was already Iran, even back then).

It takes less imagination to appreciate the Temple of Hephaestus, which dominates the agora. It is one of the best preserved ancient Greek temples. From here, you have a magnificent view of the Acropolis, just a few hundred meters away . . . but not yet—you can consider this the passionate embrace in the hallway outside her door. First, go check out the Roman Forum, notable (according to the guidebooks) for the Tower of the Winds, by which the Greeks of the Roman period checked out both the time and the weather, and likewise notable (according to me) for the large public latrine, with its banks of toilets—essentially, long slabs of marble with numerous holes in them, underneath which flowed running water in a continual flush. Oh, those tidy Romans.

Now she opens the door, fumbling with her keys, and you enter her apartment.

You approach the Acropolis via a shady path, olive trees all around. The olive trees hide the Propylaia, the monumental building that served as a gateway to the sacred rock, until you're pretty much there (she's gone inside to get into something more comfortable, then suddenly appears nude in front of you . . . and here I'll drop the metaphor out of gentlemanly discretion, although you're free to engage in a little fantasizing along the same lines between now and the end of the dispatch).

That's it. I'm going to stop describing the Acropolis. I know that some are disappointed when they see it. "It's just a bunch of ruins," I've heard them say. Shame on them. Have they no imaginations? The Acropolis was the center of Greek, and therefore Western, civilization in its time; it was a crowning achievement of the ancient world. If you go, read all about it beforehand. Read about the chryselephantine statue of Athena that stood in the inner sanctum of the Parthenon, the ultimate masterpiece of Pheidias, and perhaps the greatest sculpture in history. Stand there and imagine . . . imagine. Then be sure to refocus your eyes on the present, and become incensed at the stupidity of mankind: in 1687, the Ottomans used the Parthenon as an ammunition dump (!?), and during one of the ceaseless wars men have waged over the ages, the site was bombarded and the Parthenon blew up, leaving it the ruin that it is today. Oh, the wonders men can perform, and the stupidity to which they are prone.

That's enough of that, though. Experience it all for yourself, but study it first. What you won't be able to study beforehand is the presence of Zvouros and his companions, for the Parthenon is their territory, and they defend it well.

Zvouros is one of the six or seven cats that lives among the ruins. He's a big black-and-white cat and is apparently the ringleader; the top cat, if you know what I mean. I ran across Zvouros when he was confronting a dog. (Note that Athens is full of sleeping dogs. You run across them all over, generally lying around, breathing real fast.) This dog had climbed up on some of the rubble and was kind of checking Zvouros out, but Zvouros would have none of it. He stood his ground magnificently, didn't even deign to hiss at the dog, just bristled up to about twice his natural size and *stared* at the offending canine, with the columns of the Parthenon backing him up. The dog couldn't take the moral pressure and slunk off towards the Temple of Athena Nike.

I have three cats, but it must be said that none of them is as majestic, as *classical*, as Zvouros. Plus, none of them has anywhere near his balls (to tell the truth, none of them have any balls at all, if you get my drift).

I learned Zvouros's name from a couple of the guards who sit in their little booths and make sure no one tags the place, or whatever. According to them, the dogs come and go, they are "visitors," generally begging for food from the tourists. (Shortly thereafter I saw one dog, who had evidently long practiced his pitiful/friendly look in some doggy mirror, scrounging a good long pet-on-the-head and some scraps of food from three elderly American tourists.) The cats, however, live there, and don't you forget it. The guards feed them.

"So the Parthenon is their territory," I said.

"No, the Parthenon belongs to Greece," they replied, rather incensed, and pointed out that there were a lot more important things for me to be writing about than cats. I looked around, noticed that from there I could see, far below, the Theatre of Dionysus—essentially, the world's first theatre, where Sophocles, Euripides, Aeschylus, Aristophanes and others first presented their plays.

I looked at the Parthenon towering above, pictured the Erechtheion right behind it, marveled at the industry of mankind, and figured they were right.

But if you take a long look at Zvouros, sitting like a sphinx among the columns, it's easy to imagine that he disagrees.

Zvouros, the Clawed Guardian of the Acropolis

MILLER, YOU'RE ASLEEP!:
L'ÎLE D'ARZ, FRANCE

Too much sun is bad for you. This is why not all French people flock to Corsica every summer (that, plus it's expensive and bombs are known to explode when the independentists get restless). What's more, many French people lack the foresight to marry someone from a Corsican family, and therefore do not benefit from the family house on a hill overlooking the sea. These people have only themselves to blame.

For those French people who do not head south for the summer, there is another holiday destination available that shares two, and only two, characteristics with Corsica. First, people there were forced to learn French over the last couple of hundred years, and second, it is (mostly) surrounded by water. In every other respect, Corsica and Brittany are pretty much opposites.

As I've pointed out in other dispatches, despite living on an island, Corsicans have no great love for nor tradition of the sea. Bretons, on the other hand, were apparently crafted not from the clay God used to make the rest of us, but from the muck remaining on the flats when the tide goes out. They are very much a seafaring people. Whenever you hear about some French sailor who navigated solo around the world in a four-foot boat built out of cheese rinds, or some such nautical exploit, you can be sure he or she is from Brittany.

Brittany is the peninsula that sticks out of France into the Atlantic like a finger pointing at America. It is rocky and windy and wet, and like many rocky, windy, wet places full of sailors, it possesses a haunting, misty beauty. A holiday in Brittany is a holiday during which one risks being rained upon. This doesn't seem to bother people from Great Britain overmuch, and thus many Brits holiday in Brittany.

For that matter, the similarities in the names of Brittany and Britain are not coincidental. Brittany is considered one of the six Celtic nations, along with Ireland, Wales, Scotland, Cornwall and Boston. The local language, which was strongly "discouraged" by the French government ever since Louis XIV, is a Celtic tongue not dissimilar to Irish, but most closely resembling (so it would seem) Cornish. Like all Celtic languages, it is completely impenetrable to me, but I can safely report that it has lots of *K*s and *R*s in it.

One of the nicest spots in Brittany is the Gulf of Morbihan, which is a wide gulf dotted with islands on the southern coast of the peninsula. One of these islands is l'Île d'Arz, also known as the Island of Captains, since it has a tradition of producing captains for the French merchant marine. It just so happens that my wife's best friend is the descendant of one of those captains, and her family owns a windmill on the island.

Wind and tide used to provide a lot of energy in Brittany, since the region enjoys an overabundance of both (the choice of the verb "enjoys" as opposed to "suffers from" is a question of taste). For many centuries, therefore, wheat was milled on l'Île d'Arz by two windmills and one tidal mill. One of these two windmills stands near the only town on the island, smiling down on it and being insufferably quaint. The other mill was transformed into a residence about 100 years ago and serves as a summer house for my wife's best friend's family—and the luckier of their acquaintances.

There's something disconcerting about living in a cylinder, however stunning and white and picturesque it may be. The walls curve, there are no angles, it's really . . . *round*. After a couple of nights, though, it just becomes *cool*. You lie in your bed next to the curving wall, after having climbed a narrow curving staircase that resembles nothing so much as a ship's ladder, listening to the wind as it comes flying in from the sea to beat against your window, and you could swear the floor is rocking with the waves.

One day, while staying in our friends' cylindrical abode, we all decided to take a walk out to see the tidal mill, known as the Mill of Berno. It was a day typical of Brittany: wet, with a driving wind blowing in from the west. We put on thick rubberized sailors' clothes, complete with tight-fitting hoods, bent our heads against the nearly horizontal rain, and set out across the barren fields of the island toward the mill.

Weather like that in a place like New York is nothing but misery, but in Brittany it comes with the territory. It's a land shaped by wind and sea, where the flora hugs the ground—as do the buildings, made of strong gray stone. It's a land of gorse and lichens and low, sturdy bushes near buildings that were made to last, mostly out of granite.

The tidal mill stands in the middle of a curving stone causeway built across one of the island's bays. The bay is long and shallow, and the tide comes rushing in and out with great force. Five hundred years ago, the island's residents built the causeway, leaving a narrow gap through which the tide is forced to run. In this gap, they put a waterwheel and a small mill. The wheel ran the machinery to grind the wheat, thus feeding the island.

But time and tide wait for no man, and when the mill fell into disuse in the nineteenth century, both conspired to wear it into a ruin. Both it and the causeway gradually succumbed to the elements, until they were just heaps of jumbled stone. A few years ago, a number of local volunteers decided to rebuild it, stone by stone, despite the fact that flour, and indeed fully cooked bread, is now readily available on the island's Kwik-E-Mart. Call it a labor of historical love. The volunteers toiled in the muck for six years, and eventually the causeway and the mill rose again. In 2000, the wheel turned once more, and produced flour, which was then sold as a kind of souvenir to help raise funds for maintenance.

It doesn't turn anymore. It's not the wind and the waves that have done it this time, it's the taxman. It seems that there's some weird regulation about having to pay a salt tax if you use seawater for purposes of grinding, or some such nonsense. This was explained to us by the caretaker/guy-who-gives-tourists-information, once we had pushed our way through the rain to take shelter inside the mill. He was surprised to see us. L'Île d'Arz doesn't get many visitors on days like this. In fact, his boredom had reached such levels that he hardly wanted us to leave, and gave us a detailed overview of the mill's history in an attempt to retain us. It began by being charming, but gradually turned to "numbing." Come on, there's only so much you can say about a flour mill on a tiny island, particularly when there's precious little historical documentation on the subject. He must have realized this, so he switched to a discussion about the genealogy of the island's families, in which our friend, at least, had a stake. The rest of us hung around primarily because we appreciated not being rained on for a while.

The waterwheel turns a lonely grindstone in a great wooden box. Wheat is poured into the top and flour comes out the bottom. It turns out that flour dust is highly flammable, and if the wheel turns too fast, or if there's not enough flour to counterbalance the friction, the whole thing can go up in flames. (Hence the little medieval song that warns millers of this lurking danger, and that every French child knows: "*Meunier, tu dors, ton moulin ton moulin tourne trop vite/meunier, tu dors, ton moulin ton moulin tourne trop fort.*") In order to guard against catastrophes of this sort, there's an ingenious little mechanism that causes a small bell to ring if the mill gets out of hand.

After learning far too much about this kind of thing, we headed back out into the gale and made our way through the weather to the mill in which we were staying, clear on the other side of the island (i.e., about a half mile away). This time, the wind was at our back, but after a few minutes I turned into it once more to look at the lonely little mill sitting out in the bay, perched in the middle of the causeway like a sock on a clothesline that someone forgot to bring in out of the storm. In the distance, a sailboat bobbed violently on the waves, dragging its inadequate anchor as the wind pushed it back. The next morning we would find a multitude of small craft beached on various bits of the island. "Tourists," spat our friend's husband. "They think that just because the Gulf of Morbihan is not the open sea, they don't need to take care when they moor their boats. It might be a gulf, but it is Brittany, after all."

That's for damn sure.

GIRL WITH LOTUS FLOWER:
SAIGON, VIETNAM

hen I was a boy, I knew that one day I would go to Vietnam. It was a sure thing. When you reached a certain age, there was something called "the draft" and through it you would become a soldier and go to Vietnam to fight the communists and stop them from taking over California. My friends' big brothers went, as did some of their younger uncles. Most of them came back, but they didn't talk about it.

As a kid, it didn't occur to me that the war would, or even could, end. It had always been there; we watched it on TV every night. My grandfather had gone off to stop the Germans from taking over his adopted homeland (he emigrated from Sicily) and I would go stop the commies. In the meantime, we played with our plastic guns and tried to train up as best we could.

I was perhaps eight when my grandfather, who generally displayed the kind of ardent, grateful patriotism that only immigrants demonstrate, reacted strongly one night to a discussion about my inevitable tour of duty in Vietnam (I suppose he, too, figured the war would never end) by saying, "No, you'll go to Canada." I was shocked, and somewhat disappointed, but he was adamant (my grandfather, who was a man of few words, made proclamations with the moral authority of Moses). His face took on a hardened expression and unspoken wartime memories flashed in his eyes. "You will never know war," he said. And that was that.

By the time I reached the age of 18, the war had been over for nearly seven years, and I had become an ardent anti-militarist anyway. However, come to Vietnam I did, albeit only now, at 43—not to fight, but to teach a graduate class.

Not that it wasn't dangerous. Don't misunderstand: Ho Chi Minh City (as Saigon is now known) has very little crime; the danger comes from crossing the street.

While on a trip to Singapore a few weeks before my Vietnam foray, a friend of mine who had lived in the country for several years gave me some pointers about how to cross the street. "What you have to do," he explained, "is walk slowly, and don't vary your speed. Just keep walking and they'll adjust, in all probability missing you." It was the "in all probability" that stuck in my mind, but when it comes right down to it, you don't have much of a choice, unless you want to restrict your movements to the one square block on which your hotel is located.

It's not the cars, of which there are relatively few, it's the motorbikes; the 50 to 100 cc bikes that swarm around like frenzied locusts, ridden by helmetless individuals, or even entire helmetless families, in a pattern reminiscent of India. (Incidentally, if you ever do want to get your family of four on a small motorbike, there is an invariable technique to it: the smallest child sits in front, his chin over the handlebars; next comes the man, who drives the contraption and tries to make sure the littlest child doesn't fall off; next comes the second child; then comes the woman, who tries to make sure the second child doesn't fall off.) The difference is that here they probably *will* miss you if you walk slowly and steadily across the street. The same cannot be said for India. Still, it's best to keep your eye on the traffic and vary your pace a *little* as you wade through the oncoming wheeled death.

And you'll want to walk. Most of what you'd like to see in Saigon (I'll keep calling it that, as it's more practical and more poetic than Ho Chi Minh City, and the locals call it that anyway) is within walking distance. And the city, despite the pollution constantly being spewed by all those motorbikes, is pleasant enough. Lots of trees.

Which brings us to the War Remnants Museum (actually, it doesn't, but I'm at a loss for a segue here). Until a few years ago, this was called the War Crimes Museum, but Vietnam has changed a lot over the last few years, and the museum was recently repositioned and redesigned.

Here, I got to see what I missed by not being born a few years earlier. Here, I saw just a little of why my grandfather had wanted to send me to Canada.

This is no balanced view of the atrocities committed during that sad conflict. It is propaganda, to be sure. But it was far less blatant than I had expected. There are tanks and planes and guns outside, almost all of them captured American equipment, and there are various objects in display cases, but the museum's real impact is the photo gallery. I certainly expected to see pictures of Americans doing horrible things, and some of the things are too horrible to imagine, but there were also a lot of pictures taken by Western correspondents of Americans just trying to survive: American medics trying to help their comrades, American soldiers writing letters, or smoking a cigarette, or sheltering from enemy fire, or just staring at some distant point, stubble on their chins and incomprehension in their eyes. You feel for these guys, they are all too human, and it's good that the Vietnamese have put these photos here.

Still, it's the photos of the Vietnamese that hurt the most. I walked, and looked at them. I don't know what expression I wore. I sat down near a bunch of photos showing napalm victims, all civilians. I won't describe these photos to you. After a few moments I sat nearby and considered the faces of the people who came to look at the pictures.

The Vietnamese stared at them with no expression, then they moved on. The Westerners all stopped and almost all of them took on the expression of someone looking into the sun—squinting, trying to keep out the light. A young woman put her hand to her mouth. Her hand trembled. A tall man, perhaps 20 years my senior, wearing a checked shirt and a white baseball cap, came up to the wall with the pictures on it. He was accompanied by his wife and a young Vietnamese woman with a name tag, who appeared to be their guide. The man stopped. He slowly took off his hat and stared at the pictures. His wife said something, but he seemed not to have heard. Eventually, the two women backed away and left him there alone.

He was American, of that I am sure (trust me, after a few years of living abroad, you can tell Americans). I couldn't shake the conviction that he had fought in that war. Perhaps he had been a pilot. Perhaps he had dropped bombs. I was briefly tempted to try to interview him but I was luckily overcome with a sense of reason and common decency. He took a few steps to his left, to look at a fragment of a bomb casing displayed under the famous Pulitzer-Prize-winning picture of a naked young girl who had been napalmed. He bent over and touched the bomb casing, then he stood up and looked at the picture. He stayed there for a long while then moved on slowly.

The war museum is an emotionally taxing experience, one that requires a good long walk afterwards. The fine arts museum can be emotional, too, in a much more subdued way. Here, in a refurbished colonial building, are paintings and sculptures by various Vietnamese artists, and here you get a look beyond the propaganda at the impact that a thousand years of conflict can have upon a nation. So many of the paintings and the sculptures touch on war and loss, even if it's only in the eyes of a young girl.

One of the young girls in question was painted by Nguyen Dang Khoat, a 55-year-old artist based in Saigon. The girl in the painting sat in white mist holding a lotus flower. The painting was on the ground floor, where the museum was holding an exhibition of work by four artists from the south of the country, with some of the work available for purchase. I found the painting beautiful, and it was on sale for a reasonable amount of money. Although I'm not prone to impulse buying (except in matters pertaining to music or literature), I suddenly decided to leave with *Girl with Lotus Flower*.

It turns out that I could only pay with cash, and I didn't have that much cash on me. The woman at the entrance to the museum explained via a mix of English and sign language that I should go with her colleague, an elderly Vietnamese man wearing a floral print shirt. I assumed that in some other part of the museum, they had some kind of facility for paying with credit cards, but it turned out that the facility in question was across town. The old man took me out to the parking lot (where there were only motorbikes parked) and gestured for me to get on the back of his bike.

What the hell.

And so I found myself careening through Saigon, helmetless, behind the Vietnamese gentleman. I comforted myself by thinking that if he had managed to reach his evidently advanced age, then he had so far avoided any major accidents and must therefore be possessed of a high level of skill in these matters. I adopted my usual mad-ride-in-a-motor-vehicle defense mechanism, which is to close my eyes. In that case, the gentle (actually not so gentle) swaying, starting, stopping and honking can actually be relaxing, in a high-adrenaline kind of way.

So I acquired *Girl with Lotus Flower* and walked it back to my hotel in a makeshift cardboard container. It was not easy getting her from there back to Paris, but after a few more adventures we both made it home, where she now adorns my wall, forever contemplating her flower and whatever she sacrificed to find it.

DRUNKEN ANGELS:
ISLAY, SCOTLAND

It's said that you have to give the devil his due. In Scotland, though, it's the angels that take their cut, because once a spirit is distilled it must spend at least three years maturing in barrels inside Scotland before it can be called Scotch whiskey. During that time, each barrel loses around two percent in alcohol and volume per year. This is known to the distillers as "the angels' share."

Nowhere are the angels more inebriated than over the island of Islay.

Islay (pronounced "eye-luh") is just off Scotland's western shore, separated from the rest of the country by cold gray waters and a taste for peaty whiskey. The island is inhabited by around 3,000 people, myriads of sheep, a few cattle (some of which are the long-haired, long-horned Highland variety) and eight working distilleries.

After having headed to the area near Inverness a few years ago to sample whiskies and pretend that we were rootless adolescents once more (see my column on Dalmore), my best friend and I decided to renew the experience by heading to the home of the world's earthiest, wildest whiskies: Islay. So we met up in Glasgow, rented a car and drove to the tiny port of Kennacraig, then sailed over to the edge of Scotland.

It is evident even from the boat that Islay is a forbidding

place. The Hebrides (of which the island is a part) are sparsely inhabited for a reason and the rocky coastline seems to be baring its teeth to any boats that may want to land there. Luckily, over the centuries the inhabitants of the island have managed to carve a few ports into the coastline, where white buildings sport black gutters, adding to the overall black-and-white impression that you get from much of Scotland's more weather-beaten regions. (It should be noted that all of Scotland is weather-beaten, but it shouldn't be surprising that an island standing some way off into the Atlantic is doubly exposed to the elements and I can't help but think that if all filmmakers had been from the Hebrides they would have just kept on filming in shades of gray. But I digress.)

After having settled into our B&B in Port Ellen, we went off to rent a couple of bicycles from the local bicycle rental emporium. Our unimaginably hospitable hosts had already booked the bikes for us, and we were furnished with an address that turned out to be that of a tiny row house with a sign on the door saying "Bicycle rental. Open door and shout for Mick."

Mick is a short, round, one-eyed, gray-haired fellow who was also painfully kind and who led us through his tiny house to his tiny backyard, where we entered his tiny garage and found five bicycles for rent, all of which we could try out until we found the bicycles that best tickled our fancy. As my best friend tinkered with seat and handlebar adjustments, trying and discarding a variety of wrenches, Mick leaned against the door and told us how his son had gone off to live in Pennsylvania to design outdoor clothing for a large company over there in the United States, and weren't we from the United States, and we were free to keep on adjusting the bicycles, about which he knew nothing, and we didn't need locks, no one would steal them on the island, although we should perhaps be careful if we were to ride them to Bowmore, as once, someone had stolen one bicycle out of four that he had rented to a group of Swedish bird watchers, although come to think of it, they *had* locked the bicycles up and the thief (who undoubtedly hadn't been from Islay, of course) had unlocked them somehow, taken one bicycle, then locked them back up again, which was rather perplexing when you think about it, but that was a couple of years before.

As Mick took a breath, we assured him that we wouldn't ride the bikes as far as Bowmore and we waved goodbye while he said that if we were going to Ardbeg to eat then perhaps he'd see us there since he needed a new bottle from the distillery and they served good soup.

Mick may still have been talking when we turned the corner, but he waved all the same.

I won't describe all the distilleries to you, nor all the distillery tours. Suffice it to say that the creation of whiskey is a rather simple process. (In a nutshell, you distill beer a couple of times then let it sit for a few years in a wooden cask.) All distilleries in Scotland follow the same basic process, but they end up with notably different whiskies. The distinct nature of the whiskies come from differences in how they malt the barley, the water they use, the shapes of the stills, and the types of barrels in which the spirit is aged.

Most of the Islay whiskies are renowned for their peatiness. They are smoky, rich, wild whiskies, and the wildest of the lot is Laphroaig (pronounced "La-froyg").

It is said that one either loves or hates Laphroaig, but I think it's a question of mood. There are times when I'd never drink it, and other times when only a Laphroaig could possibly work. Thanks to the latter sentiment, I've been a member of the "Friends of Laphroaig" for some 12 years now, which means that I have an official deed for one square foot of peat bog near the distillery. I am therefore entitled to show up at the distillery at any time, visit my land, and claim rent from the distillery.

I know it's a marketing ploy, but it's a nice one, and the distillery itself is a pleasant little place overlooking the sea, so my friend and I rode over on our bicycles and took the tour, which was nifty enough, but what I was really waiting for was the chance to go out and find my square foot of bog.

Upon being informed that I was a long-standing Friend of Laphroaig, the manager explained how to find my parcel, number 64193. It turned out that the number indicates a certain distance from a certain post over in the bog across the road. I needed only find the post then take a prescribed number of steps south and a different number of steps east. I was provided with rubber wellington boots, a rather silly hat, strings to tie around my trouser legs so the stoats don't run up them, and a small American flag, which I could plant on my land so as to stake my claim.

My friend and I stomped across the road and after some difficulty, found the post. I then started striding south, then east, carefully counting each step. South was OK, but east began leading me into ever deeper bog, so that I was worried the muck would suck the wellies off my feet. I managed to find the spot, though, just before the goo got above welly-height, and I proudly stuck my flag into plot number 64193 (or thereabouts), where it promptly began to sink.

After exricating myself from the peat, we stomped back to the distillery and collected my rent, in the form of a dram of whiskey.

Laphroaig is neighbor to two other distilleries, all of which are within a couple of miles of each other: Ardbeg and Lagavulin. These, along with Caol Ila, on the other side of the island, are the tall, dark strangers of the whiskey world, full of peat and bravado.

Far less peaty, but perhaps the most amusing distillery I've ever visited is Bruichladdich (pronounced, roughly, "Brookladdy"). This distillery had closed down for a couple of years before being purchased by a partnership of very fun guys, who are pretty much the Ben and Jerry of the whiskey world. All of this was explained to us by Mary (pronounced, roughly, "Meeerry"), who informed us that unlike many distilleries, Bruichladdich intended to do everything locally, from growing the barley to bottling the whiskey, and that all the employees had shares in the company, and all were having a rip-roaring good time. She also explained the still out front as you drive up, which is an old, out-of-commission still that has a pair of feet sticking out the top. It would seem that a few years ago, the U.S. Department of Defense actually monitored the newly re-opened Bruichladdich, since the stills had a shape that seemed ominous to some intelligence analyst with a vivid imagination and a stick up his ass. (I will make a deliberate digression here to point out that distilleries tend to have four to eight stills, which are beautiful shiny copper things shaped like stretched-out teardrops, usually about 10 feet tall.) The distillery was therefore monitored by the same clever fellows who ensured us that Saddam Hussein had model airplanes armed with nuclear weapons aimed at Coney Island. When they learned of this, the owners decided to come out with a bottling called "WMD" for "Whiskey of Mass Distinction" and they stuck a couple of boots in the top of the still near the entrance, took a picture of it, and labeled it "Weapons inspectors at work." It made the round of the local papers and gave everyone a good laugh.

I bought a lot of whiskey from Bruichladdich.

Islay isn't only about beautiful white distillery buildings with quaint little piers in front, it's also about the aforementioned cattle and sheep and gorse and bluebells and strikingly empty hills that roll down to the sea. In fact, we ended with such a hill, as we drove back from the Bunnahabhain (pronounced with difficulty) distillery. Bunnahabhain is located on the northeastern shore of Islay, on the channel facing the island of Jura, which is one of Western Europe's most pristine places, with a population density of roughly one person per square mile. The road from Bunnahabhain follows the channel between the two islands, and after a while we stopped and strode out across the heather toward the water.

It was only upon approaching the edge that we realized that we were, in fact, on a tall cliff. A vista opened up before us: some three or four hundred feet below us was the slate-gray sea, moving swiftly in the channel; across it was Jura, enormous and stretching off into the distance, the peaks of her mountains lost in the haze; on either side of us were the browns and yellows and grays that make up these islands, subdued in the mist. Nowhere was there any sign of man or of his constructions, it was all as it must have been millenia ago when men themselves were new in this world and the angels were sadly sober.

TAXIS

Not too long ago I stumbled out of a taxi in Shanghai after one of the more harrowing cab rides I've ever experienced. The cab had brought me careening from the airport to Nanjing Road, in the middle of town, and when my foot touched the pavement I nearly wept with joy. The cabbie (who of course spoke no English) had driven like a Formula One driver on coke, making sharp turns to change lanes, cutting off cars, trucks, busses, and even police vehicles with a kind of maniacal nonchalance that was somehow even more unnerving than if he had been chuckling and wiping imagined cobwebs from his face. Furthermore, while *he* attached his seatbelt once we got onto the highway, I did not have the benefit of a seatbelt. It's amazing how naked and vulnerable you can feel in the back of a speeding car without a seatbelt.

I'm sure that many readers are wondering why I didn't ask him to slow down. Despite his lack of English and my lack of Chinese, it undoubtedly would have been possible to make myself understood. The answer, of course, is that I'm a man, and the vast majority of men are cowards when it comes to this kind of thing. That's why we never ask for directions. A woman wouldn't have hesitated, but then women are far more courageous than we are (which is a good thing, because having been present at two births, it has become clear to me that if women were not braver than men, they would never agree to give birth and we'd all be extinct by now). In the end, I resorted to my ultimate line of defense in the back of taxis . . . I closed my eyes.

It was only later that I realized that I've amassed a fair number of harrowing taxi stories, what with all this traveling, and that they were probably worth a dispatch.

New York

I had come back for a visit with my wife and a couple of friends, and we had gotten into a taxi at JFK to head into Manhattan. The driver was a sullen man who tried to turn on the meter when we got in the cab (which he should not have done, since there's a fixed fare from JFK to Manhattan) and then decided to drive as closely as possible to whatever car had the misfortune of being in front of him. On the Long Island Expressway, one of those cars decided to stop short and he skidded to within a couple of inches of it. You could tell he wasn't actually from New York, because he didn't swear at his windshield but instead mumbled something to himself as the smell of burning rubber invaded the cab. We sat in the back and swore in French, making comments about his poor judgment and his mother's career as a prostitute (a French insult). This was one of the few times I actually did ask a cabbie to slow down, to which he grunted but didn't change his driving habits. It was only once we arrived that he turned around and complained about his lack of a tip . . . in perfect French.

Cergy

I used to live to the northwest of Paris, and whenever I arrived at the airport, I would either ask my habitual cab driver to come and pick me up, or I would just take a cab from the queue. In the latter case, I would sometimes cause some grumbling, since I lived pretty far outside Paris (at least in the estimation of Parisian cab drivers), but it was slightly less expensive. Once, a cab driver asked me to get into the front seat, since his dog was in the back seat. Of course, I should have just waited for the next cab, as this is highly unusual, and unusual in the case of cab drivers often means psychotic, but I have sometimes suffered from periodic bursts of bad judgment. Anyway, I got in and the cabbie started driving off, at a reasonable pace, while talking to one of the plastic apostles on the dashboard. While I had explained where we were going before entering his temple to the odd, he apparently hadn't really grasped the distance involved, and as we drove along he became increasingly agitated, so that by the time we had gone about half the distance he was actually yelling at the apostles about how it was totally unreasonable for him to be going all the way out here and how the phone numbers didn't even start with a zero-one out here (which wasn't true) and how it would take him forever to get back to Paris and how bad the weather was. All this yelling caused the dog to begin howling. I instructed the driver to stop at an intermediate point, at which I got out and called my habitual driver, who was happily free and who came and collected me, explaining that this was exactly why I should always ask him to come and pick me up at the airport.

Istanbul

I was returning to Paris on a Friday night after a few days in Istanbul, and it was only at the airport that I realized that I had forgotten my passport at my hotel in Besiktas. I had an hour to get to the hotel, pick up my passport, and return to the airport, which should be impossible if one constrains oneself to the habitual laws of physics. However, mine was the last plane out, and as much as I love Istanbul, I didn't want to stay for that particular weekend. I therefore found a cab and explained in a mix of English and German (which sometimes works well in Istanbul) that if the cabbie could actually manage this, I'd give him an extra five million lire. (Note: the lira has since been devalued, and back then this was not quite as impressive as it sounds, since there were *coins* for 250,000 lire, but it's still a good tip.) The driver set off like Han Solo, zipping between cars, driving on the shoulder (and even the grass), his hand on the horn the whole way, TIE fighters shooting laser beams past our wings. As we flew back from the hotel (through even heavier traffic), I gave up and tapped him on the shoulder, explaining that I'd give him the extra five million anyway, but that he should slow down since I really do enjoy my life and would like it to go on a bit more, but by then this had become a *challenge* for him, and to give up would have been some kind of affront to his manhood (one does not affront the manhood of a Turk lightly). I made it to the airport with time to spare and a persistent heart murmur.

Bangkok

On my first visit to Bangkok, I decided to take the tuk-tuks wherever I wanted to go. These are little three-wheeled contraptions that I think I've mentioned in some other dispatch. They are open to the breeze and driven by very eager proprietors who have a tendency to drive along slowly beside any obvious foreigner, offering to take him or her to whatever destination they like. I quickly discovered, however, that giving a destination to a tuk-tuk driver did not by any means ensure that this was the point at which you would be deposited. As it turns out, many of them get free gas if they deliver a tourist to some shop, most of which sell either jewelry or clothing. I once got in a tuk-tuk with a colleague and explained that we wanted to go to a particular restaurant near the river. The driver said, "Fish restaurant! Good fish!" and headed in exactly the opposite direction. I reiterated that we wanted to go to a very specific restaurant, and gave him the restaurant's card, telling him that we were meeting people there. "Yes! Good fish! Good fish restaurant!" he replied as he continued going the wrong way. Despite my pleading, he ended up bringing us to a local place with a number of tuk-tuks parked outside. "Better fish here!" he exclaimed, as he asked for payment . . . which was not forthcoming.

Agra

Lastly, there was the taxi I took, with a friend, from Delhi to Agra in

1999 or so. We had decided to make the journey by cab, then return via third-class train (which is a story in itself). As the taxi, an Ambassador (If you've never seen one, the Ambassador, built by Hindustan Motors, is the archetypical Indian car. It has been continually produced since 1957 and redesigned ... well, never.), pulled up, we got our things and prepared to board. The driver opened the trunk, and here you should note that the Ambassador, which is a fine automobile, does have a slight inconvenience in that when the trunk is open a bit of it sticks backwards. I, of course, banged my head against this protruding bit just before we entered the car. I immediately began to bleed profusely, since I had nicked that part of your eyebrow that just loves to spew blood. The driver realized I was bleeding once we all got in the car, as I held a handkerchief against my head and it rapidly turned a bright crimson color. "Oh please don't die in my car," he begged me. "I shall take you to a hospital—please, please don't die in my car." I explained that I was not going to die in his car and by no means did I want to get stitches in an Indian hospital. This sent him into paroxysms of indecision, as on one hand he didn't want to anger a paying customer and on the other, he was convinced that I was going to bleed to death in the back of his Ambassador, which I assume would have created an administrative nightmare for him (not to mention seriously bad karma). As we bounced over the 253 kilometers between the two cities, the poor man continued to plead with me and with any number of gods that I should be well and healed and live a long and prosperous life (at the very least until I got out of his car).

Despite all of these rather harrowing experiences—and believe me, this is only a small sampler—it must be admitted that so far I have indeed led a pretty prosperous life. Maybe the Indian cab driver's fervent prayers were heard.

FORGOTTEN HEROES:
LONDON, ENGLAND

Immediately upon appearing online, this column generated mail from punctillious Brits who pointed out a number of errors:

1. *It's not the Canadian embassy, but the Canadian High Commission; since Canada is part of the Commonwealth, they don't have an embassy.*
2. *Charles was not beheaded where the statue stands, but outside the Banqueting House at the other end of Whitehall.*
3. *Charles's statue was erected by his son, who had become king.*
4. *Distances to and from London are not measured from Trafalgar Square but from Charing Cross.*

The first point reinforces my impression that Canadians (who apparently don't warrant an embassy) like to accentuate their independence from both the United States and Great Britain. The following points mean that the kindly, very English gentleman who appeared so very proper and correct was apparently wrong about a number of things (although he did get Harry Havelock right). I confess a mixture of disappointment and relief—I'm disappointed that a seemingly perfect representative of British respectability could have been so mistaken, and relieved that such a seemingly perfect representative of British respectability was indeed so mistaken. It does wonders for my New-World inferiority complex.

I'll also add that when it originally appeared, I attributed the Battle of Trafalgar to 1815, not 1805. This was a slip of the metaphorical tongue (it was, of course, Waterloo that took place in 1815). I begged the editors of McSweeney's to change it, since that 1 stared off the screen accusing me of ignorance to the entire world.

I have a strange relationship with London. I go there often, to the degree that sometimes when I enter the UK the passport officials, after leafing through my passport stuffed with UK entry stamps, suggest that I need a work permit (if you spend more than something like 30% of your time working in the UK, then you need a work permit). I point out that I'm never there for long, but I think it's only the prospect of spending hours tallying up entry and exit times from the myriad of disparate stamps that buys me entrance in such times. Most of the time my destination in the UK is London . . . and yet I've never written about it.

Why not? I suppose that part of the answer is that my time in London is generally boring. I know that London is a wonderful place to live and that it's a fascinating city to visit as a tourist, but I've never lived there and I've very rarely gone as a tourist, in which case it's just a city, you know? What's more, it's all spread out, it goes on forever, and I'm never quite sure where to start.

All that being said, the glaring absence of a dispatch about London has weighed heavy on my consciousness, so I recently decided that the time had come to write about London, which immediately begged the question of where to begin (and end, for that matter).

I had long harbored ideas about Speakers' Corner, that small bit of Hyde Park where (generally crazy) people set up a soapbox and rant on about this and that. The problem is that every time I've set off to do a bit of field research, there's been no one speaking at Speakers' Corner, in which case it's just a corner.

I eventually decided that if you're going to write about a city then a good place to start is in its center. I therefore recently went to Trafalgar Square, which houses the dead center of London, in that all distances from London are measured from it. It also has a big column in the middle, dedicated to the hero of Trafalgar, Admiral Lord Nelson. (A brief aside for those of you who slept through your history class: the Battle of Trafalgar was the decisive naval battle of the Napoleonic Wars, fought in 1805 between the British fleet, under Nelson, and the combined French and Spanish fleets, under Admiral Villeneuve. The British won, although Nelson lost his life, passing into martyrdom as he asked for a kiss from his friend Captain Hardy and gaining himself a square in London and a highly phallic column on top of which perches his statue. His ship, the HMS *Victory*, has been preserved and sits in Portsmouth and must absolutely be visited. If I get back there one day then I'll write about it too . . . but I digress.)

Nelson shares the square with four enormous bronze lions, two fountains, and the statues of Charles Napier, King George IV, Harry Havelock, Admirals Beatty and Jellicoe (they only warrant busts) and a fellow named Cunningham.

The fountains are populated by a variety of merpeople and dolphins. The dolphins spout water from both their mouths *and* their blowholes, which is kind of cool. The lions are almost inevitably carrying tourists on their backs, most of which are posing for photos. Trafalgar Square is prime tourist-photo territory. I watched one African family line up their children on the pedestal supporting Nelson's column: one boy and four girls, the three youngest girls all wearing identical pink shirts. The eldest girl had evidently outgrown the pink-shirt phase and wore more adult clothing, with earrings. The parents carefully arranged the children then got down in front of the pedestal with the camera, at which point all the children sang "cheeeeeeeese" as they were immortalized in pixels. The parents then went back up, arranged the children in a different order (What were their criteria? Hard to tell.) and then went through the whole process again.

I was at Trafalgar Square with a Canadian friend, who pointed out that they might as well call it "Canada Square," since the Canadian Pacific building flanks it on one side and the Canadian embassy on another. (I find it charming how Canadians have a tendency to point out things about Canada to Americans, probably in an attempt to remind us that theirs is an entirely different country . . . and for all you Canadians out there, yes I know that Neil Young, Pamela Anderson, Keanu Reeves, Alex Trebek, Robbie Robertson and all the Barenaked Ladies [as in the rock group, not actual bare naked ladies] are Canadian.) What's more, it would seem that last year there was a big celebration in Trafalgar Square for Canada Day, on July 1.

"Doesn't that celebrate your independence from Britain?"

"That's right," she replied. "In 1867."

"Kind of ironic that they'd hold a celebration here, don't you think?"

There are no Canadian heroes at Trafalgar Square, though, only the statues of British ones, such as the aforementioned Harry Havelock, of whom I had never heard. The pedestal of his statue bears a plaque stating: "Soldiers, your labours, your privations, your sufferings and your valour will not be forgotten by a grateful country." I decided to test this out by finding out how many British people had ever heard of Havelock, let alone his soldiers.

This proved a daunting task. I went around the crowded square trying to find British people to ask if they had ever heard of Harry Havelock. I quickly discovered that on that particular August day there were precious few Brits to be found in the square. Upon the question, "Are you British?" the vast majority of the people I approached either answered that they were not, or in some cases didn't even understand the question. I eventually did manage to come up with some Brits, who apparently have a tendency to travel in packs of four (at least around Trafalgar Square), and I discovered that none of them had the slightest idea who I was talking about. When I explained that his statue was right behind me and that as citizens of a grateful nation they were supposed to remember him, they shrugged. One young man did respond in the affirmative. "Sure!" he said. "I've heard of him." A little leery of his cavalier manner I asked who, exactly, Harry Havelock was, and he was stumped.

"You don't really know, do you?"

"Why are you asking about Harry Havelot anyway?"

I explained that I was a writer, at which point he immediately asked me to proclaim his name to the world (Dean Kay-Barry), confessing that although he didn't actually know who Harry Havelock was before I told him, he was a nice chap all the same, which seemed true enough.

I was running zero for nineteen before my Canadian friend spotted an older gentleman who was so British you could hear his Oxbridge accent in the swish of his trousers. I didn't bother asking if he was British, but immediately asked if he had ever heard of Harry Havelock. He raised his eyes, pursed his lips, and said "A soldier, I believe. Indian campaign, what."

I congratulated him, explaining that he was the first of 20 British subjects who apparently hadn't forgotten a man whom they were all encouraged to remember, at least according to the plaque on the statues.

"Ah, well, you see I collect Staffordshire figures [whatever they are] and they have a figure of him, you know."

He then informed us that in front of Trafalgar Square is the exact spot from which all distances are measured in London: the plaque commemorating Charles I, who was beheaded on that very place, just in front of where they later erected a statue to him. We thanked him and headed over to check it out. I have to confess that I do find it strange that a country would behead its king and then erect a statue in his honor on that very spot 26 years later. You'll see no statues of Louis XVI in Paris (although the French did build a couple of fountains on the places in which they guillotined old king Louis and his cake-eating Austrian wife).

We were about to leave Trafalgar Square (which, I might add, was strangely devoid of its famous pigeons. I wonder what the Brits have done with them.) when I noticed yet another plaque in the ground, stating that neither would the nation forget Admirals Beatty and Jellicoe, whose busts are set into the north wall of the square. Of course, this meant that I had to do one last bit of research to determine whether these two had also slipped into the fog of history, so my friend and I approached another foursome of Brits to ask whether they had ever heard of either of the two sailors. None of them had.

"Who were they?" asked one young man.

"Admirals. Their busts are behind you."

At this news, he slapped his hand against his forehead. "Admirals! My father would kill me. He spent 20 years in the Royal Navy!"

I assured him that *his* name would not appear in print.

"I do know something, though—Nelson's statue was set up so that Nelson is facing Napoleon across the Channel. Where's Nelson anyway?"

"Up there," I responded, pointing to the top of the column looming over us.

"I knew that! Really. Of course. Christ, my dad would kill me."

I don't know what Nelson himself would think of all this. It's been almost 200 years, after all (although even I know that Jellicoe won the battle of Jutland, in 1916—which may not be yesterday, but neither is it ancient history). Maybe he would take solace in the fact that his square is full of people of every nation, none of whom are enemies at all.

THE WORLD'S OLDEST
FERRIS WHEEL:
VIENNA, AUSTRIA

I once had a friend from Vienna. Whenever he met a woman, he
would click his heels, bend slightly at the waist, take her hand
very lightly in his own, and say something eminently civilized.
You could tell that he would have liked to kiss the air a millimeter
above her skin, but he was sadly restrained by the uncivilized era in
which we live. One day I ran across him in the street in Paris, where
we were both living, and I mentioned to him that my wife and I were
going to the ballet that night to see Sylvie Guillem dance (I think it
was in *Gizelle*, or some other extremely classical ballet). He hadn't
known that Sylvie Guillem had come back to dance in Paris that evening and said that he would meet me there. I pointed out that it had
been sold out long before, but he sniffed at the news and said that he
would meet me "under Egypt, at the first intermission."

Only he could have said such a thing. On the first floor
mezzanine of the Opéra Garnier there is a series of carved wooden
shields bearing the names of the great civilizations of antiquity, one
of which represents Egypt. These are written in Greek. My Austrian
friend not only assumed that I knew what he was talking about, but
also that I could read enough Greek to identify the shield representing Egypt. He also assumed that he could somehow get into a

show long sold out. Despite all this, at the first intermission there he was, sipping a glass of champagne underneath Αἴγυπτος. As we approached, he, of course, clicked his heels, bowed, took my wife's hand and exclaimed how charming it was to see her again.

This, to me, is Vienna personified—gracious, old world, unsmiling.

Vienna has always struck me as being pervaded by a certain sadness. I'm not really sure why. Vienna was once a great center of power, the seat of a vast empire, and today it sits in the middle of its former glory, seemingly gazing ever at the past. It is a monumental place, with monumental palaces, broad avenues and refined cuisine, where the elderly are stately and the young are behaved. It is a city of formality, where it is common to see people strolling in the evening in full formal dress, going to one of the numerous balls to waltz the evening away to the strains of the innumerable great classical composers who once graced the city. In a nutshell, it's a place in which the nineteenth century seems to be sorely missed.

I therefore decided to find a center of amusement in Vienna so as to revise my impression of the place, so I headed off to the Prater. What better place to find laughter and gaiety than in an amusement park?

The Prater is a park very near the center of old Vienna, and in it is the Wurstelprater, an amusement park. The amusement park is full of the expected rides and stands and games and things. They are small by American standards, but the park is free (although each attraction charges its own fee) and there are a lot of attractions and you can walk there from the center of town, which can't be said for most amusement parks.

Unfortunately, I went there in December, when most of the attractions are closed. This, therefore, did nothing to alleviate my impression of Viennese sadness, for what could be sadder than a closed amusement park? Perhaps a fully closed amusement park retains a certain mystery, but there is no gate to the Prater; you can still go in despite the late season, and some of the attractions do remain open. You wander deserted paths, crossing the occasional couple, or a mother with a young child who gazes at the stilled merry-go-round or the chairs-on-chains that should be swirling overhead but are instead hanging limply in the winter air. This does nothing to dispell a mid-winter Viennese sadness.

The only advantage to going to the Prater in the winter is that the lack of crowds (the lack of anybody, to tell the truth) makes it easier to strike up conversations with the people who work there. So it was that I met Fredo Nemec, owner of the Prater's oldest merry-go-round. This consists of a series of little blue boats in a covered enclosure. A few zombies and skeletons line the walls to scare the children as they go around and around. Fredo informed me that he was the fourth generation to run the ride, which was built in 1903. "It's the original motor," he explained, "and most of the little boats are original as well." He also informed me that the rides are all owned by individuals, who lease their spots from the city. These individuals come from a very small number of families, many of which have been at the Prater ever since the amusement park was opened at the end of the nineteenth century. "The haunted house over there [boasting 'Jack the Ripper/Sensationen/Thriller Tunnel/Exit Elevator/Action House'] belongs to my aunt, and the ride across the way belongs to a cousin."

I desperately wanted to get a tour of a closed haunted house—after all, I did used to be a little boy and what little boy wouldn't want to get shown around behind the scenes of a haunted house? Unfortunately, this was impossible and I headed off to find something that was open.

I discovered that while the rides and shooting stands and the like were closed, the casinos were very much open. I expected gaming tables, but in reality the casinos consist solely of rows of electronic slot machines. In one of these I found 30 or so customers sitting at stools in front of the machines.

These were dimly lit places, devoid of all warmth and charm, where solitary individuals huddled over their machines and pushed the same buttons over and over again, oblivious to everything except the flashing lights in front of them. I asked a few questions of the staff, but my German wasn't really good enough to get any answers, so a burly waiter suggested that he would get the manager. The manager in question turned out to be a slick looking individual wearing an impeccable suit and tie along with a thin-lipped, suspicious smile. This wasn't really surprising—after all, here's this foreigner taking notes under the dim lights of his gambling establishment. Once we got to chatting, though, he opened up a little and was very polite (but then again, he is Austrian, and politeness comes naturally). He suggested that I head over to the Riesenrad.

I had actually been saving this for last. The Prater is almost defined by the Riesenrad, which is the world's oldest Ferris wheel and stands near the entrance of the park in all its antique glory.

The Riesenrad kind of looks like a humongous bicycle wheel with subway cars studded around the rim. The wheel was built in 1897, just a year after G.W. Ferris himself died. It was the brainchild of Walter Bassett, a lieutenant in the Royal Navy who wanted to help the Austro-Hungarian empire celebrate the 50th anniversary of the accession of Franz Josef II to the throne. He also wanted to make a pile of money, since Ferris wheels were very new to the world and the two or three that had already been constructed in the United States and the UK had raked in the dough. The Riesenrad didn't dissapoint him, as it raked in lots of dough until the First World War saw the confiscation of property belonging to British citizens. The wheel was then auctioned off to an Austrian who wanted to tear it down and sell it for scrap. Luckily, he couldn't come up with the money to fund the demolition, so after it was used as an observation post for the army, it ended up just going around and around again, full of paying Viennese.

From the start, the wheel attracted a varied assortment of

artists and wackos, including one woman who hung from a wagon by her teeth and another who managed to coax a horse onto the roof of one of the wagons and took a spin while in the saddle. (I can only assume that it was an exceedingly calm and perhaps sedated horse. Or maybe it was simply a very polite Austrian horse that had clicked its hooves together when it had met her and thereafter acceded to her wishes.)

There was no one hanging by their teeth or sitting on a horse when I went to the Riesenrad. In fact, there were precious few people there at all, since it was, after all, in the middle of winter, but the wheel was operational all the same. I struck up a conversation with the fellow who checks your ticket before you go through the turnstile, whose name is Anthony and who is originally from Nigeria.

"Do you miss Nigeria?" I asked. "I mean, it's really cold here, after all."

"True," he replied, "it is a cold country. And pretty boring. In Nigeria, for instance, Christmas is a big deal, family comes from all over and there's a great feast. I'm one of eight children in my family. When we get together. . . ." Anthony smiled. "Here, though, you don't know the difference between Christmas and any other day."

"So why do you stay?"

Anthony shook his head. "It's safe here. I was in import and export in Nigeria; it's a dangerous business. Everything's a dangerous business there; you tell the truth, you can get shot. Here, nothing is dangerous." He looked around and spread his hands to indicate just how safe his Ferris wheel was. Indeed, the last gunman around here was tracking Orson Welles in *The Third Man*.

It was at this point that the slick-looking casino manager ran up to us, much to my surprise.

"I thought you might be able to find some good information in this book," he said, giving me a handsome picture book with images of the Prater through the years. I thanked him profusely and then considered how much trouble he had gone to in order to find me.

This may be a defining Austrian trait: an aloof, distant attitude on the surface hiding an extraordinary hospitality underneath. One must simply never seem unduly enthusiastic about it, I suppose.

Nigerians have no problem showing enthusiasm while being hospitable, and Anthony eagerly escorted me into the little display area before the entrance to the Riesenrad to explain the display cases (it must be said that he had precious little else to do, since I was the only visitor).

Each display case has a diorama inside showing various scenes from Viennese history. One re-creates a battle between a bunch of heavily armored toy knights and a horde of toy Ottoman soldiers, each of which sported a thick toy mustache. The knights seemed to be having a better day than the Turks. Other dioramas showed the Riesenrad at various points in its history, including one bleak case portraying a burnt and blasted landscape with a big scorched Ferris wheel in the middle. This was a tableau of the Prater just after the Second World War.

"How'd you get your job?" I asked Anthony.

"Through a friend of my wife's. I had already worked in tourism, and I think they wanted to show diversity in the work force."

The Riesenrad itself loomed high above me as I walked out of the display area, leaving Anthony waving at me from inside the doorway. After mounting a few steel steps I showed my ticket to a stone-faced man who opened the door to one of the cars.

Inside, I got the impression of being in a small old-time trolley car. Everything was made out of wood, with simple windows on all four walls, windows you could raise or lower with a push. There was a long flat bench in the middle, although why anyone would pay to go on the Riesenrad and then sit down, with their eyes pretty much under window level, is beyond me. You get two goes around, at an altogether stately pace, during which you can appreciate the Viennese cityscape. If you look at the other cars, you'll see that some

are decked out with formal tables, and in fact, you can rent a Riesenrad car for dinner. I'm a hopeless romantic, and I can't help but think
that there can be few more romantic occasions than renting a car
fitted with a single table for two and gazing into soft eyes as you slice
up your Wiener schnitzel while slowly spinning over Vienna.

Of course, that would have to be when it's a hell of a lot
warmer, because the cars are not heated and I was freezing my ass
off. Freezing your ass off, alone, 60 meters over an empty amusement park is not romantic in the least.

When I got off the wheel, I stopped by again to say goodbye
to Anthony and then headed back into the center of town. I confess that even a ride in the world's oldest Ferris wheel hadn't infused
much joy into me. I made my way toward St. Stephen's Cathedral,
noting the streetlights. Most cities have streetlamps on posts, but
many Viennese streets have their streetlights right down the center,
suspended via a complicated system of wires and cables running
from the façades of the buildings. I have no doubt it's more efficient
but it somehow seems less charming.

Or it may simply be that I wasn't in a mood to be charmed. Vienna impresses me, it teaches me, it sings to me and provides beauty
to be admired, but it has never charmed me, and even its amusement
park had much the same effect. I confess I don't even like Sacher-
torte, the extremely refined and rather unexciting (according to my
taste buds) chocolate cake you're supposed to love. But who knows?
Try out Vienna for yourself and let me know if there's some deep un-
dercurrent of warmth that has somehow eluded me. You might try a
romantic weekend, including a trip to the opera and a dinner on the
Riesenrad (in summer). Come to think of it, that would probably do
the trick.

CHRISTMAS CHEER IN BRONZE:
BRATISLAVA, SLOVAKIA

To many, Slovakia is a suffix. Formerly, it was half of Czecho-slovakia but then the two climbed out of their sheets of vel-vet and got divorced. Before then, I wouldn't be surprised if many people outside of Eastern Europe just assumed that "oslo-vakia" means "land of" in Czech. But no, Slovakia is a country in its own right, with its own people and its own language (which, admit-tedly, is a whole lot like Czech), and its capital is the charming little city of Bratislava.

Let it be said from the start, Bratislava is definitely a city to be visited just before Christmas. You know those picture books you used to read when you were little, in which Christmas elves would sneak into some downtrodden cobbler's shop and make classy pumps out of snippets of satin and magic thread? Remember the pictures of the streets, with low, pretty stone buildings and windows all lit up through the cold night air, and a bit of frost on the glass? Remember thinking how appropriate it was that elves should live in such a place? Not those goofy elves who live at the North Pole and assemble PlayStations. I'm talking about real elves, the size of your foot, who live in hollow trees and giggle a lot. Well, Bratislava is that place . . . or at least the very center of it is, because all around the center is a sprawling city sporting an unfortunate mix of modern architecture and Soviet-inspired monolithic apartment blocks.

What kinds of elves would live there?

Fear not, though. You can easily stay in the center, which is big enough to allow you to while away at least a couple of days.

But it's not the days that are the most interesting, it's the nights that hold all the charm, because in the weeks leading up to Christmas, Bratislavans enjoy a wonderful tradition whereby they fill the two main squares of the town with Christmas markets.

The market consists of rows of small wooden booths, each selling its various wares. Mostly, these consist of Christmas baubles, many also made of wood. There's a nice, seasonal woody smell that comes from all this lumber, although for the most part it's masked by the overwhelming smell of cooked meat.

The Christmas market doesn't seem to be about shopping at all; it seems to be about eating, drinking and meeting up with friends. In the cold (because it's damn cold out). The eating and drinking is facilitated by countless wooden stands selling all kinds of meats and other assorted goodies. Holding a treasured place among these are lokshe, which are crepe-like things containing nuts or something that was explained to me but that I didn't quite get.

To wash all this down there is, of course, beer, but in order better to face the frigid winter evenings, the Slovaks have come up with all kinds of warmed spirits, to warm your spirit, as it were. These include:

> Medveda krv: hot wine with rum
>
> Demanovka, or hot herbal wine . . . imagine warm wine with herbal cough drops. Actually, it's better than it sounds (and this was distributed for free out of a thermos by two charming young women for reasons that are still unclear to me)
>
> My favorite, medovina, which is a kind of honey

wine that is probably awful when cold, but when it's just on the near side of hot, it slides down like satin off a woman's shoulder. Delightful.

Of course, all of this was imbibed with the sole purpose of carrying out research for you, my readers. Nevertheless, it left me in a festive mood, to say the least, and to a certain degree it probably impeded the smooth functioning of the rest of my research plan for the evening in question, for which you must forgive me in advance.

But it wasn't only the heated spirits that got me all festive like that, it was a generally contagious atmosphere of celebration. Both of the markets are set up in perfectly charming squares, surrounded with the aforementioned elvish buildings. The booths create a kind of U shape, and in the center of this are long, high tables, sheltered by open-sided structures that hold up pleasant little roofs. You can stand at these tables eating your lokshe and drinking your medovina.

A Slovak friend explained to me that the residents of Bratislava often take advantage of the Christmas markets to arrange meetings with old friends with whom they've fallen out of touch, and it certainly did seem that the people standing in the biting cold with their steaming drinks had a lot to talk about. But then, Slovaks tend to be a pretty convivial, talkative bunch.

Even the bronze residents of Bratislava seem as though they'd like to strike up a conversation. Most European cities are dotted with statues of impressive individuals, many of whom wield swords, some mounted on fierce horses staring down the enemies of old (who almost never warrant statues of their own). There are a few of these in Bratislava as well, but the most interesting statues in the city are the unusual life-sized bronzes that show up in unexpected places. One of these represents a man, apparently named Cumil, who is popping up out of an open manhole, resting his elbows on the street and considering the world from a mouse-eye vantage point with one of those ironic Slavic smiles on his face. My Bratislavan friend said that there had been a story about a guy who lived in the sewer some years ago, or maybe it was supposed to be a homage to sewer workers, or maybe it's just meant to be surprising and kind of funny, but one way or another, it would be hard to imagine Cumil in any other city.

Another statue, not too far away, is of Schöne Naci, who livened up the streets of Bratislava some 100 years ago, always dressed in a rather shabby set of formal wear, greeting people in the street and opening doors for them. He was a beloved eccentric and his statue radiates loopy good will. There are also statues of a Napoleonic soldier (Perhaps Napolean himself. It's hard to tell.) and another of a paparazzo peeking around a corner with a monstrous telephoto lens.

Pretty much out of nowhere I'll mention that one of my favorite bronze statues in Europe is in the new St. Pancras Eurostar terminal in London. It's a 30-foot-tall bronze of a couple who's about to kiss. You can find it upstairs, under the really big clock. The thing weighs 20 tons and it's not really the kind of thing one expects to see in stolid old London. It was sculpted by Paul Day and was modeled on him and his wife. The original plan was to have the couple actually kissing, but the even more stolid old London and Continental Railways decided this would be "too risqué." Since the thing is so enormous . . . and rests on a pedestal . . . and the woman is wearing a skirt . . . I'm kind of surprised they allowed it at all, but one thing's for sure, it can't be missed.

The statues of Bratislava are far more discrete, but this is appropriate—Bratislava is a subtle place; it wears its charm in little things: doorways and Nativity scenes and small bronze markers in the cobblestone indicating the path taken by the newly crowned royalty of the empire (emperors were always crowned in Bratislava). You need to look for these things, but it's well worth the look . . . especially in winter, when the city hosts its Christmas markets and crowds of talkative friends run into each other again amid the smell of sausage and the heat of their drinks and the warmth of their conversations.

THE TRUMPETERS
OF CRACOW, POLAND

Let's face it—Warsaw is not a pretty place. It's not the fault of the inhabitants; the city was completely razed in the Second World War and only rebuilt under the heavy architectural hand of the Stalin regime. I think it's safe to say that few Poles would defend their capital's beauty, but they will all immediately tell you that if you really want to see Poland, you have to go to Cracow.

Cracow was the capital of Poland for . . . OK, here I'm going to stop the overview of Polish history, because Polish history is really, really complicated—too complicated for an overview. Let's just say that Cracow was once the capital of Poland, during one of those intermittent periods in the past when Poland was a country. The capital was only moved to Warsaw in 1596 when Wawel Castle burned and the king put the entire court on a raft and floated down the Vistula to Warsaw, where they set up camp and then apparently forgot to return.

The castle, which dominates the old town, was rebuilt shortly after the fire, and in many respects it is the focal point of Polish history. All Polish kings but two were crowned here and most of them are buried in large, ornate sarcophagi housed in the cathedral in the castle's center. It should be noted that this cathedral has a number of very cool things about it, the most unique of which may be the three very big old bones hanging by chains in front of the entrance.

When the cathedral was built in the thirteenth century, the bones were discovered and thought to come from the dragon of Cracow. Turns out they are primordial remains of a mammoth, a whale and a rhinoceros.

Have I mentioned that I love dragons?

Wawel Castle is built on a hill overlooking the Vistula River. At the base of this hill, nearly on the riverbank, is a cave. In this cave the dragon used to live. In order to appease it, the inhabitants used to feed it every day with (details vary according to who's telling the story) cows, pigs, sheep and a virgin (it's the mix of animals that varies . . . the virgin is always served for dessert). After a while, almost all the virgins were used up, and the last one remaining was the king's daughter, who was, of course, the most charming and fair damsel in the land (you didn't really expect a fairy tale with a pustulant hag for a princess, did you?). Anyway, the king decided to offer his daughter's hand to whichever knight could slay the dragon. All the knights of the land tried, and all were fried, until a local cobbler asked to have a shot at it. He got some (variously) sheep or pigs or cows or whatever and inside their carcasses put smoldering lamps. The dragon ate them readily, but then came down with a serious case of heartburn, which made him thirsty . . . so thirsty that he went down to the river and drank and drank until he burst. The cobbler married the princess and they, of course, lived happily ever after.

Every Pole knows this story, and near the entrance of the cave there is a bronze statue of the dragon. This statue breathes fire every few seconds. I think that's cool. I had a guide in Cracow, who explained that the statue was put there in the '70s. "I was a kid then. My parents had me stand in front of the dragon to take a picture. When it breathed fire high over my head I nearly shit my pants."

It must be said that it's an impressive statue.

Cracow is chock full of winding little streets and beautiful architecture. It has one of the oldest universities in the world, dating from the twelfth century, and the buildings are still used by students.

Any city that can make such a claim is bound to be beautiful (just consider Paris, Bologna, Prague, to name just a few). The central square is the second largest market square in Europe (after Venice's Piazza San Marco) and it is not only ornate, impressive and extremely pretty, it is also *alive*. That centuries-old university has been joined by others, and Cracow is most definitely a university town, which means lots of cafés and restaurants and bars and bookshops and heated conversations.

In the center of the marketplace is the city's watchtower. This is over 80 meters high, mind-numbingly old, and home to one of the most charming city traditions I've ever come across.

Every hour of every day of every year, a trumpeter appears high up in the tower and plays a little tune out of the window. He does this four times, out of four different little windows, each facing in a different direction: he plays for the king out of the first window, which faces the castle; for the civic leaders of the city out of the second window, which faces the town hall; for visitors out of the third window, which faces the city gate; and for the fire department out of the fourth window, which faces its headquarters, for the trumpeters are members of the fire department. At each of these windows, he waves a few times at the people far below in the market square after he's finished his tune. According to legend, the number of times he waves at a visitor indicates the number of times the visitor will return to Cracow.

If you've ever read any of my other columns, it should be immediately apparent that this is *exactly* the kind of thing that I can't just leave alone. Luckily, my guide has contacts among the close-knit circle of Cracow trumpeters and he went over to a small door at the base of the tower and held a conversation with an interphone that then buzzed us in.

"You don't mind stairs?" he asked, as we started our way up a small, stone spiral staircase.

"Not at all," I replied.

"Good," he said. "There are 400 of them."

And as I was soon to learn, no two are identical. After the ancient spiral staircase, we came to a rather modern (as in, probably less than 100 years old) wooden staircase that was soon replaced by a series of different wooden stairways that sometimes seemed more like ladders than stairs. As we made our way up, clinging to various beams and braces to keep from clattering down, I couldn't help but think that these stairs constituted one of the most unique commutes in the working world.

The stairs end in a tiny room crisscrossed by massive beams and surrounded by these famous windows, out of which the trumpeter blows his trumpet. The room has a number of amenities, including a microwave, a radio, a small TV, a computer, a tiny table with a few chairs and a trumpet. There is also a toilet behind a door. "That was a big improvement," my guide informed me. "It was added in the '20s. Before that, the trumpeters had to go all the way down and back up again when they wanted to pee."

There are seven trumpeters and they work in shifts. Firefighters have fulfilled this almost sacred duty since the fourteenth century, when mention of it first appears in written documents. According to them, not an hour has been missed in over 500 years.

The tune is a short but complex one. Up in the tower there is one line of staff music on the wall just in case a trumpeter forgets. I tried to find out what the origin of the tune is, but no one seems to know. They did tell me why it's cut off suddenly in the last note. It would seem that centuries ago, when Cracow was suffering one of its periodic Tartar invasions, a trumpeter took an arrow through the throat as he was blowing the last note. Ever since then, his successors have paid homage to his dedication by cutting off that particular note. Personally, I'm not convinced. I know the Tartars were extraordinary archers, but the tower is over 50 meters tall and that would have been a hell of a shot even for one of the Great Khan's fearsome warriors.

This crossed my mind as I looked out one of the windows from which the trumpeter plays his tune. There were no Tartars in the market square, but there were a whole lot of revelers. It seemed a shame for the trumpeters to be shut up here, looking at the endless party going on so far below, but they don't seem to mind.

Next to the window of my contemplation was a large cone-shaped device, which looked a lot like an old gramophone speaker. I asked about this and was told that it was actually a kind of microphone. It seems that the Polish national radio station broadcasts the call of the trumpeter all over the country every day at noon, live. Once again, this is a fact that is apparently known to every Pole. "You can even hear his footsteps as he walks from window to window," my guide informed me. This was substantiated by a couple of friends from Warsaw who were with me. The trumpeter was a kind, uniformed man who explained through my guide that the microphone had never been changed, that it was the same one that had been installed there in 1927. It looked it.

Traditions are one thing, but I also learned that the trumpeters all play in local jazz bands. I find that indicative of the city as a whole, a mix of medieval tradition and cool nightlife.

Cracow's charms aren't only to be found 50 meters high. There is also the Wieliczka Salt Mine nearby, in which you can plunge hundreds of meters *under* the ground and marvel at the chambers and sculptures carved by the miners into the salt over the centuries. These go from salt donkeys to an entire salt cathedral. This is not a model cathedral; it's a real cathedral, in which people get married, then celebrate in the cavernous reception area nearby.

When it comes down to it, the salt mine is probably worth a column of its own, but then there are many things about Cracow I haven't even covered . . . like the pope. I'm sure the inhabitants of Cracow will be sorely upset that I've written about their city without even *mentioning* John Paul II, but fear not . . . the trumpeter waved to me seven times, so there may yet be another six columns about the city, through which I can begin to do it justice.

THE WEST

"We've all come to look for America."
—Paul Simon

In 2008, my family and I embarked on a five-week trip through the American West. Apart from a couple of brief trips to Los Angeles and a trip or two to Dallas or Phoenix, I had never crossed the Mississippi, and even those trips had been confined primarily to hotels. The time had come to discover my own country, outside the boundaries of the East Coast.

I had realized that I knew the rest of the world better than the land of my birth, and you can't really know the United States if you haven't seen all those purple mountains' majesty and the amber fields of grain. I was not disappointed. The United States is really, really big (that was lesson number one) and the sheer beauty of it was astounding.

The following four vignettes, none of which have appeared in McSweeney's, recount our travels.

ROCKY MOUNTAIN HIGH

It seems to be a right of passage of sorts to go driving around the American West for some extended period of time. Maybe it has something to do with the myth of the West, or maybe it's just that the sights are supposed to be spectacular, or maybe it's just the idea of all that *space*, but one way or another, there is a distinct drive to head out west, either camping one's way across the continent or moteling it from state to state.

If this impulse is universal, how much stronger is it for an expatriate American travel writer? For several years, I had been waiting for the right moment to uproot everyone and head across 3,000 miles of sea and sundry states to discover America. I finally got around to it, gathered up my family and dragged along a family of friends, flew to Denver, rented two RVs and set out for a five-week circuit through every national park we could hit.

The very first question was, of course, which music to play. One of my first purchases was one of those devices that allows you to play your iPod through the radio (what will they think of next?), but by the time we got into Wyoming it was clear to me that I couldn't play just anything. From a U.S. perspective, I'm very much a New Yorker, and I had never seen anything like the great, rolling, empty spaces of Wyoming. Let's face it: Lou Reed is just out of place out there. I therefore concentrated on the Allman Brothers, The Outlaws, The Band, the Eagles, Pure Prairie League, Creedence, etc. But there's a whole lot of Wyoming to cover, and I needed more ammunition.

By the time we got to Cody, which is a temple to that great American buffalo and Indian exterminator, Buffalo Bill, I realized that I needed to update my music library. We headed to a Wal-Mart (my American readers will here be amazed to learn that this was my first foray into a Wal-Mart) to buy various provisions, and I noticed they had a bin of discount CDs. These consisted entirely of "best of" albums, which I generally avoid at all costs, but here we were talking about musicians I was purchasing purely out of geographical necessity. I therefore scooped up a few CDs (John Mellencamp, stuff like that) and headed for the checkout, where my wife and family and friends were paying for several gallons of milk and wondering where American grocery stores keep their wine.

I couldn't quite leave, though, because there was one CD I had refused to purchase, but that was calling to me from across the store saying, "You know you need me." I therefore scurried back and bought it, hiding it in a paper bag on the way out.

So it was that I listened to John Denver as we made our way into Yellowstone. I immediately made up for it by compensating with a brief dose of George Thorogood (the archetypical nice boy followed by the archetypical bad boy), but Lonesome George was really out of place amidst the wonders of Yellowstone . . . which I won't go into here. (Ha! Take that, all you other travel writers! Go to Yellowstone and only describe what was on your radio!)

The trip from Yellowstone, through pretty much all of Utah to Bryce Canyon probably would have been best accompanied by the Mormon Tabernacle Choir, but I do have my limits. As it was, I discovered that Simon & Garfunkel and James Taylor served nicely, although nobody really conveyed the emotion generated by swimming in the Great Salt Lake. This emotion has much to do with slime, since the lake smells awful, is surrounded by muck, and is populated by zillions of tiny shrimp that spend a great deal of energy either fighting with each other or copulating (as is often the case in the animal world, the two activities are almost indistinguishable). We all tramped into the lake, checked out its renowned floatability, and then played a little Ultimate Frisbee. This was cool. What was even cooler was that as I did research for this dispatch (while sitting in the lobby of Ruby's Inn, at Bryce Canyon, under a stuffed puma and amid a horde of tourists [almost all of whom were, ironically, French] simply because this was the only place I could get an Internet connection upon which to do research … but I digress), I discovered that the Great Salt Lake brine shrimp are actually sea monkeys! I assume most of you know about these mystical creatures; you clip out a black-and-white advertisement from some third-rate publication touting the wonders of sea monkeys, which, according to the ad, will build little cities and fight little wars with their little tridents right in your bowl if you just cough up a few dollars. You send your money, receive a tiny pack of what looks like pepper, add water and salt, and presto! Of course, this never works, but if it did, you would apparently end up with a colony of fighting/screwing brine shrimp.

It was as we approached Bryce that I decided to widen my musical exploration a little. I had made it a rule as we drove around the West that only American artists would do, but I had a bit of inspiration, and tried out KT Tunstall, who after all *sounds* really American (she's Scottish). She worked out pretty well for the the next hundred miles or so, but it was another European who really nailed it: trust me, if ever you go to Bryce Canyon, put on Joe Strummer and the Mescalaros well before the Red Canyon, then stick with him all the way through.

Music took a back seat to art once we were actually in Bryce. The other family that came with us are so French that the man of the family is a bona fide cheese-eating artist. The two of us snuck off for a reconnaissance trip into the canyon itself as soon as our RVs were parked, while our families did more familial things. Laundry, I think.

The Paiute Indians say that the hoodoos, strange colossal forms that nature has sculpted into Bryce's sandstone, are actually the Legend People, who were so wicked that Coyote transformed them into rock. As we hiked down from the rim into their midst I felt like an ant at the feet of ancient beings and could well believe the Indians. My companion, the French artist, fell into a kind of trance, running from spot to spot to take pictures.

"I won't paint," he told me. "I didn't bring my things, because it would have been a pain in the butt for you." This was an excuse for stopping to take vaste numbers of pictures. I don't take pictures. Ever. "Sublime" was a word that passed his lips at least two or three times per minute.

"Look at this dirt!" he exclaimed, bending over on the trail to crumble some reddish-yellow soil in his hands. "And over there, look at that dead tree! See how it spirals?"

True, it was very attractive, as dead trees go.

But it was the vistas that really got him. "Sublime!" he said, as he looked over a forest of hoodoos at a crenelated ridge with gaping holes in the rock. "Look at this bush, it's so *green*, and the rock behind it, all red, and the gray-blue clouds behind that!" He took some more pictures. "It's a shame there's not a real thunderstorm over in the distance there," he indicated the Escalante range, about 30 miles away. "That would have given us some superb contrasts."

I don't think of things like this, but every exclamation about dead trees or clouds or fluorescent greens was true, and as I stood and tried to find words for it all, it wasn't words, but images that floated in my mind. How different the world must be for painters.

I eventually managed to drag him back out of the canyon to rejoin our families. They were all excited about the local squirrels and chipmunks, the former being rare and the latter being nonexistent in Europe. I tore them away from their rodent ecstasy to sit everyone down for their English lesson—having carefully explained my linguistic theories to them (see my column "Useful Phrases") I was teaching them some useful English phrases (that evening we were working on "There's no squid on my head"). My wife, who theoretically does speak English, was working on pronunciation, repeating the word "chipmunk," which still sounded a hell of a lot like "sheepmuck." Our academic endeavors completed, my friend and I retired to our respective corners, where he took out his watercolors and I tried to capture it all in words that are once again, alas, too small and colorless and bland to describe the visions that nature had placed before our eyes.

OH, TO LIVE ON SUGAR MOUNTAIN

Bryce Canyon is not really a canyon. It's the eroding edge of the Colorado Plateau. Upon leaving Bryce, we headed into *real* canyon country, going from Zion to Glen Canyon to the grandaddy of them all.

As Joe Strummer gave way to Neil Young on the iPod player thingy, we drove farther into southeastern Utah, where the land is slashed with canyons big and small. The first, and in some ways the most stunning of them, was Zion. Here, the Virgin River has sliced its way through eons worth of rock, cutting a gash through ancient deserts and seas and leaving a wonderland of color painted onto soaring cliffs. If nature used a set of finely wrought tools to carve the delicate shapes of Bryce, it used the brute force of its considerable muscles to create the cliffs of Zion.

We hiked out to the end of the trail and sloshed our way up through the river toward its distant headwaters, accompanied by a vaste horde of tourists, the majority of whom were French. This is odd. We had first encountered this at Bryce, where the lodge was stuffed with French speakers, but here at Zion it became downright eerie. I had come back to my homeland accompanied by a bunch of French people who felt less out of place than did I, at least by purely linguistic standards. Perhaps this has something to do with the wonderful work of the current U.S. administration, which has managed not only to create a considerable economic differential with Western Europe, but which has also succeeded in bringing the dollar to a level at which a Camembert wrapper is more valuable. But one way or another, this was clearly a year for European tourism. Why the French were more heavily represented than their European colleagues is a bit of mystery (not that we didn't hear a lot of German, Dutch, Italian and even Oxbridge English), but at least it keeps the tourist trade alive.

This became even more evident once we reached Wahweap, on Lake Powell. We stayed here a few days, lolling in the sun and boating our way around what used to be Glen Canyon, before the construction of the Glen Canyon dam turned it into a giant aquatic playground for the Southwest. Just about everyone we came across was from France, including a well-known television anchorman who impressed us with the fact that in reality, he's about five feet tall (you only ever see him sitting down during the eight o'clock news in France). He, like us, had rented a motorboat, but he evidently wasn't lucky enough to discover our own sinuous branch of Labyrinth Canyon, which we navigated only with difficulty, as one member of our group sat on the bows with a paddle, pushing us off of the canyon walls. At the end, we found ourselves in a tiny alcove, a fully flooded canyon all to ourselves, affording isolation, warm waters, and a walk up to the desert, where after a score of steps one could turn around and discover that the canyon containing our boat, not to mention our children, had mysteriously disappeared, replaced with rolling petrified dunes criss-crossed with mysterious bovine tracks. Navajo Mountain loomed in the distance and, like the lizards, modern man with all his works had scurried back into some kind of time hole.

It was from our base at Wahweap that we headed into Page to take a tour out to Antelope Canyon with a Navajo-owned company. This consisted of bouncing across the desert in a makeshift vehicle with Marvin, our Indian guide, out to the entrance to Antelope, which is a slot canyon not too far away, pictures of which you have surely seen, even if you're not aware of it. Antelope Canyon is never more than a few feet wide, although it's over 100 feet deep at points. Its walls curve and plunge and fold themselves into forms that are weird and wonderful, mirroring the nature of the violent waters that have shaped them. Ours was the last group of the day, and Marvin, who can't be more than 20 years old, led us through the canyon with care, pointing out the more surprising forms and colors, which, of course, caused my French artist friend to squeal with delight and snap pictures in every direction, ever bemoaning his lack of painting materials.

For my part, I talked to Marvin, who regretted the loss of his people's language. Even those of his own generation tend not to speak Navajo, he explained, as he caressed the rock.

"Does this place have a significance to your people?" I asked.

"No," he replied, "now it is dead. Look at how some have defaced the rock, they have chipped it, or even carved into it. Navajo should not do that."

Nevertheless, he did say that sometimes he comes to the canyon alone, often at night. At those times, the place can indeed seem alive. "At night," he explained, "it can get creepy—sometimes you can hear the spirits."

Partly on the basis of Marvin's suggestion, we decided to spend the evening at Navajo Village, which was touted as an opportunity to have Navajo traditions explained and demonstrated to us. Upon arriving there, we discovered a fenced-off area near the highway, behind an RV wash. This reeked of a tourist trap, and if Marvin hadn't mentioned that there is upwards of 60% unemployment among the Navajo, we probably would have left.

We were immediately shunted into a small group that was going from point to point within the motley collection of reconstituted shelters, each area presided over by a Navajo who was explaining a particular aspect of his or her people's history and culture. Our first guide was a young man training to be a healer. He seemed rather shy, but he pointed out the significance of stones and sticks and even grains of sand to us. His very timidity began to win us over, and by the time we got to the next point of instruction we were much more receptive. Here, we met an elderly woman who demonstrated traditional rug-weaving techniques. She went into detail, continually referring to her mother-in-law, who apparently is a master (it should be said that her own skills seemed masterful to me, but what do I know?). We were thoroughly charmed by the time we were called to dinner, where an elderly man explained to the group what, exactly, we would be eating. When he had finished, I approached to ask him a question about traditional Navajo agriculture. This earned me not only an answer, but a half-hour private tour through the nearby desert, where he pointed out the identity and uses of every plant he laid his eyes upon. I would have written every one of them off as barren scrub, but each was a treasure trove of food and medicine, and even a tool chest of sorts. The old gentleman walked among this cornucopia with the aid of a painted walking stick, and his explanations were animated and passionate, to the point where I began to worry that no food would be left by the time he finished, but this was not to be missed. He did finally answer my original question, explaining that his people considered the spiral to be sacred and that traditional Navajo cornfields were always planted in a spiral pattern (which he illustrated by drawing in the sand with his walking stick). This is why hands are likewise sacred, since each finger bears the symbol of a spiral in its imprint. He laid one sacred hand on my shoulder and led me to get some food.

After dinner, a troupe of dancers demonstrated a series of traditional dances. This would normally be the point at which I go cringe in a corner, but it was entrancing and engaging and even with my travel-worn cynicism and dread of all tourist-oriented activities I found myself participating, as requested, in a friendship dance. Afterwards, as we left the enclosure with Native American rhythms pulsing in our veins, my French artist friend pointed out that they hadn't even tried to sell us anything. "They don't even understand marketing," he said. "Normally, they would have led us to a gift shop or something, but here they just smile and shake our hands and thank us. No wonder half of them don't have electricity." I must confess that for my part, I do know about marketing, and I couldn't help thinking that he was right, and I was selfishly grateful for it.

The next stop was the Grand Canyon. Lord knows I had seen images of the Grand Canyon, read stories about it, was fully prepared. I therefore wasn't *surprised* by what I saw, but that didn't stop me from being overwhelmed.

Actually, I think there's something wrong with me. As our entire troop slogged its way to Bright Angel Point, on the North Rim, I couldn't help but push a little harder and arrive before the others. The overlook is like the prow of a ship jutting out into the canyon, with a nice secure metal rail around it. I climbed up onto the rock, where there was no nice metal railing, and sat perched on a boulder. Despite the crowds below, reading the placards to each other, discussing the weather, taking pictures in every direction, I found that my will had been sucked up by the immensity of what was before me; it had trickled down into the canyon, swallowed up and insignificant, leaving me paralyzed on my rock, unable to move and barely able even to react to my family and friends as they showed up below. I just kept *looking*. I didn't think anything, I just looked, vaguely motioning to the others that they should go on, that I would catch up. There I stayed for about a half hour, unable to do anything else.

The Grand Canyon is too large to exist, and too wonderful to be imagined. It invites one into it, and so I once again left my group of loved ones to hike down into it and be swallowed into the earth. There I saw hummingbirds and squirrels and brilliant yellow birds with black wings and horned lizards and great towering cathedrals of rock. I felt as though I was penetrating into the intimate regions of the planet and when I climbed back out again I couldn't help but think that maybe the idea of rebirth isn't as wacky as I had always thought.

I'M LEAVING LAS VEGAS

The next stop on our western odyssey was markedly different from all that had preceded it: we left behind the wonders of nature and headed to Las Vegas. Yes, this was my first trip to Sin City, and I greeted the occasion with both trepidation and an admittedly significant degree of titillation.

I'll assume that many of my readers are far more familiar with Las Vegas than am I, and I'll make it clear that I bear no judgment for anyone who enjoys the place. After all, I, too, have had pleasant visits to a number of spots created by the Disney corporation. I was unprepared for the sheer scope of Las Vegas, though.

From a musical perspective, the billboards clearly announce the kind of place you're entering as you first penetrate the city: Wayne Newton, Cher, Donny and Marie Osmond, and Barry Manilow were all headlining there during my visit. These are not musicians who figure on my iPod, and Sheryl Crow was the best I could do to get a real Vegas feel to the music (and she was warmly welcomed).

I spent a day alone, wandering among the casinos, trying to take it all in. It struck me that it's a shame one can't conjugate adjectives in English, for surely the words "tawdry" and "kitsch" do not suffice in themselves to describe Vegas—they need some other forms; plurals and tenses and such. Being in Vegas is like being an extra in one of Donald Trump's wet dreams, complete with surrealistic segues and stained satin sheets.

My favorite place was probably the Venetian hotel/casino/ resort, which sports a canal on the second floor under an ersatz evening sky. The canal leads to a scaled-down reconstitution of Venice's Piazza San Marco, eternally frozen in summer twilight (without the pigeons and the risk of floods). On the canal, gondoliers pole their way along, transporting paying guests and singing American versions of Italian songs.

The first time I was in Venice was almost 25 years ago. I was accompanied by a tall Englishwoman with hair down to her waist. She was perhaps the first true love in my life, and we had taken the train from Paris despite the fact that I was penniless. We stayed in a rented room that contained few amenities but that did have a large

soft bed. We spent our days walking through the tiny streets, paus-
ing on the bridges, chasing the pigeons, and we spent our evenings
riding the vaporetti, strolling through the *piazze*, eating sparingly
in sidewalk cafés and making love in the large soft bed. Venice was
magic, it was the breath hanging between our lips, it was the song I
wrote for that girl. The Venice they have reconstructed at Las Vegas
is a sanitized, scaled-down fascimile of someone else's tame impression of a real, magical place, and seeing it was like seeing a nude cari-
cature of someone you once loved, drawn with a fat red crayon.

Vegas was created to allow people to gamble, but gambling
seems a lonely sport. The great majority of the "players" seemed to
me to spend most of their time sitting alone in front of a machine,
putting money in, pressing a button or pulling a lever, and then hoping that money comes out. At least in Monte Carlo there's a lot of
posing and strutting involved, but how does an overweight woman
wearing shorts and a UCLA T-shirt strut? Even the tables lacked the
pizzazz I had seen in my very rare forays into European casinos.

Of course, European casinos don't have roller coasters running through them. Nor do they have Disneyesque representations
of foreign cities lining the distant walls . . . nor do they have the sheer
size and bulk of the lowliest of the Strip's venues. Nor, for that matter, do they incorporate vast shopping malls in their innards; shopping malls with giant animated fountains and clouds painted onto
the ceilings. (Note: a number of casinos all enjoy eternal Italian mid-
summer evening lighting. It's actually very impressive, I have no idea
how they manage that.) I discovered, though, that while you can't
spit without hitting some store in which you can easily drop a thousand dollars, getting something to read is quite a different matter.

My day of exploration included a lunch break, and as I was
alone it was imperative to have something to read before sitting down
to eat. This is a rule of mine—when eating alone, I read. I had failed
to bring along any reading material, and therefore set out to look for
some while in the forum of Caesars Palace (allow me to mention

here that I won't even begin to complain about the blatant historical travesties extant in such places). Anyway, despite the wealth of stores, not one of them sold anything with words on it (except "small," "medium" or "large"). A security guard suggested I try a place over in *that* direction (third fountain down, stay on your left). The place in question sold cigarettes, cheap souvenirs, one book (yes, one copy of one book... a third-rate romance novel), and magazines. The magazines, though, were purely of the "men's" or "women's" variety ("six-pack abs in three weeks" for the former, and "seven secrets to a happier sex life" for the latter). There was also *Playboy* and *Penthouse*, but these were out of the question. Few things strike me as more pitiful than the image of a lone man sitting in a Vegas casino reading *Playboy* while munching a veggie wrap, even if he isn't turning the magazine sideways. I finally gave up and figured I'd just take some notes.

Such as this: for centuries, historians have proffered the theory that the Roman Empire fell because of its decadence. I, for one, have always disagreed, but it struck me as I sat there that whoever dreams up this shit ("I know, let's have gondola rides on the second floor!") would have found ready employment as a party organizer for Caligula. As such, what does this augur for the future of the American empire? After all, Vegas is clearly designed to suck dry those who visit: financially, sexually, and spiritually. The streets are lined with people wearing T-shirts advertising "hot babes" who want to meet you and are ready to do so in your room within 20 minutes. These micro-pimps try to shove little flyers into your hand, even if you're walking along with your 13-year-old son. Is this the summit of civilization? Is this what all human knowledge and endeavor has been striving towards? Did Ben Franklin and Thomas Jefferson foresee this? And evidently, it's not enough . . . despite a deepening economic crisis, the city is alive with construction: more casinos are needed, more sidewalks for T-shirt-wearing pimp proxies. I'm very, very far from a prude, but all of this *energy* devoted to the seven deadly sins seems a bit excessive, especially as it is particularly brainless. I'll take 10 Marquises de Sade over one $50-million street show with exploding ships manned by half-naked "sirens" who sing a dance tune that goes *thump-thump-thump* and proclaims, "Let's go all the way, baby."

Happily, this particular tune did not figure on my iPod, which washed away the sticky aftertaste of Vegas with some good old-fashioned Beach Boys as we headed to California (with an achin' in our hearts).

I LEFT MY HEART IN SAN FRANCISCO

The Norse had Valhalla, the Romans had the Elysian Fields, Buddhists have Nirvana—many dream of paradise, but New Yorkers have a tendency to dream of San Francisco. I don't know how many old friends I have from New York who have ongoing fantasies about living in San Francisco. Many of them have never actually been there, but they are convinced it's the only place in which their true inner selves can be expressed, thereby proving them to be inherently nice people (their inner nice person having been irremediably hidden through all those years of living in the grind of New York, with all its resident assholes). San Francisco, therefore, serves the purpose of allowing New Yorkers to imagine themselves as pleasant, flower-child-like blooms of happiness instead of gruff, hot-dog-munching mumblers.

I had always guarded against this naïve utopianism when I was actually living in New York, particularly since San Francisco, as enticing as it sounds, is unfortunately located in California. The problem with people from California (as the eastern stereotype goes) is that they think they come from the center of the universe, whereas we all know that's impossible, since New York is the center of the universe, and the universe can only have one center. (I know,

I know, the Big Bang happened everywhere, and everywhere is the center of the universe, but I'm speaking from a metaphorical and social perspective, not a cosmological one, and I've already digressed way too far as it is.)

Where was I? Ah yes, San Francisco.

So I finally ended up in San Francisco. This was not my first time in California—although for many years I had steadfastly refused even to cross the Mississippi, I had ventured into Southern California from time to time—but I had never knocked on the gates of utopia itself to enter the hilly domain of Saint Francis. Once I did, I had to admit that I finally understood why the city had such appeal.

It's a wonderful place! A beautiful place! It's full of little houses that display exactly the right mix of homogeneity and quirky little differences; with their bay windows on the upper floors and their different colors and their little doors; and there's no graffiti, and the streets are wide and sunny and the clouds scurry low and fast over the bay, where pelicans and seagulls and cormorants fly and dive and fish and squawk. I'm quite ready to believe that when good New Yorkers die, they end up in San Francisco (which raises the question of where the bad ones go . . . maybe Newark?).

I had been warned against Fisherman's Wharf, but I went there anyway and a good thing it was. First of all, there are ships to be visited, and I love visiting ships. As will be evident to any who have been religiously reading these dispatches (a group of people close to my heart), I'm a bit of a history buff, and old ships (like old castles, buildings, cities and people) are dear to me. In San Francisco, you can visit a WW II submarine, a Liberty ship from the same era (one that actually sails around from time to time), nineteenth-century sailing ships, a tugboat and a paddle-wheeled steamer. You can even get into the engine room of the Liberty ship and play around in the maze of ladders and narrow passageways. It's like an iron version of snakes and ladders.

Right next to all this is the Musée Mecanique, where dozens of old nickelodeon contraptions clank and whir and play tinny music at you for the paltry price of a quarter. There are little peep shows, at which men in top hats gawked at stereoscopic images of the 1906 earthquake, or for the more daring, enjoyed a voyeuristic look into a "lady's dressing room" ("approved by New York censors"), in which a less-than-entirely-proper lady apparently hesitated about how to arrange her undergarments, thereby affording glimpses of the underside of a breast or the top of an inner thigh amidst the folds of lace . . . nineteenth-century soft porn that is still surprisingly enticing. There are working dioramas of farms, sawmills, carnivals, and horses. There are machines at which you can test your strength by arm-wrestling mechanical strongmen or squeezing handles. There are mystical booths that will tell your fortune or test your ardor, and there are games of skill in which you manipulate clockwork athletes to shoot baskets or box with each other. The noise is glorious and the place makes you wonder why no one makes these things anymore—are we really better off manipulating electrons than feeling heavy gears grind under our hands?

Near all this is Lou's, a blues club and restaurant. We didn't try the food, but I went back a few times to listen to remarkably proficient bands play Fender guitars, covering people like Buddy Guy and Al King. I've played a lot of blues in my time, but it struck me there just how many blues songs incorporate the words "I woke up this morning. . ." after which all kinds of catastrophes rain down upon the poor musician. Mornings are particularly hard on bluesmen. At Lou's, the waitresses shimmy between the tables and very old people dance with very young people while fat, bearded guitarists egg them on and motorcycles pass by on the street below.

Nearby you can find a beach. It's nice having a beach in a city (see my comments on Rio and Barcelona). As I sat near the beach engaging in some auditory and alcoholic detoxification, I amused myself by noting down the little snippets of conversation I heard as people walked by.

"Want to toss a marble and see where it lands?"

"It is cold, man."

"So how are we doing?"

"He wanted to borrow just one of our suitcases."

"Sure enough, he dropped the money."

"How many other 17-year-olds would have done that?"

"Try a little gel."

"I got asked. I swear, he had to ask."

And one man with a thick mustache who sat down near me and began singing to himself: "Well it's a good day . . ."

It makes you wonder about the rest of the conversations; who they all are, what they're doing. Each person is a universe unto themself and all these different universes were swirling around each other out near that beach in the middle of a somewhat magical city where it was indeed a good day.

HOME

In the United States, suburbia conjures Updikean images of mowed lawns, barbecues, a couple of cars in pristine driveways, and perhaps a bit of wife swapping. In France, "the suburbs" (*banlieux*) generally means rundown housing projects and perhaps a bit of rioting in unkempt streets. The suburb in which I live, though, on the western fringe of Paris, while not very American in atmosphere is all the same unmistakably bourgeois. There are driveways (although they don't front the streets, but run up to pleasant houses from iron gates) and old-fashioned lampposts. There are lots of trees, a couple of castles nearby, and a sixteenth-century church that rings in the hours as we lie in bed in the morning, meaning that you don't have to look at the clock when you wake up, but rather can just count the chimes (an altogether more pleasant way of discovering how late you've slept). The town is squeezed between the Seine and the Forêt de St.-Germain, almost 9,000 acres of carefully managed forest crisscrossed with nice firm paths upon which one can run, bike, or just stroll along looking at deer and the occasional boar.

It beats the South Bronx.

The only bad thing about my town is its name, Le Mesnil-le-Roi, which is absolutely impossible to spell out to a non-French speaker. Many's the time that I've had to give my address to someone in English and it's a trying experience. It's not just the pronunciation, it's also the fact that it's four separate words. Try explaining that to someone from Topeka.

At last we recently had the opportunity to change our street address. A couple of years ago we built a house roughly 20 meters from our previous home, on the same street. However, since the new house is on a corner, we were given the choice of an address on our old street, or on the new cross street. The new street is la rue des Graviers, which means, roughly, "Street of Gravel." While this may not sound particularly poetic, our old street was la rue des Poilus, which means, roughly, "Street of Hairy People." There's a reason for this: the French have always used the word *poilus* as a kind of affectionate nickname for the infantrymen who served in the First World War (because they tended to have beards, not because they were otherwise hirsute), so the street was a tribute to them. Nevertheless, whenever we gave our address to someone in France they would always kind of check out our arms to see if any hair was curling out the edge of our shirt cuffs, and they'd giggle. After a few years of that you'd rather be identified with gravel.

By the time it gets to us, la rue des Graviers is effectively a gravel path. La rue des Poilus is no thoroughfare either—it's almost too small for cars to pass at its northern extremity, where it ends at the church. Given this, and because it is on the way to the forest, and since Le Mesnil-le-Roi is a very horsey town, there are more horses that use it than there are cars. This means that as you lie in bed on a weekend morning you're likely to hear the *clip-clop* of horses' hooves as you listen for the church bells to find out what time it is.

That beats the hell out of the South Bronx.

Living in a town like this, far enough in spirit from the city that one might as well be in the Burgundy countryside yet close enough that the buildings of Paris can be contemplated from our front gate, it's something of a mystery why I'd want to travel at all.

But then, if I hadn't been born with this wanderlust I might still be living in the South Bronx. It's a drug, travel. It's the drug of discovery, and it perches on your back banging on your head if you don't feed it from time to time. Hold out to me the opportunity of discovering someplace new and it's very difficult not to go. I've reached the point in my professional career where I could effectively say no to just about any trip if it really came down to it, but give me a chance to see the Montenegran town of Kotor and I jump at it (wonderful place: a fortified town built into a hillside overlooking a magnificent bay).

Not that I haven't hesitated. For one thing, there aren't really that many new places left that truly interest me . . . or at least not that many that are easily accessible. Another thing is that my children are growing, and I've come to the realization that they, too, will go traipsing around the world and I won't see them nearly as much anymore, particularly if they take after me in that respect. Lastly, there's the question of mortality, which reared its hoary head not too long ago.

Mortality—or at least the fragility of one's well-being—came wrapped in a diagnosis; that of multiple sclerosis. My case is not a particularly nasty one—it is labeled "benign"—but that's akin to describing a benign pit bull; it might loll around on the couch for years, placidly licking its private parts, but then one day it jumps up and rips off your face. Upon learning that I lived with such a beast, I was tempted to shake the monkey off my back and stick around in Le Mesnil-le-Roi, enjoying the clip-clopping horses and the forest and the church bells and my family and domesticity in general. But then it occurred to me that I don't actually ride horses, that the wail of the muezzin is just as timely and more exotic than a church bell, and that I actually see quite a bit of my family, since when I'm not traveling I'm pretty much at home.

What's more, while having a potentially debilitating disease certainly does have its drawbacks, it can also serve as a sort of catalyst. It can make clichés ring true: "live for the day" and all that.

I liken it to the role of the slave who would stand behind great men during a triumph. In ancient Rome, when a great general was afforded a ceremonial triumph a slave would ride in the chariot behind him. Remember that a triumph was the ultimate honor for a Roman; they were very rare, and never offered twice to the same man. The entire city would turn out to cheer and celebrate the general's feats of arms. The slave's job was twofold: first, he held a crown of laurel over the head of the man being honored as they rode through the cheering streets; second, the slave would whisper into his ear, "Remember you are mortal."

What an idea. The reasoning behind this was that in the face of all this adulation, the man being honored might begin to take himself for a god and thus commit the sin of hubris. But there's a flip side to the statement—it could be heard as "remember you are mortal . . . so *today* have the time of your life!" Multiple sclerosis holds no laurel wreath to my head, but that insidious reminder of mortality makes itself heard through the tingling in my feet, and when it comes down to it, its not such a bad thing.

Given all that, I decided that far from settling into a more sedentary existence, I would continue to feed the discovery monkey, although perhaps with a bit more appreciation both of the destination that beckoned and the home that waited for me. This heightened appreciation has rendered both the voyages and the homecomings even more enjoyable. It is therefore time to tell you about the home to which I return.

Le Mesnil-le-Roi was something of an outpost in the St.-Germain forest, where French kings used to go hunting all those deer and boar. François I is rumored to have spent much of his childhood here and Louis XIV used to hang out from time to time. The forest actually ends at the magnificent castle of St.-Germain-en-Laye, but Le Mesnil was the more intimate, laid-back forest haunt. In the fifteenth century, when French monarchs spent much of their time in the castle at St.-Germain, the nobility started building residences in Le Mesnil-le-Roi in order to be close (but not too close) to the crown, and the town proper began to take form. When the court was moved to Versailles, a few miles south, St.-Germain and Le Mesnil both became a bit less hectic and the latter settled into the rather lazy complacency that typifies it today, discretely sandwiched between the forest, the river, and the better-known town of Maisons-Laffitte to the north.

Le Mesnil-le-Roi doesn't have much of a town center. Sure, there's the church, but there's no bakery near it. By French standards, that's not a town center. If you want a real town center then you have to go to Maisons-Laffitte, a good five-minute bike ride.

Maisons-Laffitte is even horsier than Le Mesnil-le-Roi. As an example: you know those buttons you push on traffic lights to get the light to change so you can cross the street? There are several in Maisons-Laffitte that are situated about six feet off the ground, so riders can push them without getting off their mounts. It took me a while to figure out why the damn buttons were so high. Was there a family of pituitary mutants living nearby? I only understood when I saw a horsewoman use one. Maisons-Laffitte also has a real center with a church and four bakeries, as well as butchers, a cheese shop, fruit sellers, and restaurants (but no fishmongers, although one sets up on the sidewalk in front of the fruit stand every weekend).

The town also boasts l'Epicerie de Longeuil, the store Ali Baba would have founded if he had been a grocer. Created in 1880 by a certain Monsieur Izinstein, l'Epicerie de Longeuil was purchased by Eugène DesHayes in 1924. The store has remained in the family ever since; his grandson, Bernard, handing it over to his own daughter, Nellie, two years ago.

Bernard DesHayes, who is a distinguished older gentleman invariably wearing a blue smock, still works in the store, and indeed he is as much a part of the atmosphere as the scented soap and the bags of coral lentils. He can explain the contents for hours on end, going into intricate detail about his suppliers and their own histories.

"Take tripes," he explained to me. "You might think tripes

wouldn't sell, they could be seen as old-fashioned, and it's true that women don't tend to like tripes. It's a guy thing. We sell about 400 jars a year, though. Look at this," he held up a jar of tripes. "We've had the same supplier for 30 years. First we dealt with the father and now with the son. High quality stuff. I've never actually met them, you know, I just deal with them by telephone."

M. DesHayes took me over to the dried fruit section. "See all this? We buy in bulk and then put the apricots and figs and dates and things into little packets. That way we can get better quality and maintain lower prices than if we bought it *already* in little packets. We sell three tons a year of these things. We do the same with nuts and spices." He took me to see the nuts and spices (which include smoked salt—l'Epicerie de Longeuil is the only store I've ever seen to carry smoked salt, which opens up entirely new culinary directions). "And the rice! I don't even know how many bags of rice we sell."

Across from the nuts are a variety of cookies and things, most of which hail from the UK. "It's all about suppliers," he continued, putting a box of cookies (or biscuits, as the Brits would say) in my hands. "For instance, we're the only distributors in France who import these cookies directly from the UK. You must admit, nine euros for a box like this is good—and it's a nice box."

It was a nice box. Tin. With designs and things.

Shopping at l'Epicerie de Longeuil is a fascinating experience, made all the more interesting by the fact that the store doesn't accept credit cards. *Everybody* accepts credit cards in France, but M. DesHayes stands staunch in his refusal. Given the amount one can spend in the store—especially considering the thousands of bottles of good wine sold downstairs in the extensive wine cellar—it is a little unusual to expect people to show up with wads of cash, or even personal checks. I asked about this.

"Ah! You must understand, Monsieur, that bankers are all crooks! I have a long list of stories I could tell, but they all come down to the fact that if I were to treat my clients the way they treat their clients, I'd go to jail. For instance, I don't sell you a packet of pasta (only good Italian pasta is sold there) for one price and then change the price for the next customer, do I? The bank, however, told me that to accept cards they would take three percent, whereas I know that other merchants only pay one and a half or two percent. That should be illegal! What's more, on a number of occasions they have made mistakes in their favor regarding my account. These, they never notice, whereas if there's a mistake in *my* favor it gets rectified immediately and they blame me. Once, when I complained about something like this, the director of the local agency sent one of his minions—he didn't even come himself, mind you—to see me in the store with an envelope full of cash to smooth things over! Can you imagine that? Not only won't I accept their credit cards, but since then I haven't set foot in the agency" (which, it should be pointed out, is roughly 100 meters down the road, on the same sidewalk).

"When was that?" I asked.

"1975."

Nineteen seventy-five isn't all that long ago at l'Epicerie de Longeuil, where time moves at a different pace. For one thing, the employee turnover is effectively zero. I asked M. DesHayes how often employees leave the store.

"Leave? I don't think anyone's ever left. We did take on a new employee . . . oh, 15 years ago, I believe."

I asked who had been there the longest. "Probably Denise," he said. "Let's ask her." Denise, though, was busy making change for some customers (almost all of whom greet M. DesHayes by name and ask how he's doing), so he asked a few of the other employees how long Denise had been there. None of them knew precisely. He asked a gentleman out back near the stocks: "Well, I've been here 30 years as of next April, so I'd say she's been here 35?"

"Right, you arrived at about the time we dug the cellar," continued M. DesHayes, leading to an interesting story that caused us both to forget about fixing the date of Denise's arrival.

In reality, though, the newest arrival is probably M. De-sHaye's daughter, Nellie, although that really can only be measured from the time she was an actual employee, since she's been a (very attractive) fixture at the store ever since she used to play shopkeeper there as a little girl. I asked her if it had ever crossed her mind not to enter into the family business. She paused before responding. "Yes," she said. "I did my studies and thought about doing something else with my life, but the weight of three generations cannot be dismissed lightly." She looked around. It must be said that she looked very much at home near the cheese counter across from the selection of gourmet beers.

I asked Nellie if she planned on making any major changes. "Oh no," she said. "Why would I? I mean, sometimes I do take on some new products. For instance, there's MangaJo." She held up a small bottle. "It's a drink made from grenadine. It's very trendy at the moment."

"Is it good?"

"No, it has no taste. And then there's Dr. Pepper."

I pointed out that it had always surprised me to find Dr. Pepper at l'Epicerie de Longeuil, since it's the only place I've ever seen it in France. Root beer is sold there as well, which is also highly unusual (the French, as a rule, despise root beer if you introduce it to them and wonder how on earth millions of American children can be so enthusiastic about it). "Oh, you can find both in France, but you have to look hard," she replied.

But why look hard when everything you can imagine is at l'Epicerie de Longeuil, where you can chat with M. DesHayes, who will tell you the history of just about everyone in town, or discuss root beer with Nellie, or ask Denise about recipes while you both put your purchases in a spare box (she keeps a stack of her own recipes under the checkout counter in case anyone wants an idea)?

I'm often there, because I'm often shopping for ingredients to make dinners of our own, since we have a tendency to invite friends over on a Saturday night, when we sit outside on the terrace when it's nice and chat into the breeze, or sit inside when it's cold, under the gaze of the girl with the lotus flower. And then when evening ends, and our friends have left and we're cleaning up, I watch my wife move as she carries the glasses into the kitchen. Although it's been more than 20 years since she stopped dancing she still carries herself like a ballerina, with grace and charm. We are very different; she is as practical and grounded in reality as I am impractical and grounded in nothing. Surprisingly, this makes for a perfect union. Even my sons, once they reached the age of reason, recognized this seeming incongruity. I remember one evening at dinner when my older son expressed surprise that two such different people were so very happy together. I explained that she is my anchor and I am her sails, which earned me a smile and a kiss (from the ballerina, not the boy).

In the end, wherever she is, there is my home. Perhaps it is this that has allowed me to travel so much . . . the world is far better appreciated when such a home waits patiently for your return.

ACKNOWLEDGMENTS

Although it seems almost obligatory to point out that there are too many people to be properly thanked, in my case it is painfully true. It should be obvious to those who have read this far (and I thank you: if you're reading acknowledgments it's probably either because you so enjoyed the book that you'll read anything at all to prolong the experience or because you expect to find your name here, either of which are well worth a thank you. But I digress.) that I have traveled a lot, and met many people. I have learned from all of them, the pleasant and the surly, the kind and the malicious, and as such I thank anyone who's ever crossed my path.

Nevertheless, there are some who have played a particular role in the creation of this book, and who deserve specific thanks. There are those on the Zoetrope site who helped me not only to become a better writer, but also taught me what to do with my scribbles. I can only hope that a general thanks, particularly to those from Pia's room, will suffice to generate warm fuzzy feelings in them. Pia herself has been instrumental in her help, Sue Henderson has been like a (young, sexy) fairy godmother to me and has always pushed me beyond what I would otherwise have achieved, Roy Kesey has supplied guidance and friendship, and Bob Arter is an inspiration to me, and anyone who has ever had the honor to converse with him. I think it was Avital Gad Cykman who first suggested that I try writing a travel column (one night in São Paolo, when she gave me a mango) and, of course, it was John Warner, at McSweeney's, who offered me a chance to do so. He and Chris Monks have always been great, and have put up with me for five years now.

The second group of people that deserve thanks are those in these columns who have ever remained nameless. I'm not quite sure why, but I made it a point not to name any of my friends and acquaintances who appeared in the column; this was a literary decision as opposed to a logistical one, but I would very much like to name them here if only to say thank you. They include: Duygu Kulluk, Sami Sibai, David Xue, Xavier Picanyol Puig, Toshinori Koshinori, Ryoji Fujino, Yukiko Itoh, Katrine Bach, Antoine and Béatrice Clolus, Ken Bluestone, Florent Edouard, Patrick Firdion, Terry O'Regan, Mona Rabie, Thomas Saganiuk, Peter Markotan, Jacek Nagler, and a number who were mentioned but whose names escape me.

I'd also like to thank Jeffrey Goldman of Santa Monica Press, who took a chance by putting all this on paper and without whom this book would not be in print. And, of course, there are my sons, Nicolas and Marc, who featured in much of what is here and all of what is not. And most of all, my lovely, understanding, thoroughly remarkable half-Corsican ballerina, Diane.

Books Available from Santa Monica Press

The Bad Driver's Handbook
Hundreds of Simple Maneuvers to Frustrate, Annoy, and Endanger Those Around You
by Zack Arnstein and Larry Arnstein
192 pages $12.95

Calculated Risk
The Extraordinary Life of Jimmy Doolittle
by Jonna Doolittle Hoppes
360 pages $24.95

Dinner with a Cannibal
The Complete History of Mankind's Oldest Taboo
by Carole A. Travis-Henikoff
360 pages $24.95

The Disneyland® Encyclopedia
The Unofficial, Unauthorized, and Unprecedented History of Every Land, Attraction, Restaurant, Shop, and Event in the Original Magic Kingdom®
by Chris Strodder
480 pages $19.95

The Encyclopedia of Sixties Cool
A Celebration of the Grooviest People, Events, and Artifacts of the 1960s
by Chris Strodder
336 pages $24.95

Exotic Travel Destinations for Families
by Jennifer M. Nichols and Bill Nichols
360 pages $16.95

Faces of Sunset Boulevard
A Portrait of Los Angeles
by Patrick Ecclesine
208 pages $39.95

Footsteps in the Fog
Alfred Hitchcock's San Francisco
by Jeff Kraft and Aaron Leventhal
240 pages $24.95

Free Stuff & Good Deals for Folks over 50, 3rd Edition
by Linda Bowman
240 pages $12.95

Haunted Hikes
Spine-Tingling Tales and Trails from North America's National Parks
by Andrea Lankford
376 pages $16.95

James Dean Died Here
The Locations of America's Pop Culture Landmarks
by Chris Epting
312 pages $16.95

Just Doing My Job
Stories of Service from World War II
by Jonna Doolittle Hoppes
344 pages $24.95

L.A. Noir
The City as Character
by Alain Silver and James Ursini
176 pages $19.95

Led Zeppelin Crashed Here
The Rock and Roll Landmarks of North America
by Chris Epting
336 pages $16.95

Letter Writing Made Easy!
Featuring Sample Letters for Hundreds of Common Occasions
by Margaret McCarthy
208 pages $12.95

Mark Spitz
The Extraordinary Life of an Olympic Champion
by Richard J. Foster
360 pages $24.95

The 99th Monkey
A Spiritual Journalist's Misadventures with Gurus, Messiahs, Sex, Psychedelics, and Other Consciousness-Raising Experiments
by Eliezer Sobel
312 pages $16.95

Pop Surf Culture
Music, Design, Film, and Fashion from the Bohemian Surf Boom
by Brian Chidester and Domenic Priore
240 pages $39.95

Redneck Haiku
Double-Wide Edition
by Mary K. Witte
240 pages $11.95

Roadside Baseball
The Locations of America's Baseball Landmarks
by Chris Epting
336 pages $16.95

Route 66 Adventure Handbook
by Drew Knowles
312 pages $16.95

Route 66 Quick Reference Encyclopedia
by Drew Knowles
224 pages $12.95

The Ruby Slippers, Madonna's Bra, and Einstein's Brain
The Locations of America's Pop Culture Artifacts
by Chris Epting
312 pages $16.95

Self-Loathing for Beginners
by Lynn Phillips
192 pages $12.95

Silent Traces
Discovering Early Hollywood Through the Films of Charlie Chaplin
by John Bengtson
304 pages $24.95

The Sixties
Photographs by Robert Altman
192 pages $39.95

Tiki Road Trip, 2nd Edition
A Guide to Tiki Culture in North America
by James Teitelbaum
336 pages $16.95

Tower Stories
An Oral History of 9/11
by Damon DiMarco
528 pages $27.95

Vanity PL8 Puzzles
A Puzzle Book Where You Solve the Vanity Plates
by Michelle Mazzulo
96 pages $8.95

"We're Going to See the Beatles!"
An Oral History of Beatlemania as Told by the Fans Who Were There
by Garry Berman
288 pages $16.95